Teaching Together, Learning Together

Studies in the
Postmodern Theory of Education

Joe L. Kincheloe and Shirley R. Steinberg
General Editors

Vol. 294

PETER LANG
New York • Washington, D.C./Baltimore • Bern
Frankfurt am Main • Berlin • Brussels • Vienna • Oxford

Teaching Together,
Learning Together

WOLFF-MICHAEL ROTH,
KENNETH TOBIN, EDITORS

PETER LANG
New York • Washington, D.C./Baltimore • Bern
Frankfurt am Main • Berlin • Brussels • Vienna • Oxford

Library of Congress Cataloging-in-Publication Data

Teaching together, learning together / edited by Wolff-Michael Roth, Kenneth Tobin.
p. cm. — (Counterpoints: studies in the postmodern theory of education; v. 294)
Includes bibliographical references and index.
1. Teaching teams. I. Roth, Wolff-Michael. II. Tobin, Kenneth George.
III. Series: Counterpoints (New York, N.Y.); v. 294.
LB1029.T4T415   371.14'8—dc22   2005007979
ISBN 0-8204-7911-X
ISSN 1058-1634

Bibliographic information published by **Die Deutsche Bibliothek.**
Die Deutsche Bibliothek lists this publication in the "Deutsche
Nationalbibliografie"; detailed bibliographic data is available
on the Internet at http://dnb.ddb.de/.

Cover design by Lisa Dillon

The paper in this book meets the guidelines for permanence and durability
of the Committee on Production Guidelines for Book Longevity
of the Council of Library Resources.

© 2005 Peter Lang Publishing, Inc., New York
275 Seventh Avenue, 28th Floor, New York, NY 10001
www.peterlangusa.com

Printed in the United States of America

Table of contents

Preface   vii

Introduction   ix
Wolff-Michael Roth and Kenneth Tobin

PART I: THEORETICAL PERSPECTIVES   1

Introduction: part I   3

1   Coteaching: from praxis to theory   5
     Wolff-Michael Roth and Kenneth Tobin

2   Becoming like the other   27
     Wolff-Michael Roth

PART II: COTEACHING/COGENERATIVE DIALOGUING IN PHILADELPHIA   53

Introduction: part II   55

3   Coteaching/cogenerative dialoguing in an urban science teacher   59
     preparation program
     Kenneth Tobin and Wolff-Michael Roth

4   The role of coteaching in the development of the practices of an urban   79
     science teacher
     Jennifer Beers

5   Cogenerating culturally and socially adaptive practices   97
     Sarah-Kate LaVan

6   Coteaching as a site for collaborative research   121
     Beth A. Wassell

7   Exchanging the baton: exploring the *co* in coteaching   141
     Kenneth Tobin

PART III: COTEACHING: ADDRESSING GLOBAL PERSPECTIVES   163

Introduction: part III   165

8   Developing wisdom-in-practice through coteaching: 169
     a narrative account
     Donna Rigano, Stephen Ritchie, and Trish Bell

9   Coteaching in a science methods course: an apprenticeship model   187
     for early induction to the secondary classroom
     Charles J. Eick and Frank Ware

10   Coteaching as an approach to enhance science learning and   207
     teaching in primary schools
     Colette Murphy and Jim Beggs

11   Gender issues in coteaching   233
     Kathryn Scantlebury

Epilogue   249
Kenneth Tobin and Wolff-Michael Roth

Contributors   265

Index   271

Preface

This book on coteaching and cogenerative dialoguing arose from many conversations that the authors had both in their institutions and at conferences with others who had also experimented with coteaching. In some instances, such as at the University of Pennsylvania, we have had a long-standing dialogue, which provided new researchers with an environment in which to learn what coteaching and cogenerative dialoguing was all about. One day, we (the editors) thought about bringing together a number of the scholars working on coteaching or cogenerative dialoguing to produce a volume featuring the practices as they evolved in one of our original experimental sites at an urban high school in Philadelphia and how they have been implemented and have evolved in other sites. At about the same time, in part mediated by our extensive collaboration with students from urban schools, we had an idea for a title that we ultimately abandoned, *I Got Yo' Back and You Got Mine*. For readers less familiar with our culture, this title is short for "I got your back covered, and you have my back covered," which means we cover for one another, especially in trouble, when we are vulnerable to threats that come from behind where we do not see it coming. At the same time, we also worked on some videotapes. We played around with some of the offprints, and one of them eventually was included in our cover design. It represents a situation where two teachers are standing close to the chalkboard, the more junior one interacting with the students in a whole-class session, the other one recording important aspects of the conversation or providing another notation (e.g., writing $CuSO_4$, which stands for copper sulfate, the chemical the other teacher was just talking about).

This edited volume brings together authors from three continents (Australia, Europe, North America) and four countries (Australia, Canada, Ireland, USA) who describe and theorize coteaching or cogenerative dialoguing as these practices have been implemented and evolved in response to problems and contradictions. Our introductions to the three parts of the book and our introduction and epilogue articulate similarities, differences, and salient issues between the different chapters. All studies also share sociocultural and cultural-historical underpinnings, which allows us to present a cohesive set of studies that improve our understanding of the coteaching and cogenerative dialoguing practices, and the constraints and contradictions they may face when implemented in various settings.

Particularly exciting about *Teaching Together, Learning Together* is the appearance in science education of the latest microanalytic methodologies (including conversation and discourse analysis, analysis of prosody) and technologies (including video processing and voice analysis software). These new methodologies and technologies provide science educators with new tools to the study of teaching and teacher education. Most importantly, these methodologies and technologies allow the documentation of practices that are produced and reproduced largely through unconscious means and processes.

We, the editors, consider this volume the continuation of a conversation that started with discussions of our *At the Elbow of Another* book and initially included the chapter authors in various groupings. The book is intended as an invitation to our readers to participate in this conversation and to try coteaching in their own institution and with their partners who work in various school settings. The different authors provide existence proofs for coteaching and cogenerative dialoguing for diverse settings, including the frequently difficult urban settings, and do not shy from articulating problems and contradictions that emerged in their own first attempts.

Wolff-Michael Roth and Kenneth Tobin
April 2005

Introduction

Wolff-Michael Roth and Kenneth Tobin

Coteaching has come a long way since we have started this practice during the early 1990s in a classroom in Vancouver, where pairs of teachers, a specialist in science and a resident elementary teacher got together to provide more interesting science lessons, to accord with a request from the students in the school. Working together, at each other's elbow, the coteaching pairs not only provided more interesting and challenging science classes, but also learned to teach science to young children. Some of the learning arose from the teachers' conscious reflections during debriefing and planning meetings. Much learning, however, occurred at the unconscious level, such as when one teacher slowly began to change her ways of questioning children, such that the latter moved from providing yes/no and one-word answers to elaborating issues of longer stretches of discourse. At the same time, the second teacher more familiar with the scientific content was less familiar with the children and had less experience with pedagogical issues. Her partner stepped in whenever the questions seemed to become too difficult and therefore too challenging for the children; that is, the partner had covered her back. Together, they not only brought about a tremendous learning environment for the children, but also they learned from one another. Since then, we have conducted many other studies of coteaching both in Canada and the USA and others have taken their inspiration and conducted their own coteaching research in other parts of the country and the world (e.g., Roth & Tobin, 2002).

Coteaching: consequences for agency, emotionality, and motivation

Coteaching differs from team-teaching, in which two or more teachers are assigned to teach together to decrease the workload, to create opportunities for each teacher to teach in his or her specialty, or to provide resources at the planning stage that teachers would not have otherwise. Coteaching, on the other hand, practically grounded in more than a decade of praxis and theoretically built on and supported by constructs of cultural sociology and social psychology, explicitly brings two or more teachers together to increase what they can offer to the students; they teach all the while providing opportunities for the participants to learn to teach. This orientation toward the opportunities to learn to teach while teaching is apparent in all contributions to this volume. Coteaching therefore means both optimizing learning opportunities for students by drawing on the expanded room to maneuver that arises from the collaboration of teachers *and* optimizing the learning opportunities for the teachers themselves, who thereby actively expand their possibilities rather than in completing their education once they received their teaching diploma. Coteaching (and the associated cogenerative dialoguing practice) are therefore as much about learning, that of students and teachers alike, as they are about teaching.

In an era of a culture of increasing individualism and focus on what the individual can and wants to do, coteaching explicitly is grounded in and draws on the strengths of the collective. When two teachers begin working together, and, in this, share full responsibility for planning, teaching, and reflecting on lessons, there automatically is a greater range of action possibilities. Each individual teacher therefore experiences a greater room to maneuver than he or she would experience working alone. The collective activity therefore constitutes possibilities for development, for any individual can now enact teaching practices not available in individual teaching.[1] Because the individual stands in a dialectical relationship with the collective, individual development automatically means collective development, entailing renewed opportunities for individual development. Coteaching *is* colearning, constitutive of individual and collective development (Roth & Boyd, 1999). It is this aspect of learning together that we have always highlighted and why we used the term coteaching rather than teamteaching, focusing on opportunities to teaching through division of labor. This book therefore is about colearning as much as it is about coteaching.

Fundamental to critical psychological and activity theoretic approaches to human activity is the dialectical notion of agency or capacity to act. This concept is dialectical in two linked senses: First, there is a agency|structure dialectic; second, agency never just means that an individual has—always concrete— action possibilities, but that these individual possibilities stand in a dialectical relationship with generalized action possibilities at the collective level. It has been shown that emotionality, rather than being simply an add-on to knowing and learning, is central to the phenomenon of agency (Holzkamp, 1985). Similarly, motivation is not an add-on to human activities, but is a central aspect of the object of activity, which, in our context, assisting children and students to learn. This is so because motivation, the capacity to pursue goals cannot be separated from the content of the goal—I can pursue a goal in motivated manner only then, when it is possible for me to anticipate that in realizing the goal my own possibilities expand and my life conditions improve. Coteaching, which inherently comes with the expansion of action possibilities for the individual that arises from collective activity, therefore also has implications for motivation and emotionality. In a time, when many teachers, especially those working in difficult schools or conditions, consider leaving the profession, providing an institutional structure that allows them to develop emotionally and regain lost motivations has great potential for leading to a renewal of teachers, individually and collectively.

Positive emotionality and motivation are supported and enhanced in coteaching not in the least because individuals no longer are and feel alone, abandoned to cope with difficult, emergent issues on their own. In addition to having available a greater room to maneuver collectively, they also know themselves to be in a situation where they can find consolation during inevitable moments of failure. Not in the least because of the emotional connection, coteaching has possibilities for transcending the isolation and loneliness that many teachers experience in their work.

Overview

In the present volume, we bring together a series of studies conducted on coteaching and with or by coteachers in different parts of the world. All of the studies deepen our understanding of the coteaching and associated cogenerative dialoguing practices, in part because they provide detailed ("thick") descriptions of different arrangements involving a variety of individuals in (dialectically related) coteaching and cogenerative dialoguing practices. The book is divided into three parts: "Theoretical Perspectives," "Coteaching/Cogenerative Dialoguing in Philadelphia," and "Coteaching: Addressing Global Perspectives." The chapters in each part are preceded by brief editorial introductions in which we suggest ways of reading or show strands of similarities and difference between them.

Overview: part I

In the two-chapter part I, theoretical and methodological foundations for studying coteaching and cogenerative dialoguing are introduced. In the first chapter, "Coteaching: from praxis to theory," we (Wolff-Michael Roth and Kenneth Tobin) provide an articulation of some of the major theoretical tenets of our co-teaching approach. We evolved coteaching and cogenerative dialoguing to respond to the need of teachers inexperienced in one or another aspect of teaching to learn to teach at the elbow of another. As our praxis of coteaching and cogenerative dialoguing unfolded, we developed a theoretical framework that afforded continuous expansion of coteaching and cogenerative dialogues and their fine-tuning so that participants could attain an expanding trajectory of goals. In this introduction, we present some core theoretical ideas that go with coteaching and cogenerative dialoguing. These ideas are rooted in our reading of cultural-historical activity theory and critical psychology. The resulting framework is particularly suited for analyzing and theorizing complex practices such as teaching and learning in schools for several reasons. First, it requires us to take a first-person perspective on the actions of individuals and groups. Second, it theorizes actions available to an individual as concrete cases of a generalized action available at the collective level. Third, we understand all actions to be mediated by the tools (language, curriculum theory), rules, community, and division of labor characteristic of the situation. Fourth, because this approach explicitly theorizes context, it is an excellent tool for articulating and removing structural contradictions. Fifth, the approach assists us in understanding the contradictions within a system in a positive way, namely as opportunities for change and growth. Finally, the framework explicitly focuses on the cultural-historical changes that occur for individuals, their community and tools, and the reigning division of labor and rules. In the second chapter, Wolff-Michael Roth provides multilevel analyses to articulate how participants in coteaching are becoming like the other. He focuses in particular on the complementary coverage of space and on the prosodic features of voice in support of the concept of entrainment, which denotes a process by means of which the practices of two or more individuals lock into one another. This chapter lays out a theoretical foundation for explaining why and how coteachers come to practice like the other.

Overview: part II

All studies in the five-chapter part II took place in Philadelphia and were conducted by teachers and graduate students enrolled at the University of Pennsylvania, all of whom had taught or conducted research at the same school to which we refer as City High School (CHS). Over a seven-year period, we not only implemented coteaching at CHS but also conducted an extensive research program at the site. The changing nature of coteaching over this period is provided, in chapter 3, as a background against which the other four studies are to be read. It is also the background against which the earlier chapter 2 is set. In chapter 3, we

(Tobin and Roth) provide descriptions of the changing nature of coteaching and cogenerative dialoguing, as one might expect this to occur in any attempt to implement a practice at a broader level.

Jennifer Beers had begun coteaching during her teacher preparation at the University of Pennsylvania, where she also took her science methods courses from Kenneth Tobin, and participated in our studies on coteaching at CHS. In chapter 4, "Teaching at the elbows of others: The role of coteaching in my development as an urban science teacher," Jennifer provides a mesoscopic analysis of the impact of coteaching on her identity as a teacher and the continuing development of her teaching over the last four years. Using a sociocultural theoretical framework, she explores the coherences and contradictions associated with her participation in two forms of coteaching in two different urban high schools. This chapter draws on autobiographical data from field notes and personal reflections as well as interviews from stakeholders involved in her coteaching arrangements. The research describes Jennifer's initial experiences with learning to teach through coteaching in a team of three teachers and highlights how this arrangement afforded her the agency to begin developing her teaching. The chapter explores how coteaching through collaborative research with students and a university researcher has informed her identity as a teacher and transformed her practices as she became a more effective teacher who taught in ways that were culturally adaptive.

For several years, Sarah-Kate LaVan has conducted research together with Jennifer Beers in the latter's classroom, focusing, among others, on the inclusion of high school students in the evolution of understanding and theory for the purpose of bringing about change in practices. In chapter 5, "Cogenerating culturally and socially adaptive practices," LaVan argues that cogenerative dialogue has become a catalytic force for building "collective responsibility" for classroom events and learning to successfully interact with participants (in this case researchers, teachers, and students) selected because of their social and cultural otherness. Her critical ethnography draws on cultural sociology and the sociology of emotions to examine the catalytic and transformative potential of cogenerative dialogues in high school science classrooms where teachers are learning to teach students who differ from them culturally, socially, and economically. Sarah-Kate analyzes how practices and schema, developed in the field of cogenerative dialogue, can inform the structures of different fields, such as science classrooms, and serve to foster resonances that facilitate positive and productive interactions and communication. Cogenerative dialogues allow participants to develop culturally and socially adaptive practices that can then be enacted in different fields, such as in building more effective learning communities. The questions Sarah-Kate addresses in this chapter are (a) How can cogenerative dialogue allow all stakeholders to take an active role in creating classroom structures which are more conducive to meeting individual and collective goals? and (b) How does participation in cogenerative dialogues with students and coteachers afford structures for the teacher to learn science and how to teach science?

LaVan describes how the stakeholders in a classroom engage in cogenerative dialoguing, where they evolve collective responsibility for the events. Cogenerative dialoguing can therefore be understood as a form of action research, initiated and conducted by all stakeholders, not just coteachers. Beth Wassell takes these ideas further (chapter 6). In "Coteaching as a site for collaborative research," she examines the experiences of two student teachers who cotaught a physics class. Using concepts from cultural sociology as a theoretical lens, she describes the coteachers' practices in four sociocultural fields: coplanning sessions, huddles between participants that took place during class time, debriefing sessions after a lesson was enacted, and formal cogenerative dialogues in which several members of the class community took part. Beth contends that these fields were fostered through the coteaching arrangement and enabled the student teachers to continuously reflect on their practices as they were being enacted. She discusses implications for the coteachers' first year of autonomous teaching that stem from their shared experiences.

In chapter 7, "Exchanging the baton: exploring the *co* in coteaching," Kenneth Tobin examines how coteachers exchange the baton, that is, how they exchange the lead frequently without having to talk about it. Productive coteaching is characterized by synchrony, itself made available and registered unconsciously, through pitch and voice intensity. Smooth handoffs and synchrony are qualitative mesolevel descriptors for what can be observed, whereas pitch and speech intensity are the corresponding descriptors of microlevel processes that bring the mesolevel events about. Tobin contrasts his description of exchanges during productive coteaching with detailed accounts of dysfunctional coteaching, where one or the other teacher does not produce the kind of resources that allow the other to act in an appropriate way. For example, he describes how one teacher "withholds the baton" and keeps on teaching although there are signals that the other teacher has something to contribute; he also describes how one or the other coteacher seizes the baton in a high-energy takeover of the lead role and how the coteachers pursue different agendas. The author concludes that the prosodic features not only are resources that actors use in an unconscious way to signal differences, but also are means for the analyst to document synchrony or the lack thereof.

Overview: part III

The early work on coteaching and cogenerative dialoguing had occurred in our Canadian and Philadelphia sites, the setting for all of the studies in the first two parts of the book. In the four-chapter part III, researchers inspired by this early work report on their efforts of making coteaching work in different parts of the USA (Delaware, Alabama) and abroad (Australia, Ireland). In "Developing wisdom-in-practice through coteaching: a narrative account" (chapter 8), Donna Rigano, Stephen Ritchie, and Trish Bell provide a description of the application of a coteaching model to teaching science inquiry in an Australian elementary classroom. In this study, the authors draw on data sources from the experiences of a classroom teacher and two university-based researchers as they cotaught science lessons to a class of six- and seven-year-old students during a year-long study. In particular, the authors bring into the foreground the experiences of the researcher, who had not previously undertaken a teaching practicum. The authors employ interpretive and self-narrative techniques to demonstrate how coteaching creates opportunities for the development of wisdom-in-practice. As they focus on the particular challenges posed by working with very young students the authors describe how difficulties were addressed and resolved. They also contemplate the potential application of the coteaching model to teacher preparation and professional development in the field of science inquiry teaching. This is the point where Jennifer Beers' study begins.

Chapter 9 ("Coteaching in a science methods course: an apprenticeship model for early induction to the secondary classroom") is also concerned with coteaching as a means of enculturating new teachers into the profession. Charles Eick and Charles Ware investigate the benefits of coteaching in becoming a science teacher, which, as they argue, can begin early in the preservice education program. The approach to coteaching utilizes an apprenticeship model where methods students are peripheral participants in their assigned cooperating teacher's classroom. Methods students learn to teach through a gradual process of observing, assisting, coteaching, and teaching—with most of their time spent in coteaching. They do not coplan with their teachers but follow their teachers' lessons and practice when it is their turn to take the lead role in coteaching. Enacting another's practices can limit methods students' ability to test their preferred teaching style that helps to develop teacher identity. The program requires practices to incorporate a framework of national standards and teaching through inquiry. Learning to teach using this approach requires cooperating teachers who frequently model inquiry-based practice with strong management skills. Following coteaching, dialogue on practice focuses on helping methods students better enact modeled practice. This feedback on their performance is important to them as they need to feel comfortable and competent in technical practice before they can begin to reflect more critically on practice. In this model, cooperating teachers maintain their traditional role of mentor while they continue to teach their chosen curriculum. This arrangement has allowed methods students to spend time and teach in another's classrooms. Time in practice allows student teachers to begin developing their technical and practical teacher knowledge for enacting inquiry-based practice.

In the chapter "Coteaching as an approach to enhance science learning and teaching in primary schools," Colette Murphy and Jim Beggs explore the experiences of student teachers, classroom teachers, science teacher educators, and children in coteaching contexts in Irish primary schools. The model of coteaching adopted enabled student teachers (science specialist), classroom teachers, and university tutors to share expertise and work as equals, without mentoring, supervision or assessment to effect exciting learning opportunities for the children and for each other. Coteachers planned, taught, and evaluated lessons together, and were encouraged to experiment with different learning and teaching approaches. The opportunities for all concerned were many. Students discussed the massive increase in their confidence to teach. They highly valued the more equal relationships they had developed with the teachers and university tutors. The tutors also appreciated the improved relationships with students, the increased dialoguing with both students and classroom teachers about science and the opportunity to reflect more on their own practice. Classroom teachers appreciated the opportunity to reflect in diaries that they kept and greatly valued their own increased confidence in teaching investigative science. A survey of children carried out six months after the student placements evidenced their improved attitudes to school science and showed fewer gender differences. Coteaching constraints included the individual concerns of some students and teachers about their respective roles. The opportunities offered by coteaching arose from processes such as the sharing of expertise, individuals working together with the same objective of enhancing children's science learning, the participation of science teacher educators and the science workshops that took place in the university.

Kathryn Scantlebury is concerned the relationship of gender and socialization during internship. In her chapter "Gender issues in coteaching," she explores the contradictions that arise when teachers, high school and university, experienced and beginning, male and female share the teaching space in high school science classes and university courses focused on learning to teach. Scantlebury describes how coteaching was implemented in the science teacher education program at the University of Delaware and, simultaneously, at one local high school where three teachers (chemistry, coordinated science) cotaught with university interns. It soon became evident that there were problems arising from a variety of factors. Most importantly, the male interns participated in established social networks existing of male teachers, leading to the fact that they had a lot of respect for male cooperating teachers but much less for the female counterpart. Scantlebury uses the concept of respect and lack thereof to explain what has happened at the high school. She concludes that coteaching warrants a particular attention on gender issues because more than the normal, solitary experience, teachers have to work together to make coteaching work. Gender constitutes an important aspect that contributes to the production and reproduction of teachers.

In the epilogue, we (the editors) identify some of the key issues of coteaching articulated in the different chapters. Our discussion is intended to make these issues more salient because we believe that they are of particular interest or suggest particular needs in science educators' work with preservice and in-service teachers.

Notes

1. Scholars who focus on learning often use similar ideas for the asymmetrical relation between a teacher and a student to theorize the opportunities for learning available to the student. In these situations, the salient concept is the *zone of proximal development* (Vygotsky, 1978). In this, the opportunities for learning constituted by collective activity are not articulated. In our work on coteaching, we have frequently had two or more new teachers teach a class without an experienced teacher present. In these situations, we also observed learning and development. A different conceptualization of the zone of proximal development is therefore needed, which focuses on the opportunities arising from activity to all members of a collective. Thus, the zone of proximal development can be viewed as the distance between the possibilities of individuals and the possibilities in collective activity (Engeström, 1987); in collective activity, individuals exceed their potential through immediate cooperation toward realizing general interests (Holzkamp, 1983).

References

Engeström, Y. (1987). *Learning by expanding: An activity-theoretical approach to developmental research.* Helsinki: Orienta-Konsultit.

Holzkamp, K. (1983). *Grundlegung der Psychologie.* Frankfurt: Campus.

Holzkamp, K. (1985). Grundkonzepte der kritischen Psychologie. In AG Gewerkschaftliche Schulung und Lehrerfortbildung (Ed.), *Wi(e)der die Anpassung: Texte der kriti-*

schen Psychologie zu Schule und Erziehung (pp. 13–19). Soltau, Germany: Schulze-Soltau.

Roth, W.-M., & Boyd, N. (1999). Coteaching, as colearning, in practice. *Research in Science Education, 29*, 51–67.

Roth, W.-M., & Tobin, K. (2002). *At the elbow of another: Learning to teach by coteaching*. New York: Peter Lang.

Vygotsky, L. S. (1978). *Mind in society: The development of higher psychological processes*. Cambridge, MA: Harvard University Press.

Part I

THEORETICAL PERSPECTIVES

Introduction: part I

In part I we provide two chapters that lay out the conceptual and empirical framework for the book. In chapter 1 we situate our initial experiences of coteaching in Michael's research in Canada in the early 1990s. From the outset coresponsibility and corespect were central features of coteaching and so too were conversations about the most salient features of the curriculum. In this chapter we show the characteristics of coteaching with analyses of the interactions from selected vignettes from the database of the Canadian coteaching studies. In the first chapter we show how cultural-historical activity theory (Engeström, 1987) is applied to research on coteaching to highlight the salience of historical, social, and cultural perspectives. A key advantage of using cultural-historical activity theory (CHAT) is the importance of identifying and resolving contradictions in a process that leads to the improvement of the activity. Historically, we drew on CHAT after having conducted several years of research on coteaching and cogenerative dialoguing. We did not attempt to artificially graft the theory onto our work. Rather, having developed a practice-based theory—a *praxeology* (Roth, Lawless, & Tobin, 2000)—we found that it was compatible with CHAT, perhaps unsurprisingly, because the latter was evolved to overcome the traditional theory-practice gap.

In the remainder of the chapter we elaborate our theoretical framework to introduce elements such as dialectical relationships between individual and collective, agency and structure, and the importance of collective responsibility. We emphasize the importance of agency in our work, stressing that social change is possible through the agency of participants, who can collectively alter structures and produce new culture, thereby disrupting cycles of reproduction. Our approach presents coteaching and cogenerative dialogues as activities in which participants can learn to teach and enact curricula that are conducive to the learning of students.

In chapter 2 Michael focuses on a theoretical framework that enables him to explore the dialectical relationships between agency and structure in coteaching. In a microanalysis of interactions Michael explores how coteachers position and move their bodies and synchronize their uses of space and time to produce and reproduce coteaching. Michael's methodology is innovative and allows him to explore prosody of speech and show how coteachers become like one another as they teach together. The setting for the empirical part of this chapter is City High, an inner-city school in Philadelphia, where almost all students face economic hardship and are African American. The coteachers have very different social and cultural histories from one another and from the students. Accordingly, the study is very important in exploring how coteachers create productive environments in which they learn to teach from one another and produce forms of teaching that afford the learning of their students. Michael's chapter sets the stage for later chapters in the book, notably those by Sarah-Kate LaVan (chapter 5) and Ken (chapter 7) who use similar theoretical and empirical frameworks.

References

Engeström, Y. (1987). *Learning by expanding: An activity-theoretical approach to developmental research.* Helsinki: Orienta-Konsultit.

Roth, W.-M., Lawless, D., & Tobin, K. (2000). Time to teach: Towards a praxeology of teaching. *Canadian Journal of Education, 25*, 1–15.

1   Coteaching: from praxis to theory

Wolff-Michael Roth and Kenneth Tobin

Coteaching, teaching at another teacher's elbow and taking shared responsibility for all parts of lessons, has become a central aspect of our work on teachers and teaching. Our research has shown that coteaching is a powerful context that provides new opportunities for enhancing student learning and for learning to teach. As part of our work, we developed theory particularly useful in representing the complexities of teaching and learning. In this article, we articulate a theoretical framework that acknowledges the primacy of teaching praxis and places equal value on the structural and agentic aspects of teaching. In this approach, individual human actions derive from the dialectic of agency (the power to act and make conscious choices rather than merely reacting to the context) and (social and material) structure (Sewell, 1992). We begin by providing a narrative description of one coteaching situation.[1]

Coteaching: the practical grounding

Christine, a veteran teacher with twelve years of experience, and Brigitte, a curriculum developer who had previously taught for four years, decided to take collective responsibility for teaching science in the Christine's split fourth- and fifth-grade classroom. The particular unit focused on learning concepts of science and engineering related to material properties, strength, stability, and forces while building bridges, towers, and houses from simple, everyday materials such as paper, straws, glue, pins, and so on. The two had decided to teach together because each was hesitant to teach the unit on her own. Christine, while eager to teach the hands-on child-centered unit, did not feel confident enough to bring the children to learn the science concepts without direct teaching. Brigitte initially did not know the children and felt that she could therefore not make the

best curricular decisions on her own. So they decided to be collectively responsible for teaching the unit.

Assuming collective responsibility meant that they not only planned the
curriculum together but also that they taught together, at each other's elbow so
to speak, rather than dividing up the task so that each would do only what she
felt best able to accomplish. Christine, Brigitte, and Michael (first author) felt
that doing the entire unit together provided each teacher opportunities to learn
from the other, in explicit and implicit ways. Thus, for example, they conducted
whole-class sessions together, each contributing when it appeared opportune and
of benefit to the children. As teaching was enacted each teacher experienced the
actions of the other, and those actions became resources for teaching the students and for learning how to teach. What is learned about teaching might be
beyond conscious awareness; efforts to learn about teaching from the other
might also be conscious and intentional. For example, for a while one teacher
might follow the other, experiencing her interactions with children in small
groups or one-on-one situations, and then, while the children work on their constructions, the same teacher might attempt to teach them by interacting with
them in small groups and one-on-one.

The following episode involves coteaching in a whole-class conversation
that followed a series of tasks in which the children developed techniques for
strengthening materials. The intent of the conversation was to get the children to
talk science and engineering design and, on a collective level, to create a classroom discourse in and about the topic.

Brigitte:	OK, I really liked that technique and Shannon, you used this technique as well especially on your Christmas light strengthening technique, where Shannon hung paper clips along spaghetti and put plasticene at the ends. I am interested in Shannon how you came up with that idea?
Shannon:	I don't know.
Christine:	I really want you to think about that . . . Shannon?
Shannon:	I thought about my house. I got it from my house-
Brigitte:	Sorry, Shannon, I couldn't quite hear that?
Shannon:	I just said where my dad had to climb up the roof to put it on it.
Brigitte:	Um and did you try to do something else besides plasticene at the end, or was that the first thing you used?
Shannon:	The first thing I used.
Christine:	Can I say something? ((Pause. Brigitte nods.)) What I think Brigitte is really getting at is for you to think about what makes you think of things and use it. Actually, go into your brain and think, "What do I think of?" "What am I thinking about?" Because part of this science is not just doing

your thing and doing it, but also is becoming aware of what kinds of
things help you think and what you are thinking about when you are learning and when you are experimenting.

From the beginning of the unit both teachers encouraged the girls in the design of artifacts and in talking science and engineering. Although both teachers
were somewhat hesitant to put girls on the spot when they did not volunteer to
speak, Brigitte directly addressed Shannon while talking about a particular technique she had used. Shannon, as many other girls, attempted to dodge Brigitte's
question about how she came up with the idea by saying, "I don't know." At this
time, Christine, the homeroom teacher, took the next speaking turn. She insisted
that Shannon think about how she came up with the idea for the "Christmas
light-strengthening" technique. Because Shannon responded, Brigitte could re-
enter the conversation and pursue her line of questioning. However, Shannon
provided short, hesitant answers. Christine therefore stepped in to take another
speaking turn, here to explain to the children the approach that they, the teachers, wanted to take to the unit: allowing the children to become reflexively
aware of their own learning.

When we analyze this small excerpt in terms of the heuristics for productive
coteaching developed as part of our project on learning how to teach science in
inner-city schools (Roth & Tobin, 2002), we note that many of our indicators are
present. For example, Christine and Brigitte created space for one another to
contribute to the unfolding conversation, which included the willingness to step
back, actually stepping back, willingness to step forward, and actually stepping
forward. Their interaction and contribution to the lesson was seamless, the lesson seemed orchestrated without a conductor and actions were compensatory
and coordinated. Their coparticipation was reciprocal, which we had described
in terms of playing off one another and passing the baton.

The most striking aspect of the unit was how the two teachers became so
much in tune that they picked up one another's ways of being in the classroom
without actually becoming aware of their similarities until our analyses of videotaped lessons showed striking similarity in their patterns of interacting with the
children and one another. For example, Brigitte was very good at asking productive questions, which allowed children to talk through important and difficult
scientific and engineering-design issues. "Which are the features of your tower
that you can sell me on?" or "Can you find another way of strengthening this
part of your bridge?" were typical of the questions Brigitte asked throughout the
lesson. In contrast, Christine asked questions that allowed students to answer
with "Yes," "No," or with simple fact-like statements and therefore to avoid

dealing with science and engineering concepts. Although Christine made students aware of the "great questions" Brigitte asked, she did not initially ask such questions herself. In the course of the three-month unit, however, Christine's questions became increasingly like those that Brigitte asked.

The learning was not one-sided but reciprocal. For example, Brigitte initially asked questions that Christine thought to be too challenging and risky so that children might avoid answering. In the course of the unit, the questions Brigitte asked and her timing of difficult questions become increasingly like Christine's. Furthermore, even their mannerisms became more and more alike and synchronous: little gestures or ways of moving about the room became common features of both teachers. Slowly and surely Brigitte and Christine came to teach like the other. This, we found in our extensive work on coteaching and cogenerative dialoguing in an urban school in Philadelphia, is yet another indicator of productive coteaching.

Coteaching provided learning opportunities for Christine; these arose because she experienced Brigitte's questioning, for example, which, if she had taught alone, she could not have prepared for and enacted because she was preoccupied with managing the students and the learning environment.

I could have done this unit without Brigitte and I would never be where I'm right now with those kids. And the kids would have never made the bridges they made today, because I just wasn't able to think enough you know. . . . To me the whole process of organizing them, and getting them to do what I was expecting them to do, took so much of my thinking that I wouldn't have had the time to think about the questioning.

That is, collectively Brigitte and Christine were able to organize the classroom *and* ask the kinds of questions that provided increased learning opportunities to the children. At the same time, being there with the other, provided Brigitte and Christine opportunities for experiencing actions that were, at the time, not part of their own range of possibilities.

Central to the unit were regular meetings in which Brigitte and Christine talked with the researcher and sometimes with other teachers and professors who were present in the classroom for one or more lessons. We have come to think about such conversations in the way we organize them as cogenerative dialoguing, because their purpose is to collectively generate a discourse (i.e., [local] theory) about the classroom events and to design changes that the teachers can enact the next time they teach. The critical feature of cogenerative dialoguing is for the participants to create a collective responsibility for action and a shared sense of purpose.

Brigitte:	I am familiar with the content a lot, and I think that the kids come to me about the content.
Christine:	You know what I say– Sometimes I realize that and I say, "Ask Brigitte."
Brigitte:	Yeah, I am the same.
Christine:	Because, I have never done it before. It's not common; I am not as good in it. And usually I have an answer, I just go, "fine"; and sometimes I wonder what she would say about that? I am interested to know and I say, "Go ask her."
Brigitte:	It's part how we set that up. We've been often– you have asked me in front of the kids about some concepts. So there is an atmosphere in and around the content, but I do think that they have adopted us both in different ways.
Christine:	That is true.
Brigitte:	You know that a lot of the cooperative skills that they need in order to make a structure work they come to you for, you know, I can't work this out, like Brittany and Melissa, they know . . .
Christine:	Oh yeah, probably they don't go to you for that.
Brigitte:	No, nothing related to what do you call that . . .
Michael:	Group skills?
Brigitte:	Yeah group skills, collaborative skills. Or like something is wrong and [they] need empathy and sympathy and that sort of thing.
Christine:	Yeah, I wouldn't see that.
Brigitte:	So we have taken different roles with it, which in some ways is a bit artificial. Michael [Roth] and I were talking about this how you know if it wasn't for our collaboration, you would answer those questions, and you would do it in your own ways.

In this conversation, which occurred after about one month of coteaching, Brigitte and Christine articulated the different, complementary roles that they had come to enact in relation to the children's needs. Brigitte had become the subject matter expert: the children came to ask her when they had design problems, and Christine, rather than providing a quick answer or saying "Just fine," sent students who had questions to Brigitte. At the same time, when something went wrong and children needed empathy and sympathy or needed to work through trouble with a peer, they came to Christine or were referred to Christine by Brigitte. What is important to us in the present situation is that the two teachers articulated the different roles as an aspect of classroom life at that moment in their coteaching. As it turned out, coteaching allowed both teachers to increasingly take on the roles previously enacted by one of them. In the end, both equally felt comfortable as content experts and facilitators of group work.

As these episodes show, coteaching is not just a way of going about the everyday work of accomplishing a teacher's task but equally important, it is a way of changing the way one teaches. Coteaching is not about two teachers being in the classroom together to make their job easier but about developing as teachers while teaching, that is, continuously participating in a process of becoming (a better teacher) in the classroom (Roth, 2002). This becoming in the classroom is associated with and defined by an increasing range of actions available to any individual teacher, an increased *room to maneuver* for dealing with the myriad of situations that a teacher faces on a daily basis.

As part of our work, we generate theory that allows us to understand and explain the classroom events that we experience together with the resident coteachers. In our theorizing, we draw on and adapt existing theoretical tools. It turned out that cultural-historical activity theory had available a range of concepts ideally suited to capture the complexity and changing nature of teaching and learning.

Structure of activity: cultural-historical activity theory

Cultural-historical activity theory makes hierarchical distinctions between activity, actions, and operations. (To avoid confusion, the activities that are theorized in activity theory are not the "activities" that often appear in educational discourse. Rather, they are global activities such as farming, schooling, or manufacturing.) Activities, oriented toward motives or objects, are carried out by the community; actions, oriented toward goals, are carried out by individuals or groups; and operations, oriented toward conditions, are carried out routinely and automatically by individuals (Leont'ev, 1978). In the course of individual and collective development, activities can become actions and actions can become operations. For example, for beginning teachers, creating an appropriate learning environment is a specific conscious goal, which they attempt to achieve by engaging in specific (explicit) actions. Experienced teachers no longer have the creation of learning environments as conscious goals; creating and maintaining appropriate learning environments have become implicit in their everyday (routine) enactments of teaching.

Basic elements

Human activity is fundamentally oriented toward objects, is mediated by tools, and results in a tangible outcome. The object typically exists as a vision of the outcome and it is mediated by materials or material conditions, and an understanding of the reigning social and material conditions (Saari & Miettinen,

2001). While teaching, a typical activity, teachers draw on pedagogy and curriculum materials (tools, means of production) to assist students in learning. Their use of tools affords an expansion of the range of actions available for them to mediate the learning of their students. Most importantly, though, the community of participants within which subjects (individuals or groups) are situated always mediates human activity. Thus, the motivation for schooling is at the level of the society, which through this activity guarantees its own reproduction. To understand what Christine and Brigitte do and why they do it, one needs to take into account the societal context.

Each field of activity is characterized by its members, the rules that govern the way in which they interact, and the forms in which labor is divided up among them (Engeström, 1987). Saying that human activity is mediated acknowledges that the relation between any two structural elements of a field of activity (i.e., subject, object, tools, rules, members, and division of labor) is mediated by a third. For example, how a teacher relates to other members in the community, the principal, colleagues, parents, or students is mediated by the rules of conduct that structure the field. Likewise, the roles teachers enact within the community and the hierarchical and collegial relations with the principal and fellow teachers are aspects of the division of labor in society. To provide a final example, Brigitte and Christine did not employ pedagogy and curriculum in an ad hoc fashion; their teaching roles were shaped by being in a particular field and practicing with others. Thus, the teachers' roles were mediated by the field (i.e., consisting of the community, its rules, division of labor, objects, and tools), which gave rise to, and supported, particular pedagogical approaches, here, the child-centered and constructivist curriculum. Of some interest to this paper, for example, is that the pattern of most responses to questions in science being given by male students was not under the sole control of the teachers, or for that matter the students (below we discuss the contributions from teachers and students to the reproduction of inequities in the participation of boys and girls). The potential for mediation can involve interactions between any of the elements that comprise a field of activity or interactions between the elements of intersecting fields.

An interesting aspect of the analysis of productive human activity is that the subjects in the activity do not only produce tangible outcomes that are subsequently reintegrated into the activity system (Marx & Engels, 1970). In the course of realizing the object/motive of an activity, individual subjects produce and reproduce their identities as members of the community. Thus, Brigitte and Christine not only contribute to expanding students' agency (as part of preparing them for participation in the adult world) but they also produced themselves as teachers through the enactment of teaching roles that are experienced by all members of the community (themselves and others). Because students enjoyed the science unit and attained high levels of achievement, Brigitte and Christine also projected themselves as successful teachers, recognized as such by their peers, principal, and parents, and as teachers who are liked by students.

Historical perspective

These basic elements of an activity system and the mediated relations that they bring about are constitutive of a culture. At the same time, because all relations are mediated, each element is necessarily cultural so that it makes little sense to theorize an activity system as independent of culture. An important advance of activity theory was that it emphasized the historical nature of culture and the elements and mediated relations that constitute it such that an activity system is never regarded as fixed, but as an entity that undergoes continuous change. A system in activity theory can only be understood in the context of the historical processes that led to its current state as a transition point for future states. An activity system, that includes coteaching, can best be understood as dynamic, historically and culturally situated practices that are continuously evolving.

An interesting example, elucidated through an historical approach to understanding the events, involved the difficulties Brigitte and Christine faced in implementing a more sex-balanced distribution of the respondents to questions during whole-class conversations. Because of their intent to make the unit appealing and replete with learning opportunities for boys and girls, Brigitte and Christine sought to obtain equal numbers of responses from boys and girls to teacher and student questions raised during whole-class conversations. However, the response ratio favored the boys; some discussions were characterized by approximately twenty responses from boys for every one from a girl.

Brigitte:	So this is the question I have, I have felt uncomfortable in a whole-class setting when there are five boys with their hands up, consciously asking girls. And you know that I do that "Right, Cara what do you think about that?"
Christine:	She is the girl that never gets her hand up.
Brigitte:	I know. But you know my struggle is there is something going on with me about relating to that girl. I feel uncomfortable; I have a real hard time with my wait time. I have to consciously count to five.
Christine:	Sure, I consciously do my three circles around the classroom. One visual circle, two visual circles– That's what I do, three visual circles.
Brigitte:	But I guess my question is, "Is it right to put girls on the spot in front of the class like that?" Or are there other ways to draw them out that they are

more comfortable being drawn out in? . . . Part of it is– what we are talking about is what we value in our teaching. We value kids that have their
hands up. . . .

In this episode, Brigitte talked about her discomfort in asking girls to contribute when they did not raise their hands and when, simultaneously, many boys
eagerly wanted to contribute. Although Christine suggested that she wanted to
encourage more responses from the girls, she did not actually ask more girls to
respond to her questions. Perhaps her reluctance was tacit acceptance of the simultaneous existence of multiple activity systems in which the teacher and students were participants. The students had agency, too, and in their quest for objects associated with campaigning for respect within their peer group,
responding to questions may have been regarded as deleterious. Despite repeated feedback about the sex-biased frequency of responding to questions,
which throughout the unit never became better than two to one in favor of boys,
and despite continued willingness of the coteachers to improve the situation, little changed, at least in the whole-class conversations. When prodded to talk
about the reasons for not involving more girls, both teachers brought up their
experiences as children, when they were embarrassed by a teacher calling on
them to respond although they had not raised their hands to indicate their willingness to contribute. These responses from the teachers were consistent with
their acknowledgment of an activity system having the object of maintaining the
respect of peers while simultaneously participating in an activity with an object
of school learning.

At the same time, there were other circumstances of a cultural-historical nature that mediated the teachers' efforts to attain a balance in responses to questions of males and females. For example, on one occasion, both coteachers made
a strong effort to involve girls and called on them to respond to 33 percent of the
questions. Following that lesson, in a debriefing session, several girls asked,
"Why do you always call on us when we don't want to answer the questions?"
In the groups where there were only boys, the symmetrically opposite questions
were asked, "Why do you call on girls when they don't want to respond and
when there are so many of us who have an answer?" That is, there was a culture
in which boys and girls were accustomed to an asymmetry in responses to questions. When the coteachers made a conscious effort to change their practices, the
children noticed it and indicated their discomfort with the change in their roles.
Their experiences led students to accept as normal the practice of customarily
calling on boys to answer questions in science. Such practice underscores that
changes in a cultural field are more difficult to enact than one participant decid-

ing that changes must occur, even if the person is a teacher. There was a failure to obtain a consensus among all community members for a shared responsibility for obtaining a roughly equal number of responses to questions from males and females. Getting more girls to respond may require fundamental changes of several basic elements of an activity system and the ways in which relations are mediated between pairs of entities. What happened here can be analyzed in terms of contradictions, the removal of which may lead to changes that are collectively sought. Had the coteachers discussed their vision of what might happen and why it should happen with the students, they might have bought into the idea that there is value in responding to questions and the collective responsibility of all students and the coteachers to ensure an equal response distribution with respect to sex.

Contradictions

Brigitte and Christine identified a particular goal for achieving a sex-balanced distribution of responses to questions and therefore to the learning of science. But they did not achieve this goal, possibly because of contradictions that are rooted in their biographical experiences as learners and teachers of science. Brigitte was disinclined to ask girls to respond because she remembered an incident where she had been embarrassed as a second-grade student. She also identified other contradictions such as wanting to wait five seconds before calling on a particular student to answer, but finding it inappropriate to wait that long when several boys eagerly tried to participate. We can think of the situation also in terms of a contradiction in the relation between teachers and students, mediated by the rules of interaction. Whereas the teachers wanted sex-balanced participation as a rule, the boys and girls actually conspired to enact a different rule, which led to boys responding and girls holding back. (Roth [1998b] provided an extensive analysis of the different rules that actually mediated whole-class interactions versus those that the teachers endeavored to apply as goals.) One way of overcoming this would be for the coteachers to set up a cogenerative-dialogue session as we now do in our Philadelphia studies (e.g., Tobin, Roth, & Zimmermann, 2001) with some of the students to discuss the problem, its rationale, and possible collective strategies for a solution.

Contradictions are not inherently bad. In activity theory, which embodies a dialectical method, contradictions (including dilemmas, disturbances, paradoxes, breakdowns, and antinomies) are the driving forces of change and development (Il'enkov, 1977). The identification and understanding of sources of contradictions are central to strategies for change. Contradictions do not always originate where they first appear. Individuals (the subjects in the activity system) may internalize contradictions and accept them as normal (i.e., the contradictions are hegemonic). For example, a current trend in education is for politicians, policy-makers, and administrators to hold teachers accountable for the low achievement of students. This tendency may result in teachers having to engage in special professional development courses or even being fired because of their ineffectiveness. However, the teacher cannot be the sole cause for low student achievement. Factors that might mediate the object of high achievement include a lack of appropriate curriculum resources, tracking, and inadequate physical characteristics of classrooms. However, given an ideology of accountability, teachers often internalize the contradictions, blame themselves, burn out, and ultimately leave education altogether. One of the main goals of the subject-centered methodology of critical psychology is the identification and removal of internalized contradictions.

Subject-centered perspective on agency

Cultural-historical activity theory emerged from an interest in describing and explaining human praxis and the various ways in which it is mediated by the different elements of an activity system. In our view, despite the focus on praxis, cultural-historical activity-theoretic analyses focus more on the structural aspects of praxis. This focus on the structural aspects of human activity is inherent in the way cultural-historical activity theory cuts up reality, in particular in the third-person perspective it takes on the activity system, of which the experiencing subject is but one part. However, human beings act not because of structural aspects in an abstract world (revealed by third-person analysis); rather, they act because of structures as they experience them in their lifeworlds. The subject-centered approach of critical psychology (Holzkamp, 1983) and phenomenology are resources for thinking through praxis from the perspective of the individual. The experienced world of feeling, thinking, sensing, and acting is central to this approach and the results of such a subject-centered human science are therefore not propositions about or classifications of humans but always propositions about experienced, meaningful, and sometimes generalized possibilities and constraints for acting.

Agency and subjectivity

In a critical-psychological approach, human agency is the fundamental starting point of theorizing praxis. This means that humans are not considered to be cultural or psychological dopes who *react* to situations in ways *determined* by the existing conditions, whether environmental or internal. Rather, human agency allows for more than acting in response to given conditions: it allows changes in the conditions. Agency is conceptualized in terms of the potential to act or, in other words, the range of possibilities for acting in particular situations. This range of possibilities constitutes the room to maneuver a practitioner has at a particular point in his or her praxis. Thus, in the course of coteaching with Brigitte, Christine increased her room to maneuver in a curricular sense through her increased competence of asking productive questions that allowed students to learn rather than merely providing rote responses.

The possibilities for action do not exist in and of themselves; rather, they are mediated (rather than determined) by the reigning conditions so that praxis is the outcome of the dialectic between agency and structure (described in terms of cultural-historical activity theory). In a context of coteaching, teachers expand one another's opportunities to act, and hence their agency, by their physical presence and their actions. For example, an explanation Christina gave became a resource for Brigitte, who subsequently used the explanation in her own interactions with students; a question Brigitte asked became a resource to Christina, who used the same or similar questions in future student–teacher interactions. As an explanation or questioning sequence unfolds a coteacher is presented with opportunities for action and can respond by listening, summarizing key points on a chalkboard, or even interrupting to make a clarifying statement or to interpose a question. The expanded opportunities to act are not limited just to the object of affording student learning. Coteachers also have expanded resources to support their learning of how to teach, at a level of being aware and by unconsciously appropriating new ways of teaching. Our experience shows that in coteaching, each of two teachers begins to teach like the other after about two months of coteaching. Increasingly coteachers teach responsively and we see evidence of balance in the spatial and temporal distribution of the teaching resource and of complementarity as teachers afford the learning of students through the use of the expanded resources provided by the presence and actions of the coteaching partner.

Just as coteaching provides added resources to be accessed by the coteachers it also adds resources to support the participation of students. For example, the types of questions asked by Brigitte were not only resources that Christine used, but also they were resources for the children, who used them to ask questions of their peers in whole-class sessions. A decision by coteachers to direct up to 30 percent of the questions to females rather than males can be seen as a redistribution of resources for participation. Students who customarily raise their hands and answer questions may become turn sharks as they compete with others with their hands raised to ensure that they get much the same number of responses as is normal. Similarly, students who are called on to answer but have not raised a hand are presented with an opportunity to comply. But in so doing, they face the consequent reactions of peers and the coteachers or to use the event of being called on to meet their own goals (in any of the activity systems that are pertinent at the time). It is not uncommon in such situations for students to seize the opportunity to disrespect the teacher in front of peers, therefore showing a lack of respect for authority and earning respect from peers who may admire breaches of conformity. Thus, in one situation one of the boys made a remark that diminished the accomplishments of a girl who just had responded to a question without having volunteered. Christine intervened immediately and subsequently brought the issue up for discussion during one of the cogenerative-dialoguing sessions:

We are trying to make a classroom that just encourages positive comments all the time. I mean, who was it that made some weird comment today, Daniel or something? And just instantly that was it, "You shut up kid," and I told him so, in no unclear words, "You don't say those kind of things in our class." So I think that is a kind of positive classroom atmosphere. . . . That's probably why we see Robyn responding more than at the beginning of the year, because she knows that nobody is jumping at her for stupidity.

In this situation, Christine was able to intervene before any damage was done to the self-esteem of the girl.

Individual and collective

When groups of individuals work under the same conditions, they can experience what others do and therefore emulate such actions in situations that are experienced as similar. Let us take Brigitte and Christine as an example. The year before they taught the science and engineering unit together, Christine had taught one part of the same unit. The advantages of coteaching were readily apparent when she compared the accomplishments of the children in this classroom with the accomplishments of children from the previous year. She attributed the more advanced learning during the present year to Brigitte's productive use of questions.

There is no question, I was really becoming aware of the kinds of questions [I asked]. And I was trying to use her words because I needed to put it into my being. I needed to practice what I had seen and heard before it was part of me. You know, now it has become much more part of me. . . . After watching Brigitte, I just improved dramatically. I realized that I was going nowhere fast, and I wasn't helping these kids at all with the kinds of questions.

This appears to be an example of a change in teaching that was intentional and conscious. Teaching together with Brigitte allowed Christine to experience productive questioning in specific contexts and to consciously make efforts to ask questions of the same type and in the same manner as Brigitte asked questions. Christine was aware of changes. However, the changes in questioning no doubt involved many facets beyond Christine's threshold of awareness. At a micro level of analysis we notice similarities in the frequency of posing questions, the places at which questions tend to be asked, the manner of phrasing questions, pacing, intonation, and facial expression. So when Christine claimed to ask questions like Brigitte, she is much more like Brigitte than she is actually aware. Furthermore, Brigitte also was becoming like Christine in myriad ways, some of which are conscious and intended and others of which are unconscious and unintended. By teaching together, the two teachers expanded their identities through cooperation directed toward the establishment of collective, general goals and interests (Holzkamp, 1983) and, in so doing, expanded the resources for learning how to teach while focusing mostly on improving the learning of their students.

In activity-theoretic terms, the changes in the (e.g., questioning) practices observed in both Brigitte and Christine while coteaching are attributable to a zone of proximal development arising from the increased resources, emanating from the teaching of the other, and the manner in which all actions support the unfolding teaching of both coteachers. That is, new possibilities for acting and learning arise whenever teachers teach together, thereby creating more (collective) room to maneuver and expanding the agency for all participants in the field.

This perspective on collective activity suggests that we would anticipate expanded learning opportunities for all coteachers even when they are all new (beginning) teachers or when the collective includes new and long-time teachers. This is just what we showed in a series of more than a dozen studies that involved different groupings. Thus, for example, a thirty-year veteran biology teacher learned more about genetics and teaching genetics while coteaching a unit with an intern (Tobin, Roth, & Zimmermann, 2001); two interns significantly improved their teaching while coteaching together (Roth & Tobin, 2002); and two professors learned content and pedagogical content knowledge in biology while coteaching with an intern and a regular teacher (Roth, Tobin, Zimmermann, Bryant, & Davis, 2002).

Collective responsibility

Building *collective responsibility* for the events in the classroom has become perhaps the most important and central aspect of enacting and talking about praxis in coteaching. In teaching the unit together, Brigitte and Christine each contributed to the collective responsibility for student learning, that is, expanding the students' agency with respect to talking and enacting engineering design. The two always complemented one another. When Brigitte saw that Christine's questions did not provide maximum support for student learning, she stepped forward and asked a few excellent questions then and there. Similarly, when Christine saw that Brigitte's questions pushed students too hard, thereby discouraging them, she stepped forward, interposed what she considered to be pertinent questions, and thereby expanded the learning opportunities for students. That is, both teachers acted with individual responsibility; a concrete realization of a collective responsibility to afford the learning of the students. In the following episode, Christine provides a recollection of one situation in which she had believed that Brigitte's questioning was potentially interfering with the learning of a student identified as learning disabled within the school system.

So bridges were being built, a toothpick bridge was built, a straight bar of tooth picks, popsicle sticks, straight across about this ((gestures about twenty centimeters)) wide with a couple of braces taped around it, more than one layer of popsicle sticks, it spanned a gap about this ((gestures about twenty centimeters)) big. One made it in about five minutes. He is somewhat low achieving, well really low achieving. . . . He made this thing, and what Brigitte and I have been working together on is to try to ask questions to pull out more, from the kids; you always wind up pull out more. Brigitte had asked him some questions and he had changed something underneath to make it stronger and I sort of came in and didn't know what she had talked about, and she was trying to get him to think about building a top on the bridge, and, because I knew the kid better than Brigitte did, I wanted to stop, because I thought this was enough for that kid. I thought he had done this magnificent thing, I didn't think he should do another thing to it, he is really proud of it. It carried weight, that's what we asked them to make it to do. It just needed to stop then. I probably could judge that way quicker because I know the kid so much better than you do.

Coteachers who see that something in the situation that could or should be improved immediately go about making required changes. Rather than sitting back and after the lesson talking about it or, worse, blaming the other for making mistakes, coteachers who enact their part of the collective responsibility do what can be done to improve the situation then and there.

Making the changes necessary to enact one's part of collective responsibility does not necessarily come easy. For example, in one of our projects, we taught a lesson in biology. We had planned two investigative tasks for this ninety-minute period, but because we allowed students more time to complete the first task, we made a quick decision to use the time remaining for reviewing and extending some core concepts of the ongoing unit. As it happened, the only transparency sheet available was full of writing and needed to be cleaned. (This is one of the contradictions found in urban schools: the tools for teaching exist in limited amounts or not at all. Teachers often internalize this contradiction and feel personally responsible for the lack of means and purchase materials out of their own pockets.) There was therefore a time lag while the four teachers and the class waited for the student who was cleaning the transparency to return. During the subsequent cogenerative-dialoguing session, Ken (second author) asked the lead teacher at the time why she had permitted such a lengthy transition between the two parts of the lesson. She immediately defended her actions and accepted blame. However, when we subsequently talked about the situation again, we realized that Ken, who noted that there was something wrong and that time was wasted, could have stepped forward to use the time productively. It would have been consistent with collective responsibility for Ken to immediately address the situation and use the time to further the students learning of biology.

Agency and change

Teachers often do not recognize or realize their personal agency by understanding their actions are shaped by the unfolding circumstances in a given field. They resign themselves to reacting to the conditions imposed from the outside, constraints they see as imposed by the principal, school board, or ministry of education. Such resignation, whatever its sources, necessarily means that an individual looks at situations in ways that are too general and global to see his or her own possibilities for action and alternative determinants of particular outcomes. The individual teacher's room to maneuver thereby becomes limited and restricted. For example, the teachers at the school where Brigitte and Christine taught their lessons, and elsewhere in the British Columbia, felt constrained in their actions by the prescribed learning outcomes outlined by the provincial government in the *Integrated Resources Packages* (IRPs). The learning objective and examples provided by the ministry, such as those included in Figure 1.1, constrain teachers such that doing well on an item such as "the teacher looks for evidence that descriptions are accurate, detailed, and uses scientific language with precision" (Figure 1.1) becomes the primary motivation. Thus, rather than teaching a unit in which children explore the properties of a variety of natural and synthetic materials by building bridges, towers, and other structures, many of Christine's peers at Mountain Elementary used to teach in ways so that their students "used scientific language with precision." Rather than allowing students to develop a discourse based in their experience, they told students definitions that they wanted them to memorize and repeat on a test. Many teachers felt they could not follow the recommendations of recent research with a constructivist orientation because of fears that they would not attain the prescribed outcomes, such as "students create a Venn diagram to compare and contrast natural and synthetic materials" (Figure 1.1). Their room to maneuver was mediated by the presence of the prescribed learning outcomes, in effect reducing what they felt they could do. During their coteaching experience, Christine learned from Brigitte how to ask questions so that students were enabled to show the required skills and knowledge in the context of student interests and needs (Roth, 1998b).

In our work on coteaching in inner-city schools in Philadelphia, we extended the idea of collaboration to students—participating in the collective determination of what goes on in the classroom allows students greater control over their individual conditions rather than reacting, they actively change conditions. The underlying idea is that collaborating on the creation of functional learning environments expands the action possibilities of teachers *and* students and thereby gives them greater individual control over their life conditions by contributing to the collective control over life conditions of the group.

The dialectic approach inherent in our coteaching method does not advocate change efforts where researchers infuse abstract recommendations for change that are subsequently implemented by teachers. Our very purpose for coteaching, particularly for the associated cogenerative dialoguing, lies in its potential for enlarging the *subjective* possibilities and therefore the range of *concrete actions* available to the teachers to make changes in the situation as they see it. Cogenerative dialoguing produces recommendations for concrete actions and change that teachers experience as an opening of their possibilities rather than recommendations that they know to be "possible only in theory but not in praxis." A dialectical approach depicts the current state of an activity system as a possibility space for its own transformations. Change is usually not a radical and revolutionary process but a (slow) historical evolution of the possibility spaces experienced by practitioners. This is why research that exhorts teachers to act very differently than they currently do has only limited prospects of success. Coteaching and cogenerative dialoguing, however, have great potential because learning occurs explicitly *and* implicitly and change occurs to the extent

Prescribed Learning Outcome
It is expected that students will:
- distinguish between natural and synthetic materials;
- identify some unique properties of synthetic materials that are useful to society; and
- compare the environmental impacts of using natural and synthetic materials.

Suggested Assessment Strategies
Context
Students can demonstrate their knowledge of synthetic and natural materials through a variety of written and hands-on activities. They demonstrate their ability to apply scientific skills and processes when they identify attributes and classify materials, examine consequences of using synthetic and natural materials, develop environmentally friendly options, and conduct surveys.

Skills and Processes
Students work independently or with a partner to examine a collection of natural and synthetic materials that have not previously been discussed in class. They are required to:
- describe the properties of each material
- classify the materials according to potential use
- explain how the properties of the materials make them useful to society
- The teacher looks for evidence that descriptions are accurate, detailed, and use scientific language with precision; that categories are logical; and that the explanations are logical and consistent with the descriptions.

Knowledge
- Students create a Venn diagram to compare and contrast natural and synthetic materials that could be used for the same function. (The teacher may wish to restrict this activity to materials that have not previously been discussed in class.) Criteria could include specificity, number of points of comparison, and inclusion of unique properties that make synthetics useful.

Figure 1.1. An excerpt from the Integrated Resource Package *for the fifth-grade physical science unit (http://www.bced.gov.bc.ca/irp/sciencek7/5phymat.htm) in the province of British Columbia.*

that participants are comfortable. The zone of proximal development that exists because of collective action provides a much greater space for change than would exist if teachers attempted change on their own.

Change is often difficult because it is associated with anxieties that derive partly from the extension of one's possibilities truncating an existing state of relative agency together with the proven means for coping with the demands of life (Holzkamp, 1983). Any attempt to improve one's quality of life is always linked to insecurities, such as whether the envisioned new level of agency and new possibilities can actually be attained. In this situation, support can be experienced when change is envisioned in and as a cooperative effort. The success of our coteaching experience has likely come from the support that any one of us experienced as part of collaboration. Coteaching and cogenerative dialoguing constitute a practice and mechanism that mediate the insecurity that comes with change and even with prospects of change. Other possibilities arise because the move from individual teaching to coteaching constitutes a radical change in the conditions of teaching, which open up a space for continuous teacher development to occur in a context that participants experience as safe because the responsibilities are both collective and shared.

Contradictions, change, and expansive learning

In the perspective advocated here, learning to teach is synonymous with changing participation in activity that arises from increasing control over one's life conditions through an expansion of the possibilities for acting. Learning to teach, therefore, is in some sense inherently expansive. Because of the relation of individual and society, each new possibility of acting at the individual level is also an expansion of action possibilities at a collective level. Engeström (1987) reserves the notion "expansive learning" for the outcome of changes at the collective level, that is, learning as a change of the activity system.

An important driver for learning and change are the contradictions that exist in an activity system. From the perspective of the individual subject, the expansion of action possibilities and agency are mediated by the ability to find the location and removal of contradictions. This is an important step in working toward changes because higher order contradictions, such as poverty in an affluent society, can become internalized by and understood as contradictions at a lower level, such as low achievement of a particular student. Addressing the contradictions at the lower level, while sometimes being able to deal with the symptoms does not address the root of existing problems. For example, teacher burnout is usually dealt with at the individual level—a teacher takes time off, receives counseling or other (e.g., pharmaceutical) treatment, or quits. Thus, rather than seeking to identify the contradictions at a systemic level, which could yield a lowering of teacher burnout across a system, the costs have to be borne by the individual. Instead of yielding an expansion in the range of actions available to the individual teacher, the traditional approaches to burnout are various means to mitigate the effects of contradictions rather than the removal of them. At the same time, the recognition of systemic higher-order contradictions sometimes leads to the articulation of new actions that remove the contradictions and systematically eliminates some problem.

At Mountain Elementary School where Brigitte and Christine taught, science teaching at the school improved not because individuals took more university courses or workshops but as a result of identifying and removing some central contradictions that interfered with student learning. Although the teachers had tried in the past to bring about changes in science teaching in the school as a whole, all attempts had failed. Some of the problems identified included limited access to resources for science teaching; lack of science content knowledge and pedagogical content knowledge for teaching particular units; lack of equipment for teaching science; limited budget to purchase new equipment or supplies; lack of understanding of and approaches to sex-related issues; and lack of time to prepare a class which, because of its short duration, does not warrant the amount of preparation time needed. Above all, budgetary constraints were constructed as a major impediment to reform. The engineering design curriculum responded to these budgetary constraints because it made use of everyday materials and scraps that were procured from a variety of sources; it also provided teachers with release time for observing other science classes and planning curriculum. Coteaching (involving Brigitte or Michael) not only was a temporary response to the lack of content and pedagogical content knowledge but also provided learning opportunities that brought about changes in the level of science teaching across the entire school. Christine did not just improve in her own teaching but also fostered the learning of other teachers in the school by becoming the science coordinator and facilitator of others. Other teachers in this school came to her class to coteach and in the process to expand their own possibilities for teaching science. Here, the teachers' collective effort removed systemic contradictions, with the result that science teaching improved throughout the school. Rather than focusing on shortcomings in the science teaching of one or the other individuals, the collective approach addressed a widespread problem in a systematic way.

To bring about change, the subject of the activity system (individual or group) therefore needs to better understand the structure of the activity system in order to appropriately locate the contradictions that are limiting productivity, that is, for teachers, the learning of students. Coteaching provides the conditions in which expansive, collective learning can occur. At the core of both approaches is the fundamental assumption that expansive learning and institutional change occur more easily when the subjects constitutive of the activity system begin to collectively articulate and remove existing, structural contradictions.

Together with cogenerative dialoguing, coteaching provides teachers (and students if teachers involve them) with opportunities to create new possibilities for concrete action and change.

Coteaching has considerable potential for bringing about changes of praxis. Rather than spending great amounts of money on workshops, which often bring about little change as the research on science teaching over the past four decades has shown, fewer resources are needed to hire competent science teachers to coteach with regular classroom teachers. In our experience, three months of coteaching can lead to striking changes in individual classrooms and across a school (Roth & Tobin, 2002). The theoretical perspectives articulated in this paper have the advantage over others that exist in the literature in that they start with the premise of agency as a fundamental characteristic, which allows teachers (as all humans) to change their life conditions rather than merely react to them. This perspective is more positive than the somewhat pessimistic perspective often associated with viewing schools as agents in the reproduction of an inequitable society (e.g., Bourdieu & Passeron, 1979). Coteaching and cogenerative dialoguing are appropriate vehicles and practices to change the often deplorable conditions under which learning and teaching currently occur—such as in the inner-city schools where part of our coteaching work is situated.

Notes

1. In this study, we primarily draw on data collected over a three-month period in split fourth- and fifth-grade classroom. Over this period of time, each lesson was videotaped with two cameras; children's artifacts were photographed and their notebooks photocopied. After each lesson, the two teachers and the principal investigator, Michael Roth, debriefed the lessons; these debriefing sessions intended to make sense of and plan change to the classroom environment were also videotaped. Two research assistants collected additional data, including interviews with other staff and the principal, conducted an ethnography of the site. At times, the two teachers analyzed videotapes from their own classrooms in sessions that were also attended by other individuals, for example, teachers from the same and other schools or university-based researchers. Detailed information on data collection and interpretation processes may be found in Roth (1998a).

The first author, Michael Roth, had been teaching with Christine prior to Brigitte's arrival, as he had done subsequently with other teachers in the same school. However, because Brigitte had designed the science curriculum, a decision was made to have her coteach with Christine, whereas Michael was responsible for data collection. The second author, Ken Tobin, was responsible for the teacher training and research at the University of Pennsylvania mentioned in this article. Both authors cotaught with teachers in one Philadelphia high school. This research, too, is based on an intensive database including videotapes of classroom and cogenerative-dialogue sessions, ethnographic descriptions, and interviews with students, teachers, and coordinators. For a description of the database and the interpretive methods used see, for example, one of our articles coauthored with a preservice teacher, a practicing teacher, and a student (Roth, Tobin, Zimmermann, Bryant, & Davis, 2002).

References

Bourdieu, P., & Passeron, J.-C. (1979). *Reproduction in education, society and culture.* Thousand Oaks, CA: Sage.

Engeström, Y. (1987) *Learning by expanding: An activity-theoretical approach to developmental research.* Helsinki: Orienta-Konsultit.

Holzkamp, K. (1983). *Grundlegung der Psychologie.* Frankfurt: Campus.

Il'enkov, E. (1977). *Dialectical logic: Essays in its history and theory.* Moscow: Progress.

Leont'ev, A. N. (1978). *Activity, consciousness and personality.* Englewood Cliffs, NJ: Prentice Hall.

Marx, K., & Engels, F. (1970). *The German ideology.* New York: International.

Roth, W.-M. (1998a). *Designing communities.* Dordrecht, The Netherlands: Kluwer Academic Publishers.

Roth, W.-M. (1998b). Science teaching as knowledgeability: A case study of knowing and learning during coteaching. *Science Education, 82*, 357–377.

Roth, W.-M. (2002). *Being and becoming in the classroom.* Westport, CT: Ablex.

Roth, W.-M., Lawless, D., & Masciotra, D. (2001). Spielraum and teaching. *Curriculum Inquiry, 31*, 183–207.

Roth, W.-M., Masciotra, D., & Boyd, N. (1999). Becoming-in-the-classroom: A case study of teacher development through coteaching. *Teaching and Teacher Education, 17*, 771–784.

Roth, W.-M., & Tobin, K. G. (2002). *At the elbow of another: Learning to teach by coteaching.* New York: Peter Lang.

Roth, W.-M., Tobin, K., Zimmermann, A., Bryant, N., & Davis, C. (2002). Lessons on/from the dihybrid cross: An activity theoretical study of learning in coteaching, *Journal of Research in Science Teaching, 39*, 253–282.

Saari, E., & Miettinen, R. (2001). Dynamics of change in research work: Constructing a new research area in a research group. *Science, Technology, & Human Values, 26*, 300–321.

Sewell, W. H. (1992). A theory of structure: Duality, agency and transformation. *American Journal of Sociology, 98*, 1–29.

Tobin, K., Roth, W.-M., & Zimmermann, A. (2001). Learning to teach science in urban schools. *Journal of Research in Science Teaching, 38*, 941–964.

2   Becoming like the other

Wolff-Michael Roth

People who spend time together begin to experience the world in similar ways, coming in fact to share the world. Just a few days ago, my wife and I walked through downtown Victoria to pick up a stereo amplifier from the repair shop when I noticed her head move slightly left to right. I turned my head in the direction of her gaze, and, before we began talking, I knew she was alerting me to the aboriginal people sitting against the wall asking for dimes, with faces ravaged by alcohol abuse. In fact, she was alerting me to the plight of the First Nations people in our country, their fight for self-government, and their battle against alcohol. Seconds later, we talked about just that. That is, without having talked, a simple movement of her eyes while gazing in a particular direction had communicated to me what she was presently attuned to. While walking on, I thought about what had happened. I remembered many such incidences that had occurred between my younger brother and me during a period when we had spent a lot of time together. A little movement of the hand toward the forehead by one of us allowed the other to see a person with a particular, funny haircut or hat; a slight turn of the eyes upward toward the ceiling made salient to the other of some voice that we began to overhear together.

Coming to experience the world in similar ways, or rather, coming to experience a similar world is not unique to members of the same family. A decade of research showed that people who coteach come to perceive their settings in similar ways, and they tend to act like the other. Initially, our observations were incidental: while analyzing videotapes of coteaching in the early 1990s, participating teachers, researchers, and research assistants noticed that a hand gesture by one teacher was seemingly taken up by the other; a particular stance toward the children while a teacher interacted with a small group was noticeable in the behavior of the other. However, ways of asking questions became the first phenomenon that allowed us to provide more than hunches. Extracting the questions the two coteachers in chapter 1 asked over the course of nearly three months of coteaching showed that in the beginning of the engineering unit, their ways of questioning children were rather different. Brigitte, who had a developed the curriculum asked productive questions that allowed children to articulate and develop their engineering discourse. Her partner Christine, on the other hand, who had little science and engineering background knowledge, initially asked questions that the children answered with yes, no, or other one-word responses. The analyses showed that over the three-month period, Christine came to ask questions like Brigitte.

Over a period of years of conducting research on coteaching at City High School in Philadelphia, a school serving an almost exclusively African-American clientele, Ken Tobin and I began to notice other ways in which coteachers become like the other. An initially plain and somewhat lethargic new teacher increasingly began to bounce about in the way that his coteacher did; intonations of one teacher came to be more like those of the other. However, although we had this strong sense of patterns in coteaching, it was difficult to communicate it to others, particularly in the written medium of scholarly publications. Mere description was unsatisfactory evidence, both to myself and to reviewers of articles submitted for publication—that is, until recently when new digital recording technology made it possible to convert video images into high-quality offprints and new software allowed rendering voice qualities such as pitch, loudness, and aspects of timbre in visual form.

In this chapter, I draw on such technological advances to depict aspects of coteaching that are not normally accessible to the consciousness of the participants, and that are insufficiently rendered by qualitative descriptions. Detailed analyses of alignments that occur at an unconscious level allow me to contribute to the building of a theory that explains why and how coteaching makes us become like the other, at least in those cases where the participants are inclined to work together and do not experience "conflicts of personality."

Production and reproduction of practice

Theoretically, my research is grounded in an agency|structure dialectic (Sewell, 1992), which implies that neither agency nor structure can be thought without the other: they are two sides of the same coin. Without action, neither the surrounding world nor our patterned ways of perceiving could exist; but a structured world and structured perception are required to act in patterned ways. A structured world and a structured perception coemerge with active engagement in the initially unstructured material world (Giddens, 1984). That is, structure itself is dialectical, existing both in the form of the sociomaterial world and in the schema (mental structures) that allow us to perceive the world in structured ways. Again, active engagement with the material world is required for both types of structures to emerge. To clearly distinguish the two forms of structures, schema, associated with the acting subject, are distinguished from the sociomaterial resources, associated with the setting.

This approach leads us to a dynamic model of practice, whereby engaging in teaching science, for example, inherently is linked not only to the reproduction of the practice but to the production of new forms and therefore its very change. At the outset, the fact that each action simultaneously constitutes both cultural production and reproduction may surprise—and some scholars may state this as a mantra rather than articulating the reasons for the phenomenon. Take, however, the phenomenon of lining up—in a bank, at a local supermarket, or at a movie box office. When you arrive, some people are already aligned in a way that you recognize as a line. You act by joining it at its end, although the end of the line may be very different from one situation to the next—if you do not go to the "end," you may be held accountable for it by others, or hear their comments about your rude behavior. In your act, however, you not only contribute to constituting the line, a form of cultural production, but you also engage in the reproduction of lining up qua cultural phenomenon. The dialectical nature of cultural production and reproduction is a direct consequence of the fact that human beings not just act in and react to a stable social world, but that their own actions produce this world. Lines do not exist as such; they only exist in the practical realization of lines, which requires competence in the relevant ethnomethods (e.g., Garfinkel, 2002).

Inherent in the dialectic of the production and reproduction of social phenomena (structure) is the fact that each act not only reproduces the world but also produces new variants of it, at the levels of sociomaterial resources and schema. On the one hand, this explains the drift in sociomaterial (cultural) practices over time; on the other hand, this explains how in each action, a practitioner not only changes his or her setting (conditions) but also him- or herself (Lave, 1993). Even though these changes may be unnoticeable from one moment to the next, they are cumulative so that changes in a practice can be observed over longer time spans. This allows us to understand how people become experts even with respect to the most mundane practice, through apparently, but never truly repetitive actions.

Because of the complexity of classrooms, coming to the point of reliably reproducing coteaching will take participating teachers and students some time. In our experience, more or less smooth transitions between different teachers can be observed after two months of teaching together about an hour a day. At that point, the coparticipants seemed to have come to the point that their antici-pations of their coteachers' next actions have become sufficiently accurate to make coteaching unfold in the smooth ways that our research has documented.

To understand a practice such as coteaching, one needs to take into account three mutually constitutive, that is, dialectically related, levels of activity to which the acting subject is simultaneously oriented: activity, action, and opera-tion (Leont'ev, 1978). Activity is oriented to collective (societal) motives; ac-tions are driven by goals, which the subject (individual, group) sets as part of its own concrete realization (version) of the collective activity; and operations are spontaneous, unconscious responses to existing conditions. Activity and action are dialectically related, because series of actions constitute the activity but ac-tivity motivates the selection of conscious actions and their sequencing. Simi-larly, a particular action motivates a sequence of operations, but the concrete op-erations concretely realize the action. These relations are important for understanding coteaching, because they link common orientation and motiva-tion, which are phenomena at the level of activity, with the embodied, uncon-scious operations that constitute the actions of the practitioner.

Entrainment and complementarity

It had been suggested that the alignment of practices occurred by means of the homogenization of dispositions, which operates when different individuals are exposed to the same conditions (Bourdieu, 1997). This explanation, however, is unsatisfactory because it separates the acting subject from its setting—in a dia-lectical approach, the acting subject (individual or collective) is a constitutive part of the setting. This leads to the fact that practitioners not only find them-selves in some conditions but also contribute actively to the constitution of the conditions. When the subject is a collective entity, such as coteachers and their students, each individual also constitutes part of the setting for all other indi-viduals. The actions of any individual contribute not only toward producing the lesson, which therefore emerges as a product of the enacted curriculum, but also to the constitution of the setting.

In coteaching, individual teachers therefore contribute not only to the con-stitution of the setting as they experience it but also to the setting experienced by their fellow teacher(s). When they have a common orientation and motivation, the actions of coteachers eventually become complementary. Temporal and spa-tial alignment of (simultaneous or sequential) actions is required so that the ac-tions of different coteaching individuals do not interfere with respect to achieving some common goal. Sociologists and social psychologists use the concept of entrainment (borrowed from physics and biology) to describe the processes by means of which temporal alignments in the actions of coparticipants come about (Giddens, 1987). Entrainment describes a process whereby two rhythmic processes interact with each other in such a way that they adjust toward and eventually lock in to a common phase or periodicity. The temporal patterns of individuals who are in interaction become mutually entrained to one another, that is, that they get in synchrony of phase and period. The actions of the members of a collective thereby become complementary. There is preliminary evidence, for example, that in certain situations the periodic rhythms of speech continue across boundaries of turns at talk—in other words, a speaker may conform to the speech rhythms of the preceding speaker (e.g., Auer, Couper-Kuhlen, & Müller, 1999).

It has been noted that African-American youths share particular traits, including harmony between humans, rhythm, an emphasis on emotions, and social connectedness (Allen & Boykin, 1992). We might therefore hypothesize that successful teachers of African-American students, that is, teachers who are "in tune" or "in sync" with the particular ways of being of these students, will (probably unconsciously) adjust different aspects of their prosody to be aligned with characteristic features of their students' prosody. Or rather, we might expect that harmony and social connectedness of teachers and students is expressed in and leads to entrainment at the level of speech, including prosody. When new teachers work with more experienced and successful teachers of African-American students, particularly when they are from a different cultural background, becoming like the other would mean that they become entrained into the existing harmonic relations between cooperating teacher and students.

The current object of talk, group size (e.g., small group, whole-class), and spatial arrangements mediate the nature of classroom interactions (Roth, McGinn, Woszczyna, & Boutonné, 1999). Thus, in whole-class, teacher-led situations, there is a general spatial orientation, often to the chalkboard, and a topical orientation to the issues usually controlled by the teacher with characteristic effects on who talks, when, about what, who responds, who evaluates, and so forth. When two or more coteachers conduct a whole-class session, they cannot all talk simultaneously and over stretches of time. Furthermore, because such whole-class teacher-led sessions are related to particular spatial configurations in which teachers take up particular positions with respect to chalkboard and class, we can therefore expect interactions between current teacher in the lead, his or her position, and the nature of the unfolding talk. In fact, we may hypothesize that there will be changes in the positions coteachers take up, even unconsciously, to allow their mutual participation in the interaction with the class. That is, entrainment would be produced and expressed in the complementary positions with respect to the physical and metaphorical spaces during interactions between teachers and the whole class.

In the remainder of this chapter, I provide evidence for and discuss forms of entrainment in two aspects—the complementary use of space, which inherently involves temporal alignments, and the adjustments that occur at the prosodic level.

Context

The materials for the following analyses derive from research conducted in an urban school in the American northeast. City High School is attended mostly by African-American students from families living in poverty or representing the working class. Two teachers who participated in our research for some time, and with whom we also published together, were Cristobal Carambo and Chris Dalland. Cristobal is a Cuban-African-American teacher who, after several years of teaching in Miami, had come to City High School. Although he initially experienced difficulties due to cultural differences between the students in the Miami and Philadelphia situations, he had become an effective and, by students well-liked teacher. Chris, a new teacher of Italian-American origin, was currently enrolled in a teacher education program, consisting of a one-year practicum that ran concurrent with the university coursework.

Both teachers had viewed their coteaching experience very positively. Chris in particular felt very much accepted by Cristobal. In recollecting the one-year experience, Chris described himself as having been very timid about teaching and building rapport with the students at the outset and thought that he would not be able to learn to teach the students at City High School. But in the course of coteaching with Cristobal, he had developed self-confidence and a sense of competence with respect to general and subject matter-specific pedagogy. Chris attributed much of it to coteaching: "Cristobal would often be teaching and look to me to step in, and always give me an opening, whether or not I had something to say. There were times that I had nothing to add, but he would look to pass it off to me and I would say, 'I don't have anything.' Having that opening several times a day allowed me to feel comfortable that when I did have something to say I could take it from him."

The data used in this chapter derive from the beginning of one lesson, where Chris and Cristobal first reviewed some subject matter content related to experiments for which they then, thereby constituting the second part of the introduction to the lesson, provided specific instructions.

Spatial coordination of actions

Individuals who participated in coteaching for some time come to cover space in the classroom in similar ways, which they exhibit even when they subsequently teach alone. This, I want to suggest, is the product of a process of entrainment into complementary coverage of space during coteaching. In a previous study, we provided evidence for three scenarios of how successful coteaching covers space in complementary ways (Roth, Tobin, Carambo, & Dalland, in press). (a) One person teaches alone, the other person in the wings, away from center stage where his or her actions could detract from those of the other. (b) The second person comes onto center stage, adding in talk or writing to the resources in a "helping" function without interfering with the actions of the other; he or she moves off center stage when the actions have been completed. (c) During transitions, one person moves off, the other onto center stage. If the stage is occupied but the end of the speaking turn has apparently not yet arrived, the second person moves off stage again. In the following, I focus on the micro level events in the second case, in which both teachers are in the front of the classroom where they can draw on the chalkboard as a resource to make note, capture the attention of the students, and, as recent research shows, have greater control over the discourse than if they were standing somewhere else (Roth, McGinn, Woszczyna, & Boutonné, 1999).

At the outset of this episode, Cristobal had stood to the front and side of the classroom, near the edge of the chalkboard. Chris was center stage, preparing students for the upcoming laboratory. One of the questions to be answered by students on the instruction sheet was, "Are chemicals elements or compounds?" Chris had previously told students that he and Cristobal wanted to practice note-taking skills in the laboratory, and, in preparation, wanted them to respond to the question. After several students had called out both "elements" and "compounds," Chris asked the student Ron to repeat what had said earlier, but what had been drowned in the general cacophony of responses. As the students talked, Cristobal had moved to the chalkboard and begun to record students' responses (offprint a). Chris continued to interact with the students, and Cristobal wrote a long note that covered the chalkboard to the right-hand side (offprint b).[1]

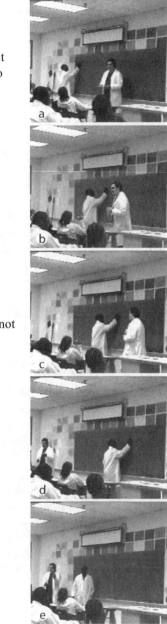

01 Chris: [a] Can you say this louder, Ron?
02 Ron: Compounds, there are two different
             substances chemically combined to
             form one.

03   [b] (1.87)
04 Chris: Chemicals are compou[::nds.
05 Joe: [They don't
             need none of them.
06   (1.48)

07 Chris: [c] Right.
08   (1.29)
09 Bill: No, it's not=
10 Chris: =Well no no that's not true, that's not
             true. They combine to form other
             chemicals, other compounds.

11   [d] (0.20)
12   ↑Right?
13   (0.52)
14   But you *ca::n't* ha:ve
15   (0.36)
16   you know
17   (0.39)

18   liquid copper.
19   (0.81)
             ((Looks toward Cristobal, who is
             writing "Cu" on the chalkboard.))
20   [e]↑Right?
21   (0.18)
22   It's a metal.

23   (1.31)
24   Things like that right.
25   (0.52)
26   So you ha::v:e
27   (0.20)
28   *co:*pper [f]

29   (0.20)
30   with some othe:r elements
31   (0.96)
32   [g] for instance...

As he wrote, Cristobal increasingly moved in on Chris, whose physical space became limited, as he had backed off until he was touching the teacher's desk (offprint c). At this point, Chris began to cross to the other side of the classroom where, because Cristobal was moving to the opposite side, there was room for Chris to stand whereas Cristobal could continue to move to the right (offprint d). Cristobal eventually finished his note and began to back off again in the direction of the space that he usually took up (offprint e). But in backing off, he came closer and closer to Chris, who again seemed to sense a lack of space, so that he, too, crossed over toward the position that he had initially occupied (offprint f). Cristobal stopped at the edge of the chalkboard, ready to contribute to the unfolding whole-class conversation or to note on the chalkboard when appropriate, while Chris continued talking to the students about the upcoming laboratory experiments (offprint g).

In this episode, the two coteachers moved in physical space. Their movements, however, were not independent. Rather, their movements were coordinated in space and time. As the supporting coteacher Cristobal moved toward the central position in front of the classroom to produce additional meaning-making resources by writing on the board, he exchanged preferred positions with the current lead teacher, who thereby made space for the actions of the other. Once the action of writing on the chalkboard was completed, the supporting teacher moved back to his preferred position, entraining the counter movement by the lead teacher. Or rather, his backing off can be seen as producing space in the central location to be taken up by the lead teacher. At this point in their work, the transitions were usually seamless and required little or no conscious attention, especially after the two had worked together for several months. At that time, the two seamlessly used the available space in the classroom in synchronized but complementary ways.

We can understand this situation as one of the microprocesses that both produce and are the result of entrainment. Chris' movement to the other side of the front of the classroom was occasioned as Cristobal encroached on his physical space. His movement not only provided more space for himself but also produced space for the coteacher. At the same time, Cristobal not only moved toward Chris, encroaching on his space, but he actively took up the space that became available as Chris crossed over. By moving in a coordinated fashion, both coteachers produced the phenomenon of entrainment as much as entrainment produced the coordination of their actions.

While Chris was interacting with the students, Cristobal captured the essence of what was said in notes on the chalkboard (see offprints in transcript). These notes were not only for the benefit of the students, but also for the actions of both coteachers. More specifically regarding the enculturation of new teachers, these notes became resources for Chris that he could deploy in his subsequent actions. For example, in turns 14–18, Chris had said, "you can't have liquid copper." As soon as the first opportunity arose, immediately following the episode, Cristobal asked a question that led the class to discuss the possibility of liquids consisting entirely of an element. Students suggested that copper, for example, could be melted, a fact that Cristobal recorded on the chalkboard (Figure 2.1). Just as this discussion ended, Chris looked toward the notes (Figure 2.1a) and began to state, "What I said before is not exactly true," and continued to articulate a more appropriate statement about the relation between liquids and solids, on the one hand, and mixtures, elements, and compounds, on the other. While he summarized, he slightly turned to his right (Figure 2.1b), pointed toward the symbol of copper sulphate ($CuSO_4$), and uttered in reference to liquids, "most of one's we're dealing with are solutions."

In this situation, the question Cristobal had asked and the conversation that followed allowed Chris to realize that his earlier comment that there are no liquid elements was incorrect. Near what became the end of this part of the conversation, Chris looked toward the notes, which allowed him to perceive the record of what had preceded. He used this as an occasion for alerting students to the incorrectness of his earlier statement and in summarizing the result of the discussion. That is, by using these resources, originally produced by Cristobal, his actions also took on aspects that one would have attributed at the outset of the

Figure 2.1. By drawing on the resources they mutually produce for one another, coteachers become also become entrained in their subject matter-related practices (content, pedagogy).

lesson to his partner only. Using the resources provided by his more experienced peer, Chris was actually entrained into using the resources at hand. Consistent with the dialectical approach taken here, the reverse is also the case. Cristobal would become entrained into acting in ways initially more characteristic of Chris or, for that matter, any other coteaching individual. That is, their mutual use of semiotic resources produced during teaching also produced entrainment into the ways of teaching and using particular resources.

In the above transcript, there are other features that we know from our database to have their origin in the coteaching experience. For example, Chris began to say "right" in particular circumstances in a way that Cristobal has done. Among other ways of using the word, the particular of interest here was always preceded and followed by pauses (turns 11–13, 19–21). Furthermore, there was a characteristic change in the pitch and even speech volume. In the past, we could only describe our sense. The recent availability of special software now allows us to represent characteristics of spoken language in a form that can be standardized across observers without having to go through face-to-face training and collaboration. In the next section, I focus on prosodic aspects that illustrate yet another level in which coteaching constituted a context for the entrainment of speech practices.

Prosodic coordination

Science educators have shown interest in classroom language since the publication of *Talking Science* (Lemke, 1990). However, their concerns have largely been with meanings or concepts presupposed to lie behind the words. There has been little interest in exploring the way in which language is used to produce and reproduce alignments and differences along the lines of gender, social class, or culture. To produce such differences, we need to investigate how language and associated features—such as manual and vocal gestures—are used in situation and thereby achieve certain effects. Prosody, for example, is a vocal gesture that speakers use (unconsciously) to signal, among other things, emotions, emotional intensity, disagreement, and alignment (e.g., Goodwin, 2000). Given the central importance of emotion and social connectedness in the culture of African-American students such as those who attend City High School, it should be of interest to science educators how prosody mediates talk in classroom interactions, on the one hand, and how new teachers, especially those working in cultural milieus different from their own, accommodate to existing patterns of interaction, on the other hand. Here, I focus on two aspects in which Chris was becoming like Cristobal. First, in the course of their coteaching experience, Chris developed certain features in his talk that were like those characteristic of Cristobal, including the verbal production of "right" and "really, really" with a particular pitch contour and pausing. Second, in the course of working with Cristobal in the classroom, Chris became entrained to align the pitch of his talk with students and his fellow teacher.

Production and reproduction of ways of talking

Twice in the episode, Chris made an assertion, paused, apparently sought affirmation from the class saying "right" with a rising inflection, followed by another, usually shorter pause. Figure 2.2 depicts the waveform, sound intensity, and pitch for this pattern of speaking at another moment during this lesson. The waveform and intensity graphs show the significant separation of the word "right" from the previous and subsequent words "colder" and "heat," respectively. The intensity graph shows that at peak height, there utterance was more than 19 decibels stronger than the background (every 3 decibels means a doubling of intensity), so that, together with the surrounding pauses, the utterance explosively imposed itself. Finally, the pitch rose by nearly 50 Hertz, first steeply then leveling off.

All of these features created a characteristic pattern, which we had found in Cristobal's teaching for many years. For example, Figure 2.3 exhibits a com-

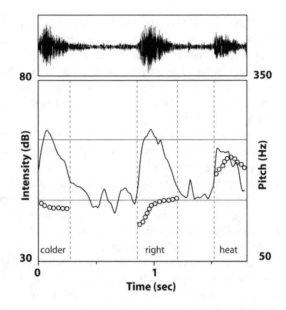

Figure 2.2. Waveform (top), intensity (—), and pitch (OOO) surrounding the articulation of "right," which Chris has developed while coteaching with Cristobal who had displayed this pattern prior to the collaboration.

parison between the ways in which Cristobal (top) and Chris (bottom) uttered this form of "right" also during this lesson. In both instances—though a little less so for Chris—the pitch contour took the characteristic shape of increasing rapidly and to level off, distinct separation of the utterance from the surrounding utterances, and the volume against background noise. Throughout this study it was apparent that Chris had appropriated a similar way of teaching and exhorting students to think about what was asserted. In fact, students also adopted this style, evidence that it is not only coteachers who become like each other by co-participating in the same situations. There are mediating circumstances that can change the particular form of an utterance, such as requirements for adjusting the pitch to previous speakers. I return to this phenomenon in the next subsection.

This form of "right" was different from its other uses. In turn 7, pauses preceded and succeeded the utterance. But these pauses were much longer than those surrounding the target utterance, there were no assertions on either end, and the pitch did not significantly change (184–188 Hz). (This was actually the pitch range at which the student had talked before. More about this phenomenon of pitch matching later.) The function of the utterance was to signal agreement with the preceding student statement (turn 5), an agreement that was revoked soon thereafter (1.29 seconds). (The pitch on "well no no" rose from 217 to 279 Hz, characteristic for statements of contradiction [Goodwin, 2000].) In turn 24, there was no change in pitch from "that" to "right" or within the utterance of the sound (108–110 Hz).

Another speaking pattern that Chris adopted from Cristobal in the course of their coteaching experience was the expression "really, really." This expression was used as a way of giving particular emphasis to some relevant feature in the situation. Thus, in the present discussion concerning the question "What happens if you heat a copper penny?" At one point, Chris said, "You have to heat it, I think it's like three thousand degrees or something really, really high." Less than two minutes later, Cristobal explained how to make the flame of a welding torch "really really hot." Figure 2.4 depicts speech intensity and pitch for both instances. In both cases, we observe the characteristically curved contour of "really, really" followed by a sudden rise in pitch during the utterance of the modified predicate, "hot" and "high," respectively. The figure also shows that the predicate was distinct from the surrounding volume either by being preceded (Cristobal) or by raising the intensity considerably above that of the preceding intensifier "really, really" (Chris).

In both instances—"right" and "really really"—the matching feature was pitch contour. A pitch contour is a melodic movement of the pitch that can be heard as a coherent whole. Analyses of pitch contour matching showed that it is the most frequent occurrence of prosodic matching (Szczepek, 2001). Such matching can, but does not have to, signal agreement or mutual orientation. The present examples also show matching to occur at relative speech volume. Furthermore, in the present situation, the speaking turns were actually separate. In fact, similar prosody was observed even when Chris was teaching by himself. The question one might ask is, "How did Chris become entrained into these patterns of speaking?" Here, being a participant in talk in interaction, that is, being part of interaction sequences may provide some clues.

Production and reproduction of pitch continuity

Pitch, pitch contours, and rhythm are periodic features, which are fundamental to the phenomenon of entrainment. Thus, when one speaker uses a certain pitch, pitch contour, or speech rhythm, theories of social entrainment predict the subsequent speaker to "chime in," at least in situations of agreement, and perhaps to differ in situations of disagreement (e.g., Goodwin, Goodwin, & Yaeger-Dror,

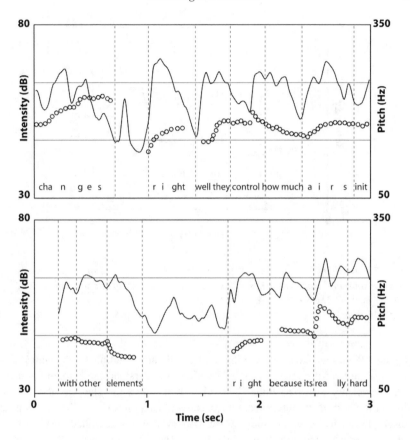

Figure 2.3. Intensity (—) and pitch (OOO) comparison of the use of "right" by Cristo-bal (top) and Chris (bottom), showing the similarity of the two contours.

2002) or lack of (cultural) attunement. Prosodic orientation may create a bridge between two turns that could not be achieved by verbal means alone. They also signal solidarity and a common mood (Damasio, 1999).

In his interactions with the students, both within and between lessons, Cristobal always seems to find the "right tone" with students whatever the situation. An analysis of pitch in consecutive turns shows that Cristobal matches prosodic features, including loudness and pitch to the preceding turn produced by a student. An example of such matching is provided in Figure 2.5, pertaining to the

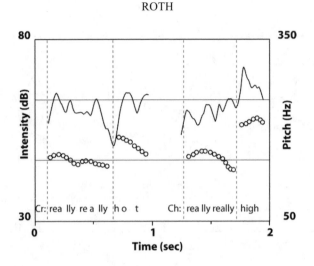

Figure 2.4. Intensity (—) and pitch (OOO) comparison of the use of "really, really" by Cristobal (left) and Chris (right), who had developed this way of talking while coteaching with the former. The similarity in the contours and subsequent step to the emphasized word is striking.

conversation about the relative hotness of candle and welding-torch flames. Following a student utterance, Cristobal queried to understand the student contribution, "When we did the candle?" (Readers will notice the characteristic rise in pitch at the end of the utterance, which is heard as a question.) Cristobal's pitch before the rise had been around 180 Hz. However, the student had answered at a much lower level, moving from 110 to 130 Hz. The plot shows that when he continued after the student, Cristobal (unconsciously) first matched his own pitch to that of the student before returning to his own preferred pitch level. Furthermore, the intensity levels show a similar pattern. The student had responded speaking with a much softer voice, which Cristobal matched before returning to a higher frequency.

Figure 2.5 also provides an example of the interaction between Chris and a student during the interaction about heating a penny. The student suggested that holding the penny in the flame for a long time would lead to a different result. The pitch plot shows that Chris matched the student's pitch both during the overlapping word "right" (a continuer, that is, an indication by the listener that he or she is listening, while indicating that the speaker may continue) and in the subsequent response, where Chris suggested that the flame has a temperature

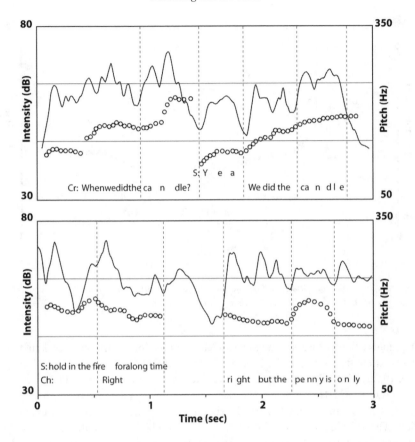

Figure 2.5. Chris (bottom) came to match students' pitch levels in overlapping and subsequent turns similar to Cristobal (top).

and however long one holds the penny, it will not exceed the temperature of the flame. Pertaining to the intensity, he picked up at about the mean of intensity for the last four words.

Here, both teachers matched volume and pitch to the levels of the preceding student. This matching contrasted, for example, the earlier mentioned rapid rise in pitch when Chris changed from an initial agreement with a statement to a disagreement. That is, the sudden rise in pitch signals an opposition between two ideas. Cristobal and, following him, Chris showed a preference for pitch match-

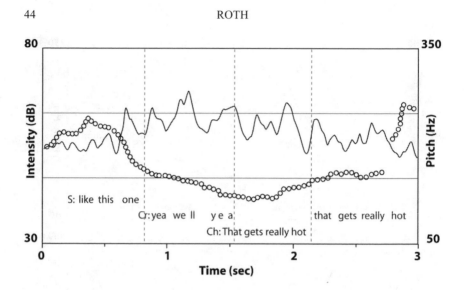

Figure 2.6. Pitch matching in turn sequences across multiple sometimes overlapping speaking turns involving the two teachers and one student.

ing unless they expressed displeasure and opposition to the current situation. Thus, at the beginning of the lesson, Cristobal called the class to order, "Excuse me! (0.20) Hey!" In this utterance, the pitch rose from about 90 Hz on "ex" to from 290 to 315 Hz on "cuse," to drop descending contour from 105 to 95 Hz. The pitch then rose from 137 to 215 Hz on "me," which is heard as an exclamation. The subsequent "Hey!" rose from 275 to 348 Hz. In both situations, the high pitch compared to Cristobal's normal pitch level between 150 and 180 Hz signaled disapproval.

A final example for the fact that Chris was becoming like Cristobal can be seen from the fact that in turns involving both and some students, the pitches were matched such as to constitute a continuity. Thus, in the multi speaker turn displayed in Figure 2.6, Cristobal initially matched the absolute pitch level of the previous student speaker. Chris, slightly overlapping with Cristobal, matched his pitch to that of his peer, who in turn matched his pitch to that of Chris. Although speakers are seldom aware of the absolute or relative pitch levels of their talk—because of resonance phenomena, we do not hear our own pitch in the same way we hear that of other speakers—matching pitches is a way to signal and produce emotional alignment and therefore solidarity.

In this situation, we observe prosodic complementation as a form producing and achieving alignment in collaborative action. A first speaker (Cristobal) has produced a contour that in itself is complete, but we might expect it to be followed by a particular contour from the next speaker. Both contributions constitute complete turns (Figure 2.6). However, although the first participant's turn signaled turn completion prosodically, syntactically, and pragmatically—Cristobal has agreed with the student, ending on a descending pitch—the second contour complemented the first both in content (semantically) and prosodically, so that the two together formed a prosodic pair. Furthermore, when Cristobal chimed in again, he confirmed the content of Chris' utterance by repeating it, and signaled and produced alignment and agreement by continuing the pitch contour. Discord and difference, on the other hand, would have been indicated and produced by producing significant pitch differences with the previous speaker (e.g., Goodwin, Goodwin, & Yaeger-Dror, 2002).

Mimesis and entrainment

In this chapter, I am concerned with the question of how coteachers, in the course of weeks and months of working together, come to resemble one another. At the outset one might assume that practices are acquired by means of a process of imitation, which, since antiquity, has been discussed under the label of *mimesis*. Here, I first suggest that mimesis may not be the main (or only) process that explains why and how coteachers become like the other and then propose the concept of entrainment as a viable and productive alternative.

Mimesis

The assumption that teachers learn to teach by a process of mimesis appears to be inherent in teacher education programs that require university students, as part of their practicum, to sit in the lessons of (more) experienced teachers and observe before actually planning some lessons and teaching courses themselves. In this way, beginning teachers are to learn about the enacted practices and, by imitating them, to get a head start in their own development as teachers. Mimesis alone, however, does not constitute a good, sufficient, or satisfactory explanation for the phenomenon of becoming like the other. If mimesis was the explanation, then new teachers could become like their mentors or cooperating teachers by sitting in the back of the classroom, watching what the more experienced colleague is doing. This, however, usually does not happen. New teachers do not develop practices by watching other teachers. In fact, our entire research program concerning coteaching at City High School, which included the requirement that supervisors, methods teachers, and researchers coteach, was in part driven by our understanding that watching others teach does not allow us to understand teaching from the perspective of the teacher. Thus, if mimesis indeed occurs, it seems to require the common orientation on the part of the coteachers toward the motive of activity and goal of current actions.

Concerned with the production and reproduction of practices, a mimetic relation between field and disposition has been proposed such that mimesis produces congruence between dispositions and field (Bourdieu, 1980). In the present study, Cristobal, the students, and the school would constitute the field to which Chris adapts so that his dispositions come to be like Cristobal's. Mimesis here would occur when a set of dispositions (Chris') copy those that are embodied in the field. This perspective is problematic, however, because the field is taken as stable and the dispositions (Chris') as malleable. The notion of disposition implies disposition for perception, so that the field itself undergoes continuous change from the perspective of the newcomer. The concept and process of entrainment helps us out of this theoretical dilemma.

Entrainment

At the outset, I suggested that entrainment might be at the heart of the phenomenon of becoming like the other that we have described at a mesolevel in previous research on coteaching (e.g., chapter 1). The concept of entrainment is due to the Dutch physicist Christian Huygens, who observed, while working on the design of the pendulum clock, that two pendulums hung near one another on the same wall eventually ended up swinging at the same rate though they may initially have swung at different rates. This entrainment is due to their mutual influence on one another. Such a perspective of mutual influence and entrainment is more consistent with our observation that not only teachers new to a situation adapt to a classroom, becoming like the other teacher, but also that teachers with many years of experience become entrained in the practices of novice teachers. Furthermore, we observed that the practices of the classroom as a whole, teachers and students included, tended to change with the arrivals of other teachers. For any actor, other individuals constitute part of the field; thus, entrainment constitutes, in contrast to the previously elaborated perspective, not merely a mimetic adjustment of a newcomer to the field, but in fact entails the mutual adjustment of field and person. In this way, enculturation entails changes not only in the newcomer, who becomes like other practitioners by adapting, as they did, to the field, but also changes to the culture itself. Such a dynamic view of mutually constitutive changes also explains the production of novel forms of cultural practices that accompanies the cultural reproduction through enculturation of new members. This, however, does not yet provide an answer to how coteachers become like the other through entrainment. That is, we still need to answer the question, "How does entrainment operate?"

To answer this question, we need to understand that coteaching is both a practice, produced in my actions, and a context, produced by the actions of my partner. It is a phenomenon that arises from participants' actions that constitute it such that it can be recognized as a phenomenon. Because there is the possibility of acting in ways that interfere with the smooth unfolding of coteaching, it is, like all social phenomena, fragile. It is fragile in the sense that if one of my actions is not in the spirit of coteaching, it does not produce and reproduce coteaching, and the situation goes awry, as it has been reported in one recent study of coteaching (Tobin, Zurbano, Ford, & Carambo, 2003). That is, smooth coteaching continuously has to be produced and reproduced in coteaching, which makes the mutual actions of the participants dependent on one another.

In the present chapter, I provide evidence for the production and reproduction of complementary actions on the parts of both coteachers. Thus, as Cristobal moved into the physical space that Chris currently occupied, the latter moved to the opposite side of the classroom. As Cristobal relinquished the space by backing off, he both moved into Chris' current space and released his partner's preferred space. Simultaneously, Chris released and moved into the available physical spaces. Here, the actions of the two coteachers were aligned in space and time, as each coteacher smoothly adjusted to the requirements of the other and made available resources. The coteachers enacted responsibility both for their own and the actions of others and therefore solidarity. Further evidence for mutuality and solidarity was observed at the prosodic level. First, I showed how Chris not only had come to use particular phrases ("Right?", "really, really") but also had come to employ the same pitch contours. Both Cristobal and Chris normally also aligned their absolute pitch with that of the preceding speaker (student or the respective other), so that there was a continuation and completion in pitch lines.

Both the mutual production and taking of space and the alignment of pitch to produce continuation and completion of pitch contours and lines shows that the individual coteacher was not and could not act completely independently of the other or the students. That is, when a coteacher produces and signals harmony (see chapter 8), shared emotions, and social connectedness, he does not act out of his own volition. Rather, actions arise from the dialectical relation of the individual and the setting, that is, the dialectical relation between schema and sociomaterial resources. The alignment and dialectical relation does not occur within independent movements, but involves itself a level of "foresight." In other words, a coteacher has to recognize intentional projections into the future such that his own actions are consistent with and harmonically linked to those that are currently in progress but have not yet ended.

Foresight is characteristic of praxis—such as when (a) jazz musicians get together for a jam session and, though they improvise, play in harmony, (b) athletes join and immediately play for a new team, or (c) researchers smoothly participate in coteaching in a school where they had not taught before. Foresight is based in practical understanding, which may but does not have to exist in a form that can be articulated in so many words (Heidegger, 1977). This practical understanding and therefore the capacity of foresight is produced and reproduced at the very same moment that a coteacher contributes to the ongoing events. Our actions do not leave us unchanged, but, while making a change in the setting, that is, in the sociomaterial resources available for subsequent actions, existing schema are changed, however slightly this might be. If this was not the case, we would not be able to explain how apparently repetitive actions, such as hammering a nail, could lead to the hammering expertise observable in carpenters or masons. In a similar way, teachers change their practices by teaching such that being in the classroom also means becoming in the classroom (Roth, 2002). Thus, we learn to teach by teaching even if we do not coteach. But in coteaching, the presence and actions of the other teacher constitute constraints that lead, by means of entrainment, to a more rapid adjustment to successful practices.

I assume that entrainment—a microlevel process—occurs when and because there is a common or compatible orientation toward existing motives of activity (historically grounded, and therefore macrolevel) and goals (mesolevel). This is so because any moment of praxis constitutes a unit in which activity, action, and operation stand in a dialectical relationship. Contradictions on the inside of this unit constitute forces that encourage movement and change. When coteachers do not experience "personality conflicts" at a conscious level, that is, when their motives and goals are aligned, any differences arising from unaligned or misaligned operations will eventually disappear as new actions, emerging from the dialectic of schema and external sociomaterial resources, not only reproduce themselves but also produce increasing adjustments. On the other hand, when coteachers experience "personality conflicts," their goals are not aligned and they realize different motives. In this context, their practices will not align at the unconscious level, for, to extent the pendulum metaphor applies, they do not share the wall or are mounted too far apart on the same wall to allow and produce entrainment.

Coda

My research on coteaching had begun with the chance observation that teachers come to resemble one another in their actions when they work together in the same classroom pursuing the same goals and concretely realizing the same collective motives. Initially, I favored the explanation that working under the same conditions, that is, finding oneself in the same field, would allow novice practitioners to become like another through processes that I introduced here as mimesis and adaptation. However, in the course of my research, it became clear to me that mimesis and adaptation could not be the main processes. Although they explain well how cultures are reproduced and how new practitioners are enculturated, they do not explain cultural renewal and change. The dialectical concept of (mutual) entrainment, however, does explain both reproduction and production of (classroom) culture, and therefore provides a dynamic explanation of practices such as teaching in general and coteaching in particular. It has provided me with a way of explaining a phenomenon, which I have known on a descriptive level for more than a decade.

The phenomenon of entrainment fundamentally involves time. Not only is speech constituted by period phenomena and unfolds in time, it also has to be coordinated with the speech of others, inherently requiring a synchronization of actions, even in the case when interacting persons disagree or find themselves in discord. Persons, who speak at the same pitch level, produce the same pitch contours, or use the same rhythm, have coordinated their own actions with those of others. In addition, spatial coordination, as shown, also requires temporal coordination in making and taking up the space for the other. This is true not only for coteachers but also for the relation between students and teachers. It is therefore not surprising to find that coteachers adopt other rhythmic features, such as in their gates or use of gestures, and to align themselves with other aspects of behavior (speech). Future research might be designed to focus on other temporal aspects involved in teaching and in the alignment of teaching practices.

Notes

1. The following transcription conventions have been used: (0.41) : time in seconds; [d] : letter in square brackets marks the moment corresponding to a particular offprint; = : equal sign shows latching, that is, two utterances are not separated by the normal pause; .,?! : punctuation is used to indicate speech features, such as rising intonation heard as a question, or falling intonation to indicate the end of an idea unit (sentence); – : the n-dash indicates stop in utterance without voice inflection indicating end of idea unit; ↑ : up ar-

row marks rising pitch; *can't* – italicized phonemes are emphasized; ((Looks)) – double parentheses enclose transcriber's comments, such as actions.

References

Allen, B. A., & Boykin, A. W. (1992). African American children and the educational process: Alleviating cultural discontinuity through prescriptive pedagogy. *School Psychology Review, 21*, 586–596.

Auer, P., Couper-Kuhlen, E., & Müller, F. (1999). *Language in time: The rhythm and tempo of spoken interaction.* New York: Oxford University Press.

Bourdieu, P. (1980). *Le sens pratique.* Paris: Les Éditions de Minuit.

Bourdieu, P. (1997). *Méditations pascaliennes.* Paris: Seuil.

Damasio, A. R. (1999). *The feeling of what happens: Body and emotion in the making of consciousness.* San Diego, CA: Harcourt.

Garfinkel, H. (2002). *Ethnomethodology's program: Working out Durkheim's aphorism.* Lanham, MD: Rowman & Littlefield.

Giddens, A. (1984). *The constitution of society: Outline of a theory of structuration.* Cambridge, UK: Polity.

Giddens, A. (1987). *Social theory and modern sociology.* Stanford, CA: Stanford University Press.

Goodwin, C. (2000). Action and embodiment within situated human interaction. *Journal of Pragmatics, 32*, 1489–1522.

Goodwin, C., Goodwin, M. H., & Yaeger-Dror M. (2002). Multi-modality in girls' game disputes. *Journal of Pragmatics, 34*, 1621–1649.

Heidegger, M. (1977). *Sein und Zeit.* Tübingen, Germany: Max Niemeyer.

Lave, J. (1993). The practice of learning. In S. Chaiklin & J. Lave (Eds.), *Understanding practice: Perspectives on activity and context* (pp. 3–32). Cambridge, UK: Cambridge University Press.

Lemke, J. L. (1990). *Talking science: Language, learning and values.* Norwood, NJ: Ablex.

Leont'ev, A. N. (1978). *Activity, consciousness and personality.* Englewood Cliffs, NJ: Prentice Hall.

Roth, W.-M. (2002). *Being and becoming in the classroom.* Westport, CT: Ablex.

Roth, W.-M., McGinn, M. K., Woszczyna, C., & Boutonné, S. (1999). Differential participation during science conversations: The interaction of focal artifacts, social configuration, and physical arrangements. *Journal of the Learning Sciences, 8*, 293–347.

Roth, W.-M., Tobin, K., Carambo, C., & Dalland, C. (in press). Coordination in coteaching: Producing alignment in real time. *Science Education.*

Sewell, W. H. (1992). A theory of structure: Duality, agency and transformation. *American Journal of Sociology, 98*, 1–29.

Szczepek, B. (2001). Prosodic orientation in spoken interaction. *Interaction and Linguistic Structures, 27*. http://www.uni-potsdam.de/u/inlist/issues/27/index.htm. Accessed February 20, 2004.

Tobin, K., Zurbano, R., Ford, A., & Carambo, C. (2003). Learning to teach through coteaching and cogenerative dialogue. *Cybernetics & Human Knowing, 10*(2), 51–73.

Part II

COTEACHING/COGENERATIVE DIALOGUING IN PHILADELPHIA

Introduction: part II

"Those were the heady days . . ." is the beginning of many a story about different times, often remembered with a little sadness because they have long gone past. Although some of our experiments in coteaching and cogenerative dialoguing have their origin in the early 1990s, when Wolff-Michael Roth and a few elementary teachers began teaching together and learning from one another, the experience at the University of Pennsylvania and some of the nearby high schools constituted the first efforts to implement coteaching on a larger scale.

An important but little used concept in Guba and Lincoln's (1989) *Fourth Generation Evaluation* is the question about the extent to which ethnographic descriptions and explanatory concepts transfer to a different situation and therefore, to some extent, are generalizable. As part of the early work on coteaching, and focusing more on students' learning, it was felt that ethnography needed to expand its horizon by testing transferability of its concepts and descriptions. Thus, "much like confirmatory factor analysis, 'confirmatory ethnography' sets out to test whether constructs derived in one situation adequately model phenomena in another" (McGinn, Roth, Boutonné, & Woszczyna, 1995, p. 172). The chapters in this section have sufficient aspects in common so that they can be read and understood from the perspective of qualitative research efforts that seek to work in the way "confirmatory ethnography" had been described. Such work is facilitated when the following conditions are met: (a) two or more team members have participated in the earlier study and thus knew both contexts, a precondition for all replication attempts in naturalistic research; (b) thick description exist for the initial context in the form of extensive video- and field note-based data corpus; and (c) new team members bring different perspectives which help to guard against confirmatory bias (Lincoln & Guba, 1985). Although each new researcher to a site brings his or her own perspective, all the researchers who contribute to this section have in common their commitment to the same theoretical framework; that is, all studies in this section not only focus on or arose from the work done in the same high school, but also they are grounded in cultural sociology and cultural historical approaches to knowing and learning.

In chapter 3, Ken Tobin and Wolff-Michael Roth provide their view on how coteaching unfolded over the seven-year span that it was practiced at the main site. This chapter provides the perspectives of the same researchers on different classrooms and different coteaching arrangements with different students over time in the same school. It provides a background description against which all other chapters in this section as well as the chapter 2 (Roth) can be read as figures. This chapter is also interesting given that it reflects not only changes in coteaching as the practice unfolded at City High School, but also constitutes a historical reconstruction of research that has undergone change.

The new teachers who worked with us at City High School eventually graduated, some taking positions in the school but most getting jobs in other schools of the same or different districts. Jennifer Beers is one of those learned to teach by coteaching at City High and then moved to Urban Charter High School. There she implemented the practice of cogenerative dialoguing with students in the attempt to establish a classroom climate that supports learning. Her perspective helps us to see and understand the trajectory of new teachers through an internship and beyond. Sarah-Kate LaVan has, metaphorically speaking, accompanied Jennifer and researched her efforts in establishing herself as a regular teacher in the new school. By drawing on microanalyses that use pitch levels and contours as indicators of emotion and on the sociology of emotion, Sarah-Kate brings new methodological and theoretical tools to the study of coteaching and cogenerative dialoguing. Such changes in methodology, as Wolff-Michael Roth showed in chapter 2, allow new phenomena to be seen and articulated.

Beth Wassell also conducted her research at City High School. Her chapter therefore can be read and understood as a different interpretive perspective on coteaching and cogenerative dialoguing at the same site where Tobin and Roth have conducted their research. Drawing on mesolevel analyses, she takes a look at one particular coteaching configuration that has not been researched before and therefore brings one of those perspectives required to guard against confirmatory bias in assertions about the transferability of ethnographic descriptions and concepts.

In his contribution to this section, Ken Tobin combines similar ultra microlevel analyses of pitch and speech intensity that are used by Roth (chapter 2) with meso level approaches to provide evidence for processes that lead to a dysfunctional coteaching configuration. At one level, the actors themselves are often conscious that they cannot work with a colleague; the microanalyses of pitch levels and contours show that the absence of harmony at levels inaccessible to unconsciousness. Readers should keep in mind that the strident differences in pitch and speech intensity not only make available sometimes-irreconcilable differences but also contribute to reproducing them.

References

Guba, E., & Lincoln, Y. (1989). *Fourth generation evaluation.* Beverly Hills, CA: Sage.

Lincoln, Y. S., & Guba, E. (1985). *Naturalistic inquiry.* Beverly Hills, CA: Sage.

McGinn, M. K., Roth, W.-M., Boutonné, S., & Woszczyna, C. (1995). The transformation of individual and collective knowledge in elementary science classrooms that are organized as knowledge-building communities. *Research in Science Education, 25,* 163–189.

3　Coteaching/cogenerative dialoguing in an urban science teacher preparation program

Kenneth Tobin and Wolff-Michael Roth

In 1997, Ken, then the director of teacher education at the University of Pennsylvania, felt certain that in any subject area a sufficient number of cooperating teachers could be found in one comprehensive neighborhood school, here referred to as "City High School." Ken was a strong advocate of learning to teach by teaching and did not value approaches to teacher education in which teachers were assumed to learn by watching other teachers before gradually assuming responsibility for teaching themselves. Instead he wanted all new teachers teaching from the very first day, learning to teach by teaching. He also expected all new teachers to have regular contact with urban youth who would advise them on "how to better teach kids like us." Experience had shown that it was essential to initiate meaningful interactions with students, not only to learn from them, but also as a sign that their perspectives were valued and a source of knowledge (Tobin, Seiler, & Walls, 1999).

When Ken became involved in the teacher education program, he was astonished to learn that several new science teachers were not given chances to teach in the first week of their assignment. He became appalled when, after an entire semester, some of the cooperating teachers still refused to allow the new teachers assigned to them to teach their classes. There was an assumption in the school and university cultures that the new teachers could learn by watching, and when they had learned enough, and only then, they could be entrusted to take over the class for short periods of time. The cooperating teacher, who was assumed to be the sole expert, carefully supervised the takeover process. A reason for not permitting new teachers to teach was a belief that the cooperating teacher needed to have established an environment that was conducive to learning before a new teacher could be successful. There was an unwillingness to acknowledge that less-than–optimal learning environments could be improved markedly through the use of additional teacher resources, in this case new teachers.

The principal of City High also was frustrated that the new teachers, which he considered to be significant teaching and learning resources, were not drawn upon more. One day, this principal had the idea that two new teachers could teach a science class during their second semester in the school without being supervised by a cooperating teacher. Since both new teachers had undergraduate degrees in science, each could obtain emergency certification and satisfy legal requirements. As a colleague strongly spoke in support of the principal's plan, Ken reluctantly agreed but argued that a careful study of the events should be conducted. Given the difficult nature of teaching at City High School, it came as a surprise that the two new teachers flourished. Not only did their teaching steadily improve throughout the semester but also their students enjoyed science, regularly participated in laboratory activities, and enacted rigorous science. This science curriculum was in stark contrast to the manner in which science was taught in the remainder of the school. At the same time, there were a variety of problems experienced by other new teachers at City High (and other placement schools). Accordingly, Ken resolved to use coteaching more extensively during the following year.

Initial rationale for coteaching

Coteaching initially was grounded in social constructivism and learning in communities of practice. The decision to enact coteaching on a widespread basis was not grounded in a theoretical rationale but in a very informal study of the first pair of new teachers enacting a curriculum that greatly increased participation and achievement in an urban high school. Ken was considerably influenced by the experience of witnessing two yet-to-be-certified science teachers teach effectively without the close supervision of a cooperating teacher. Perhaps there are certain contexts and conditions where teacher education does not have to rely on the presence of excellent cooperating teachers or on close supervision of an exemplary practitioner? Ken was well aware that many teachers in comprehensive neighborhood schools were not certified in the science subjects that they taught, leading to a shortage of well-prepared cooperating teachers. More so, he had observed teachers throughout City High struggle to teach rather than enact exemplary practice. Historically, because the best teachers were assigned to the suburbs—it was there that the prospective teachers would learn to teach. Ken was unconvinced that such an approach would lead to a future cadre of excellent urban teachers. Furthermore, he wanted to exercise radical doubt about the claim that the best place to learn to teach was in a classroom in which the culture was settled. He was attracted to the idea that the most productive environments for learning to teach would be unsettled, those where culture was visible and where adaptation and transformation were desirable and probably necessary to promote learning.

K: What is to be accomplished by placing new teachers with exemplary practitioners in suburbs? This is a complex problem to address briefly. One issue is that teachers and students in the suburbs often share more in terms of culture whereas in urban schools unexpected events unfold at a rapid rate and the experience of cultural otherness can be overwhelming; all teachers, no matter their experience, have to learn to teach students like the ones they have. Second, if a class is "settled" then the culture of that classroom can be largely invisible and practices occur without overt attention and awareness (Swidler, 1986). Students and teachers enact roles that are not dissimilar to those enacted outside of the classroom in homes and the institutions associated with life in the middle class. In settled cultures the events might be more predictable and easily manageable for new teachers who will not have to adapt their teaching to the extent necessary in urban schools or struggle to teach students new roles.

Even though urban high schools are challenging places to teach new teachers can make a significant contribution to urban students while learning to identify the students' cultural capital, create appropriate learning environments and effectively resolve problems as they emerge. Ken's personal teaching experience in urban schools suggested that the problems would unfold relentlessly even for an experienced teacher and teacher educator (Tobin, 2000). Teaching alongside another person in an urban school can provide myriad opportunities to learn to teach better, because engaging in practice alongside another allows a person to experience dispositions characteristic of practice not otherwise accessible (Bourdieu & Wacquant, 1992). Furthermore, there was a very evident need for good teachers in urban high schools, especially large neighborhood schools with a comprehensive curriculum. We thought that if "student teachers" were regarded as "new teachers," as true, legitimate, and by the culture valued resources for the learning of students, there was the potential for science teacher education to be transformative.

K: There was a tendency to regard new teachers as a burden on the academic integrity of a high school program. Teachers saw it as their duty to take a couple of new teachers every now and then as a professional obligation to induct new teachers into their profession. I was energetically opposed to this condescending idea. New teachers were a resource that could be assigned to teaching in ways that would mediate in the learning of students and change their lives forever. Every moment spent by a new teacher in an urban school was a way to make a difference in the lives of the students at that school—through education. Hence, once I had seen the two new teachers succeed even without supervision, I considered teacher education to be a transformative activity with the potential to breach the cycles of social reproduction that oppressed urban youth and constricted the quality of their social lives. Not only would students taught by new teachers learn science that could change their social lives but also the teaching culture at City High as a whole could change.

In the process of implementing coteaching, we experimented with different numbers and combinations of individuals who were teaching at any one moment. Our associated research allowed us to articulate not only what worked, but also, and more importantly, the almost inevitable and unpredictable contradictions that emerge in the evolution of new practices. Rather than viewing these contradictions as a shortcoming of our approach, we used their power to be drivers of change (Engeström, 1987). In the following section, we articulate different models of coteaching as a context for science teacher preparation that we have tried out in response to different, ever-emerging contradictions and structural constraints at City High.

Models for learning to teach through coteaching/cogenerative dialoguing

The previously described experiment with coteaching could easily have been our last. On that occasion the school principal and the two student teachers worked out the details and then presented them as a plan they wanted to try. What was not all that visible was the significance of the interpersonal relationships enjoyed by the two new teachers. They liked one another and had good interpersonal skills. Each was also highly competent in biology and had experience as bench scientists prior to coming to teaching. Although they were young and highly idealistic they brought with them a maturity to work out problems as they unfolded and an expectation that they would learn to teach from their experiences of teaching. Subsequently, however, we found out that for some combinations of individuals, coteaching did not work. In each subsequent year since we have had to deal with interpersonal conflicts; often we worked out the problems as they arose but in some cases reassignments were required. We also created new arrangements of coteaching to see whether all of these would be equally beneficial to the students and participating coteachers. In the following, we provide an historical account of how different arrangements came about in response to needs, difficulties, and contradictions that we identified in an ongoing manner.

Coteaching: the beginnings

Initially, we assigned each new teacher with a different cooperating teacher. The difference between traditional assignments and coteaching was the expectation that the two would teach *together*, at the elbow of the other so to speak. They would plan and teach together with the intention of improving the science learning of the students. Even though some cooperating teachers were reluctant to coteach, we experienced enough success with the model to continue it to the present day.

Gradually our practice evolved to assigning two new teachers to one cooperating teacher. An immediate benefit was the coplanning opportunities presented by three teachers working together. Especially if the cooperating teacher was reluctant to coteach, modeled as a contradiction in our theoretical approach, there were always two new teachers who could teach and learn at the elbow of one another. At a theoretical level, the use of three teachers seemed to be a decided step up from having one or two teachers for a given number of students. Not only are there more adults to mediate the learning of students, but also the adults vary in terms of their strengths, interests, and the personal tools they have to assist students in learning science. If one teacher could not help a given student then it is always possible that one of the other coteachers will have more success; our research shows that, when coteachers are available, students actively seek them to obtain the help and support they want (Roth & Tobin, 2002). Also, because the practices of one coteacher become resources for others to use, there exists an increased potential for learning to teach in a group of three coteachers. A question asked, a diagram drawn, a humorous anecdote—all are examples of resources that other coteachers can subsequently use in their own teaching.

The learning involved in teaching within a group can be conscious and intentional; it also can be unintentional and beyond conscious awareness as previous studies showed (Roth, 1998). By being in a community, practicing at the elbows of others, all participants have the opportunities for continued learning. Of course, from the perspective of new teachers they can learn science in new and different ways by teaching science with others, and they can learn how to teach science by coteaching with others (Roth, Tobin, Zimmermann, Bryant, & Davis, 2002). Simultaneously, students' opportunities to learn science, about science, and about teaching and learning are tremendously enhanced.

In the first trials at coteaching we noticed that new teachers divided the labor in interesting ways. For example, some coteaching groups planned in complementary ways to make it possible for each new teacher to do what he or she was best at. We emphasized nevertheless that learning to teach would only occur when they contributed to the *collective* responsibility at all times rather than splitting the work as is typical of team-teaching approaches. In planning coteaching it is necessary to carefully consider the division of labor and the tools that each participant will have to support his or her individual practices and the manner in which those practices contribute to collective action and the maintenance of the objects of activity.

Coteaching: further development through theorizing

The initial coteaching arrangements occurred without having a conscious theoretical rationale. At this stage, Ken, colleagues at Penn, and several cooperating teachers and school administrators from City High began to collaborate with Roth about his coteaching studies in Canada (see chapter 1), the theoretical frames for making sense of what was happening and, perhaps more importantly, for thinking of coteaching in ways that could lead to improved teaching and student learning. From this point on, theory became increasingly important in making decisions about the unfolding events associated with the assignment of new teachers and the maintenance of productive environments in which they learned to teach science. Although we were mostly interested to cogenerate theory with the teachers to arrive at concrete practical solutions to the problems that continuously emerged, we also drew on cultural sociology (Sewell, 1999) and cultural-historical activity theory (Cole & Engeström, 1993) to frame our work. These frames were promising because they already conceptualized culture, contradictions, tools, division of labor, and rules, which became central to our own research toolkits.

We soon began to ask, "Just how many new teachers should be placed together when they are assigned as coteachers?" Logistically it seemed as if there would be an upper limit and yet there seemed to be good reasons for three or even four new teachers to be assigned to one cooperating teacher.

Early in our research experience we also learned of the necessity to examine the roles of the participants (e.g., university supervisors, methods instructors) in the activity of learning to teach. Thinking through the notion of division of labor, which includes the horizontal and hierarchical relations of power that collaborators can enact, we argued, for example, that if a university supervisor was to have a contributing role in learning to teach he or she would necessarily coteach. His or her experience in and of praxis, involving students and the new and cooperating teachers in their context, could provide additional structural resources to students, who learned science, new teachers, who learned to teach, and to the supervisor, who learned about learning to teach. At the time, Ken made the following field note entry:

K: The idea of a university supervisor sitting at the rear or side of the class writing notes about what she is experiencing makes little sense. This note-taking ritual usually takes the form of reading and reacting to lesson plans and then making lists of strengths, weaknesses and questions to consider. My main problem with this is the supervisor has no sense of the game of teaching this class of students this topic at this time. The notes are based on experiences that are well removed from the experience being evaluated. Also, there is no sense of collective responsibility for the learning of the students and no agreed-upon division of labor with the objects of affording the learning of the students while learning to teach them. I favor a division of labor in which the university supervisor shares the responsibility for learning in a broad sense and participates as a legitimate, peripheral participant. As events unfold the university supervisor would participate as a coteacher and do whatever is possible to afford learning. Then the evaluation can occur after, in a meeting where all participants make sense of and theorize what has happened during the lesson. Within a context of a shared responsibility for teaching and learning, plans can then be made for improving the quality of learning.

Accordingly we created a rule that university supervisors would coteach when they came to review the teaching of new teachers. That is, the form of practice that we considered appropriate for supervisors involved coteaching, not in the least because the particulars of any practice are accessible only to the practitioner (Bourdieu, 1990). Similarly as we undertook research in the classrooms in which coteaching occurred—such as when Michael (Roth) came to Philadelphia to participate in the ongoing research—we quickly realized that they too had to coteach if they were to obtain dependable data about how the coteachers experienced their praxis. We knew that researchers could only understand and theorize the unfolding patterns of coherence and contradictions salient to participants if they took part in the collective responsibility for students' learning by participating in the teaching. In this way, we had as many as six coteachers in a given class. We began to realize that such a large number of coteachers was not only manageable but also could significantly enhance learning as long as there was an appropriate division of labor and a shared sense of the game. Accordingly, when the opportunity arose we were confident in suggesting that three new teachers be assigned to a cooperating teacher and that all four would coteach a class.

This approach is a major break from convention and most of our colleagues may not want to accept having this many teachers coteaching at a particular time. Given the right mix of personality characteristics we are not at all reluctant and can see how learning and learning to teach can be significantly enhanced even with relatively small class sizes. There are several interesting theoretical models (e.g., including *legitimate peripheral participation* [Lave & Wenger, 1991] or apprenticeship [see Eick and Ware, chapter 9]) that can be applied to coteaching and each of these suggests that the provision of multiple coteachers provides more central participants from whom those at the periphery can learn. However, the more individuals teach, the larger the potential for contradictions to emerge that have the potential to diminish the benefits. Such contradictions do not have to be foreseen but can be addressed as they emerge in praxis—the contradictions become the drivers of change.

Perhaps the most extreme and controversial form of coteaching is when two new teachers are assigned to a class without a cooperating teacher being present, such as what happened during the very first coteaching experiment brought about by the principal. In this situation, there is no experienced teacher available from whom the new teachers could learn—educational grounds for not continuing this practice. In addition, there are legal issues of classes being taught by new teachers who are not certified. However, every time that we had such an arrangement—e.g., when there is no cooperating teacher available to participate—the educational advantages for the high school students were evident and compelling and the new teachers concerned have been enthusiastic about being involved in this way. Collectively, our experience shows that even two new, uncertified teachers without the direct supervision by a cooperating teacher can provoke tremendous learning to occur, for the new teachers, a result consistent with other studies of significant learning occurring in groups of novices (Collins, Brown, & Newman, 1989), and their students.

Cogenerative dialoguing

As part of our initial work, we brought all coteachers to talk about their experience of teaching a particular class. Consistent with hermeneutic scholarship (Ricœur, 1991), we assume that any understanding (taken in an existential rather than purely cognitive sense) is a function of experience, that is, a person's biography. We therefore never assumed that all coteachers would have the same experiences or that different experiences could be triangulated into a generalized "essence" of the classroom events. The practice of cogenerative dialoguing evolved from earlier debriefing sessions in response to the need to articulate as fully as possible the different kinds of experiences and to explain them in and through collective interpretation, from which new possibilities for individual and collective actions emerged. These new possibilities are implemented because the actions the participants decided on are concretely available rather than existing only "in theory." To the extent possible the participants in cogenerative dialogue create a shared, collective responsibility for future activity and the accomplishment of its outcomes.

Of course, even when students and teachers get together to collectively plan next actions, there is the possibility for contradictions to threaten the achievement of planned outcomes. What complicates the issue is that many teaching- and learning-related practices are unconscious and unintended. Hence, cogenerative dialogue, a conversation between stakeholders about a shared experience, can identify and review practices that are unintended and unconscious while discussing the power relationships and roles of participants. Cogenerative dialogues need to occur with sufficient regularity that contradictions and patterns of activity are identified and their relationships to the motivation that drives the current activity (e.g., Roth & Tobin, 2002) are discussed. Issues of voice are important in cogenerative dialogue since all participants should be represented and their perspectives should inform the emerging understanding of the factors that mediate the activity of different members of the community and how those patterns of activity contribute to collective activity and accomplishment. We therefore developed a heuristic for coteachers and students to use to check whether all participants have equal opportunities to contribute irrespective of the differences in institutional power—items include "posing critical questions," "providing evidence," and "evaluating ideas and practices." The identification of contradictions is salient as is the conversation about whether or not they should be removed and best ways to remove them. Ideally, the cogenerative dialogues include thorough discussions of the rules, division of labor, and tools that apply to the activity and the manner in which different members of the community participate.

In our coteaching work, the most common form of cogenerative dialogue has been related to coplanning—the coteachers review what has been accomplished in the class, decide upon what is to happen next and the division of labor for forthcoming lessons. These meetings occur after and prior to cotaught lessons and typically involve the new teachers and the cooperating teacher. A variant of these cogenerative discussions are the "huddles" that occur any time during a lesson; teachers come together and quickly review what has happened and what they want to do next. During the lesson the coteachers and students communicate regularly to make sure that the activity is progressing in a satisfactory manner. Because of the necessity to step back from and thereby interrupt the ongoing lesson, huddles are necessarily short in duration.

At times, students participate in the above-mentioned huddles. But although this practice currently is less common, we see no reason why this should not occur regularly. Unless students begin to take their part in the collective responsibility for learning, we see little possibility for lasting change to occur. We see advantages of including students in the huddle in circumstances in which the responsibility for the success of a lesson does not seem to be equally shared between the coteachers and the students. Other forms of huddle also seem desirable. For example, cogenerative huddles between coteachers and the university supervisors or between the coteachers and school administrators can have the advantage of occurring at times when the details of a shared experience are vivid and accessible to the participants. Of course it is important that cogenerative huddles do not disrupt the collective activity in a detrimental way.

Essential to the success of this variant of coteaching, as with all others, is the coplanning that occurs and cogenerative dialogues during which discussions occur between representatives of the participants who have been involved in the enacted curriculum. A critical part of cogenerative dialogue is the negotiation of a set of collective objects, a commitment to the collective actions that must occur, and a division of labor to allow different participants to enact roles to afford those objects. Perhaps the most challenging and least accomplished goal is to develop a shared sense of responsibility for the success of a lesson. Currently, our coteachers usually assume most responsibility. Through cogenerative dialogue, however, we seek to build shared commitments and then critique the practices of all participants in relation to the current goals. Recently, as part of cogenerative dialoguing, we have had considerable success in using videotape to show all participants their practices and to create catalysts for conversations on contradictions that arise from praxis (LaVan, 2004). These participants include a number of students, whereby we found from experience that it works best when there are two students: one student alone is often too shy; three or more students change the character of the sessions in ways that make them less productive.

When students participate in cogenerative dialogue, new opportunities for learning arise for all participants in a classroom. For example, both new teachers and students can build appropriate social capital, which is a precursor to earning respect for one another. Respect is the critical currency in the urban neighborhoods of Philadelphia (Anderson, 1999); it is the most critical currency for a teacher to have before he or she can be successful (Tobin, 2000). In the absence of respect, even the most successful teachers in other (urban) contexts are likely to fail at schools such as City High (Roth et al., 2004). If cogenerative dialogues are regarded as a field in which culture can be produced, reproduced, adapted and transformed then the focus of activity in the field can be on the learning that occurs. Cogenerative dialogues can be opportunities to learn about others, who are positioned differently in social life in terms of such factors as age, class, ethnicity, and gender. When small, diverse groups are established for cogenerative dialogues it constitutes a safe place for participants to interact in a field in which the rules make it safe for risks to be taken, for interactions to fail and provide a focus for subsequent interaction on which success can build. The chapter by LaVan (this volume) points to the enormous potential of cogenerative dialogues to foster the growth of new culture that can then be applied in other fields, including the science classroom and in salient fields away from the school.

Coteaching in teacher education: catalyst for cultural transformation

Our work of using coteaching and the associated practice of cogenerative dialoguing as a context for teacher education has become a powerful context for enacting change at City High School; that is, coteaching has become a catalyst for cultural transformation. At the same time, new arrangements lead to new contradictions, difficulties, and resistance, which require further changes. For example, to deal with the problems faced by teachers and administrators within City High we developed a plan for the new science teachers to be assigned in a block to a "small learning community," which is an administrative unit combining approximately 200 students, seven teachers, and a coordinator. Each four- to five-member group of new teachers would teach general science to grade nine students for the entire year (Tracy Stickney, 2002).

In one class, one group of new teachers consisted of two females and one male; they taught half of the thirty-four students in the class. A male-female pair cotaught the other half of the students in the same room. Within a short time a critical problem emerged in the group of three coteachers. The two females became firm friends, were able to plan together easily, and made the time to do it. In contrast, the male new teacher was peripheral to the group. Although the two females found him pleasant and hard working they did not feel comfortable with his style of teaching. From their perspective he planned at the last moment and was all too ready to set his plans aside and teach according to the emerging events of the classroom. They found the constant deviations from the plan to be unacceptable and stressful and were unable to coordinate his individual practices with what they had planned as the collective activity. Within a short period it became clear that the arrangement did not work: the two females began to teach on their own. We were able to accommodate this request in a way that was not damaging to the male teacher's self-esteem by identifying another class in which his expertise was demonstrably needed. This change enabled the four remaining new teachers to operate effectively as two coteaching pairs. The problems were not due to the number of coteachers in this case; just that getting an interper-

sonal fit between three coteachers is more difficult than with two. As Kathryn
Scantlebury explores in chapter 11, it is also possible that differences in the dis-
positions of the male and two female coteachers were associated with gender.
This question should be addressed in follow-up research.

In the second classroom the division of labor was different. The cooperating
science teacher decided to play a more central role in the beginning of the semester, thereby allowing the new teachers to assume peripheral roles as the curriculum unfolded. It also allowed the cooperating teacher to "put his stamp on
this class." He wanted to be the key individual who was always deserving of the
students' respect. Hence the five coteachers planned together and enacted a curriculum initially with the new teachers as peripheral but legitimate participants.
In the course of the semester, the new teachers became more central and toward
the midpart of the semester the class was divided in two with each part being cotaught by a pair of new teachers with the cooperating teacher having a peripheral
role.

After one semester, further reassignments became necessary to respond to
emerging needs. One new teacher wanted to have a career in a private high
school and requested an experience that was less urban; although she was reluctant to leave the students with whom she had developed considerable empathy
and social capital her career goals led her to request a reassignment. Similarly
another female teacher requested an assignment to an orthodox Jewish school
because of her commitment to teach in such a school after graduation. One new
teacher seeking dual certification in science and mathematics could only find
chemistry and algebra classes to teach at times that clashed with the period one
grade nine class; he too was reassigned so that his experiences would be appropriate to his career goals. An Asian female with a disposition to be relatively
quiet asked to be placed alone so that she could teach without the feeling that
she was pushing herself forward. She felt that her own opportunities to teach
were truncated by being with forceful coteachers and, although she valued
coteaching, she realized the personal significance of having opportunities to
teach alone.

With fewer new teachers to assign to the grade nine class, some reorganiza-
tion was necessary and five new teachers and the cooperating science teacher
were scheduled to teach the grade nine class. Nevertheless, all new teachers appreciated the value of coteaching and some requested that coteaching with a new
teacher occur for all of their assignments. Others were ready to teach alone and
requested a one-to-one assignment with a cooperating teacher to supplement
their grade nine experience. It was also sensible to make individual teaching
possible, since teachers would be hired as individuals. It is therefore important

for them to teach alone in at least one class so that each teacher can assure herself and collect evidence to provide for others that she can teach effectively and teach alone.

The grade nine initiative seems to have been successful on a number of levels. The following comment by Clare Tracy, now an assistant principal at City High, is an indication of how school administrators viewed the role of coteaching and cogenerative dialogue at the school.

The immediate benefits were seen through coteaching; lead teachers learned to share power with cooperating teachers. This one element changed the dynamics in the relationship between teacher and student. The fallout effect was incredibly beneficial in producing an atmosphere for risk taking. Video clips from previous teaching days were used to emphasize areas where students' behavior prevented teaching and learning from occurring and where a teacher's use of discipline caused students to shut down. This proved more beneficial than any lecture on classroom rules. Students began to appreciate the pivotal role they played in their education and teachers adopted less reactionary discipline styles. Discussions were wide ranging. Coteachers took advantage of the information students shared about themselves and their lives when rethinking the design of the classes. The teachers involved in the ninth-grade initiative learned of the difficulties students faced at school through cogenerative dialogue. They realized a need for socialization techniques. Students learned how to express their dissatisfaction with a teacher in a more positive way. We worked with the students to help them organize their work, complete assignments on time and have tools for school with them for all classes. This was not a panacea but it did lay a foundation for students to understand their role in the teaching and learning equation.

Not all cooperating teachers accept coteaching and in some instances there have been personality clashes between a co-op and the assigned new teachers. For example, an occurrence that can create grave problems is when a cooperating teacher becomes too busy to participate in coplanning and in cogenerative dialogues. When this happens the learning environment is not as rich as it might otherwise be and it creates a situation in which the potential learning of the co-operating teacher is not realized. Furthermore, failure to participate because someone is too busy sends a clear signal to those who do participate that the activities of coplanning and cogenerative dialogue are not central to effective science education. There is no easy way to address situations like these when they occur. On the one hand courageous actions are required of all participants, especially university supervisors. Because of the inherent asymmetry in power relations between cooperating teachers and new teachers it is unreasonable to expect new teachers will bear the brunt of requesting ongoing participation of a cooperating teacher with priorities that consume his time. When such instances occur and are not quickly resolved, we endeavor to resolve problems as they emerge and we consider the educational needs of students as paramount. Changes are made as necessary to ensure that coteaching assignments afford the learning goals for the students while providing the new teachers (especially) opportunities to learn to teach. Our research in progress is focusing on how all coteachers learn from one another and over time, become like the other (e.g., Roth, Tobin, Carambo, & Dalland, 2004).

Expanding the applications of coteaching/cogenerative dialogue

Now in the seventh year of using coteaching in various contexts at the University of Pennsylvania the number of applications has steadily increased, notably as a tool for professional development in schools, as a vehicle for research, and to involve students as coteachers. It was apparent from coteaching that expertise did not reside solely with the resident teachers from a school. On the contrary, new teachers brought many resources and were resources for the professional development of peers and the resident teachers. At City High the school administrators and many of the teachers recognized that a productive pathway was to use coteaching as a resource for improving the quality of teaching schoolwide. Accordingly, there was openness to participating in coteaching with colleagues with the intention of learning at the elbow of a colleague, by teaching with the colleague and then participating in cogenerative dialogue.

A promising extension of the coteaching/cogenerative dialogue model was to our ongoing research in urban high schools. We had written about the advantages of coteaching/cogenerative dialogue in research and evaluation (e.g., Roth & Tobin, 2002) and their use became routine in classes in which teachers and students also were researchers. Sonya Martin, now an assistant professor at Queens College, was a science teacher at a magnet high school and then a science teacher educator at the University of Pennsylvania. In both of these contexts she was involved in coteaching and cogenerative dialogue. The following comment from Sonya provides insights into her experiences.

I was first introduced to coteaching and cogenerative dialogue as a teacher-researcher in my tenth-grade chemistry class when I was asked to participate in an NSF-funded study on urban science education. Sarah-Kate LaVan, a university researcher from the study, cotaught in my classroom and introduced my students and me to cogenerative dialogues. Our participation in these discussions about our classroom teaching and learning practices provided the pathway that transformed the way my students and I interacted with one another and with science. Our experiences with cogenerative dialogue were overwhelmingly positive and empowering as they provided my students and me with tools for affecting real changes in our classroom.

Although all of our collaborators have used coteaching successfully there is an increasing awareness of some difficulties that can arise when assumed collaborations do not occur as intended. The following comment from Stacy Olitsky, a researcher at the University of Pennsylvania, highlights some challenges to be considered.

I view coteaching as somewhat difficult, as it involves considerable use of nonverbal communication and the development of trust. In addition to the collective goals of teaching and learning, there are also interpersonal goals such as maintaining respect and feeling a sense of efficacy—for the students, the teacher, and other adults involved. I believe in its ideal form, coteaching can be a way for teachers to learn from each other's strategies, and for students to observe adults in the process of collaborating. Linda Loman, a teacher at Magnet High, and I (in my opinion) were successful when we cotaught, as we brought different skills and knowledge, and treated each other with respect. However, I have observed what I consider to be less successful coteaching when working with the student teachers at City High.

The use of students as coteachers has been a logical extension of our efforts to expand the roles of urban youth to include researcher, teacher educator, curriculum developer, and coteacher. Initially we focused on urban high school youth coteaching students from a nearby urban K–8 school. Although there were significant challenges in creating organizational structures to support this vision, it ran smoothly once the details were worked out. Especially when high school youths taught elementary students the learning environments were very rich. The basic model was to have groups of two to three high school youth teach five to seven elementary school children. The uses of youth as coteachers was expanded in many of the classrooms involved in our research and, as Jennifer Beers describes in chapter 4, this form of participation has produced structures to greatly expand the possibilities for action of all participants. We regard the involvement of students as coteachers as a promising direction for further research on coteaching/cogenerative dialogue.

The applications of cogenerative dialogues have been greatly expanded and continued to develop in the past two years. The following comments from Clare Tracy (assistant principal at City High) provide insights into the structure and outcomes of cogenerative dialogues in the grade nine initiative.

Cooperating teachers used cogenerative dialogue to establish relationships with students that would evolve to produce a more respectful atmosphere in the classroom. Cogenerative dialogue gives all involved information about one another over a pizza. The informality of the structure of cogenerative dialogue eliminates the need for students' use of defensive posturing that a teacher often would encounter in the more formal setting of the classroom. The teacher is not concerned with control and eliminating the dynamic of power will eventually provide those involved in cogenerative dialogue a way to understand language, and other norms that usually receive little notice, but language and idiosyncratic behavior of the teacher and students are the core in developing the classroom. Each group develops cultural toolkits that will aid in developing a successful teaching and learning environment. One lead teacher developed an awareness of his need to use the language of the students throughout his interactions with them—always concerned that they learn other discourses too—but in valuing their discourse he sent signs of respect and encouraged students to do what it takes to learn science.

As a logical extension of what we were learning from the use of cogenerative dialogues in our high school work, we extended its applications to the teaching of science and science education in college courses. Sonya Martin addresses her uses of cogenerative dialogues at the college level in the following excerpt.

As program evaluator for a Master's in Chemistry Education (MCE) degree, I had an opportunity to introduce cogenerative dialogue as a program evaluation tool in which teacher-participants and their professors coreflected on their experiences in their graduate level science courses. These dialogues were introduced to examine problems that emerge in the classroom and to involve participants in the co-construction of suitable solutions to the problems that had been identified. It has been a beneficial evaluation tool in many instances, gauging how participants feel about the program, curriculum concerns, and classroom interactions between professors and students and students and their peers. Some students have found cogenerative dialogues to be so beneficial to their development as learners in the MCE program that they have began to implement these dialogues in their own science classrooms with high school students to help provide their students with greater agency. From these discussions, students and professors have become aware of their collective responsibility to ensure the success of all students by providing all members with the ability to stimulate change when needed.

As is evident from chapter 5, in which Sarah-Kate LaVan discusses the application of cogenerative dialogues in her research, we have made extensive use of cogenerative dialogues as a research tool and regard it as a field in which all participants can produce and reproduce forms of culture that can afford successful interactions in other fields, across the boundaries of social class, ethnicity,

gender and age. The following comment by Stacy Olitsky addresses her perceptions of the value of cogenerative dialogue as a research tool.

I have used cogenerative dialogues as a research tool at Magnet High. These have been
extremely valuable in increasing mutual understanding among participants, and for providing opportunities to discuss issues of concern in depth and in an environment characterized by respect. Cogenerative dialogues were empowering for the students, fostering a
sense of collective responsibility for teaching and learning. Cogenerative dialogues need
to be a space for sharing, not just for asking students questions. It is not an interview.
Safe space needs to be established, where all participants feel comfortable speaking and
listening. This is difficult given the aspects of schooling contexts.

Conclusions

Two questions that frequently arise are whether coteachers get jobs when they
graduate and if they can teach effectively without the presence of other teachers.
We have many testimonials of success and a growing number of dissertations
that have explored coteaching and cogenerative dialogues (LaVan, 2004; Wassell, 2004). Since we began coteaching the new teachers involved have all ob-
tained positions and have been successful, some in urban and others in suburban
schools. Even those who did not seem especially effective in urban coteaching
assignments have been successful when they got their own classes and began to
teach alone. For example, one of our coteachers who struggled mightily as a
coteacher at City High became teacher of the year in his first year of teaching in
an urban school district in Massachusetts. Throughout his coteaching experiences this new teacher showed steady improvement and like all others taught by
himself for at least one class period on most days of the week in his second semester of field experience. We acknowledge that all teachers need time to teach
without others being at their elbows while at the same time stressing that having
multiple teachers is an optimal way to learn to teach and also afford student
learning. In the expansion of sites and contexts coteaching and cogenerative dialogue have catalyzed positive changes in many aspects of science education and
the organization of urban schooling. The remaining chapters in this section address many of these applications and the associated implications for the practice
of science education in urban high schools.

References

Anderson, E. (1999). *Code of the street: Decency, violence, and the moral life of the inner city.* New York: W.W. Norton.

Bourdieu, P. (1990). *The logic of practice.* Cambridge, UK: Polity Press.

Bourdieu, P., & Wacquant, L.J.D. (1992). *An invitation to reflexive sociology.* Chicago: University of Chicago Press.

Cole, M., & Engeström, Y. (1993). A cultural-historical approach to distributed cognition. In G. Salomon (Ed.), *Distributed cognitions: Psychological and educational considerations* (pp. 1–46). Cambridge, UK: Cambridge University Press.

Collins, A., Brown, J. S., & Newman, S. E. (1989). Cognitive apprenticeship: Teaching the crafts of reading, writing, and mathematics. In L. B. Resnick (Ed.), *Knowing, learning, and instruction: Essays in honor of Robert Glaser* (pp. 453–494). Hillsdale, NJ: Lawrence Erlbaum Associates.

Engeström, Y. (1987). *Learning by expanding: An activity-theoretical approach to developmental research.* Helsinki: Orienta-Konsultit.

LaVan, S. K. (2004). *Cogenerating fluency in urban science classrooms.* Unpublished doctoral dissertation, University of Pennsylvania, Philadelphia, PA.

Lave, J., & Wenger, E. (1991). *Situated learning: Legitimate peripheral participation.* Cambridge, UK: Cambridge University Press.

Ricœur, P. (1991). *From text to action: Essays in hermeneutics, II.* Evanston, IL: Northwestern University Press.

Roth W.-M. (1998). Science teaching as knowledgeability: A case study of knowing and learning during coteaching. *Science Education, 82*, 357–377.

Roth, W.-M., & Tobin, K. (2002). *At the elbow of another: Learning to teach by coteaching.* New York: Peter Lang.

Roth, W.-M., Tobin, K., Carambo, C., & Dalland, C. (2004). Becoming like the other: Learning to teach through coteaching. *Journal of Research in Science Teaching, 41*, 882–904.

Roth, W.-M., Tobin, K., Elmesky, R., McKnight, Y., Carambo, C., & Beers, J. (2004). The making and remaking of identity in an urban school. *Mind, Culture & Activity, 11*, 48–69.

Roth, W.-M., Tobin, K., Zimmermann, A., Bryant, N., & Davis, C. (2002). Lessons on/from the dihybrid cross: An activity theoretical study of learning in coteaching. *Journal of Research in Science Teaching, 39*, 253–282.

Sewell, W. H. (1999). The concept(s) of culture. In V. E. Bonnell & L. Hunt (Eds.), *Beyond the cultural turn* (pp. 35–61). Berkeley: University of California Press.

Swidler, A. (1986). Culture in action: Symbols and strategies. *American Sociological Review, 51*, 273–286.

Tobin, K. (2000). Becoming an urban science educator. *Research in Science Education, 30*, 89–106.

Tobin, K., Seiler, G., & Walls, E. (1999). Reproduction of social class in the teaching and learning of science in urban high schools. *Research in Science Education, 29*, 171–187.

Tracy Stickney, C. (2002, April). *Don't believe the hype: Getting the best from grade nine students in an urban setting.* Paper presented at the annual meeting of the American Educational Research Association, New Orleans, LA.

Wassell, B. (2004). *More than overwhelmed: How a first-year teacher in an urban high school employs agency to build solidarity in the presence of structural changes.* Unpublished doctoral dissertation, University of Pennsylvania, Philadelphia, PA.

4   The role of coteaching in the development of the practices of an urban science teacher

Jennifer Beers

The traditional view of teacher education conjures up images of a new teacher who is taking notes while sitting in the back of the classroom. In this experience, the new teacher is a passive outsider who is learning through observation and then expected to create effective and engaging lessons for the students. In an era of educational reform movements aimed at improving teacher education and the academic experiences of students in urban high schools, coteaching can be viewed as a viable alternative to the traditional model (Roth & Tobin, 2002). Through coteaching, one becomes an active participant in the daily events of the classroom and gains more hands-on experience when compared to more traditional models of teacher education. Moreover, coteaching affords a greater opportunity for developing meaningful relationships with the students and other teachers in classroom.

My own preservice experiences with coteaching provided me with a structure to learn to teach by being at the elbows of another more experienced teacher. It allowed me to examine his practices in the heat of the moment and incorporate some of his schema and practices into my own. It also allowed me to view and reflect on his interactions with students and teachers. In this chapter I attempt to chronicle my initial experiences with coteaching and the impact it has had on my practice over the last four years. Using a sociocultural theoretical framework (Sewell, 1992), I highlight the coherences and contradictions associated with my participation in coteaching in two different urban high schools. I outline the more salient aspects of my preservice coteaching arrangement and explore important contradictions associated with power, ego and professional identity. Finally, I explore how my continued use of coteaching has informed

my identity as a teacher and transformed my practice toward one that is more effective and more culturally adaptive.

Learning at the elbows of others

I was first introduced to coteaching through my experiences as a new teacher at
City High School. City High is a comprehensive public high school of 2,000
students of which 82 percent are from low-income families and roughly 93 percent are African American. The average daily attendance rate is 72 percent. In
the 1999–2000 PSSA tests, 84 percent of the eleventh-grade students scored in
the bottom quartile for math and 86 percent scored in the bottom quartile in
reading. These figures for reading and mathematics are higher than the statewide
percentages of 25 percent and 24 percent, respectively. More interestingly, percentages for bottom quartile scores in similar schools shows 70 percent in reading and 73 percent in mathematics. Thus, it appears that students from City High
are only marginally achieving in the statewide assessment tests.

City High is organized into nine Small Learning Communities (SLCs) that
focus on different themes. In each SLC, there are from 200 to 250 students and
from seven to eight teachers. Throughout this year, I learned to teach in the Science, Education, Enterprise, and Technology (SE^{2}T) SLC. While I participated
in a wide variety of coteaching activities during my year at City High, this section focuses on a large ninth-grade physical science class (thirty students) that I
cotaught with Jared, another new teacher, and Cristobal, who was the cooperating teacher and who also features with another new teacher in chapter 2.

Jared and I were placed together because we had already developed a rapport through our work with high school students during the previous summer.
We built an important relationship, which we would eventually use to create an
effective coteaching team. In SE^{2}T, we had the opportunity to work with Cristobal, a teacher of Afro-Cuban origins who had recently moved to Philadelphia
and was teaching in the school district in his first year. Prior to this experience,
he taught for five years at a high school in Miami, Florida. Thus, his schema and
practices were different from those of his students and, in the beginning, this led
to his own difficulties with teaching and in creating the necessary classroom
structures to afford students the agency to learn and do science. In this regard,
Jared and I were learning to teach as Cristobal was relearning to teach and refin-
ing his practice to meet the needs of this new student population. His philosophy
of teaching was generally based on student inquiry and guiding students through
solving problems as they related to key aspects of content knowledge. In addition, Cristobal's primary background was in chemistry; however, as the only

science teacher in SE²T, he was responsible for teaching classes in a variety of content areas. After one month of taking more peripheral roles in the classroom, Cristobal willingly handed over the duties and responsibilities for teaching the physical science class, which was out-of-field for both Jared and me.

Coplanning

The rationale for setting up coteaching at City High as been discussed in earlier papers (Tobin, Roth, & Zimmermann, 2001); however, the method for setting up an effective coteaching situation was largely left up to the key stakeholders in the classroom. In our classroom, coteaching developed almost organically through conversations prior to the official handing over of the class by Cristobal. In these discussions, we outlined the curriculum and the overall direction of the class. The practice of coteaching continually evolved as each of us found the appropriate space for providing input and expertise. We made adjustments to how we entered and exited the space at the front of the classroom. Moreover, we attempted to debrief at the end of each class and scheduled coplanning time at the end of each week.

Typically, Jared and I discussed our plans for the week and determined who would take the lead teacher role for a particular lesson or activity. When I was taking that role for a lesson, then I was responsible for organizing the lesson plan and appropriate activities. Jared and Cristobal were taking a more peripheral position by dealing with classroom management issues, keeping the students ontask and assisting those students who were having difficulty with a concept or activity. If Jared or Cristobal felt they had something to add to the lesson or wanted to present some information, then I would take a step back and create the space for their participation in the front of the classroom. Normally, coteachers in the peripheral roles would raise their hand when they wanted to add something. This not only proved to be an effective model for appropriate participation for the students, but also it served as a signal to coteachers to step back and let the others participate.

Coplanning was a major feature of the coteaching experience in the context of this physical science class. Initially, we approached coplanning more formally by meeting on the Friday before the lesson and activities were to be enacted in the classroom. We would outline our content flow, key concepts, and goals for the week ahead. This gave us an opportunity to share ideas and issues related to our teaching experiences and provided insight into how Cristobal developed his lessons. Our meetings also gave us the opportunity to discuss how to deal with problems that occurred over the course of the week.

As the semester progressed and we became more comfortable with our roles as new teachers, these formal meetings with Cristobal gave way to more informal planning. While we still maintained an open dialogue and debriefed after class, Jared and I were starting to plan individually for our lessons. During the preparation period and lunch, Cristobal offered critical suggestions concerning how to present material and the types of activities we should consider including in our lessons. Although this gave us more autonomy, the evolution of our coplanning efforts still allowed us the opportunity to gain feedback on our practice.

Learning by being with others

In the beginning, I viewed coteaching as an organizational nightmare. I generally understood why this method could be a powerful tool in the process of teaching and learning; however, I began my coteaching experience with some reluctance and skepticism. In comparing my situation with other new teachers, I felt I had the unique experience of learning to teach as my cooperating teacher was *relearning* to teach. As I reflect back on this arrangement, I realize that this experience was, perhaps, the best arrangement for any new teacher. It created a structure in which our practices evolved simultaneously and we developed a collaborative relationship that I believe was, at most times, very effective. Coteaching with Cristobal opened up the possibility for understanding the true artistry of his teaching. An artist is rarely aware of what he does or why he paints in a specific manner. Likewise, a teacher's decisions in the classroom can often occur in the heat of the moment and these crucial decisions are the result of instinct and *habitus* (Bourdieu, 1977). Working at the elbow of Cristobal allowed me to experience his instinct and habitus in action. In my experiences with coteaching, these moments afforded the greatest opportunity for learning how an experienced teacher can effectively engage the students in a meaningful way.

Jen:	Why isn't anybody writing?
Student:	Cuz I don't know what the answer is.
Kia:	Cuz I don't know it.
Jared:	Do they know what a pattern is?
Jen:	Do you guys know what a pattern is?
Andrew :	A pattern is–
Nate:	Like, takin' steps is a pattern.
	((Cristobal steps in and I explain to him what I want the students to do.))
Cristobal:	Alright, here's the question, ready. Excuse me. Excuse me. This is a skill we want you to be able to have. I need your attention. Up here. [That's how you understand something] Look this way. Put your brain up here.

	Look it, you mapped these volcanoes did you not? You placed these volcanoes here . . . eight, twenty, four . . . you placed those volcanoes, yes? On the map, right? You placed them. What Mr. Headley did was he drew dotted lines. Now, what does a line represent? What'd they tell you it is? What's a dotted line mean?
Student:	A plate–
Cristobal:	What does a dotted line mean? It's a plate what?
Derrick:	A volcano plate.
Cristobal:	No it's a plate . . . boundary–
Alan:	Boundary.
Cristobal:	This is the edge of the plate. Now, what they want you to say is, hey do you see any relationship between where they are and the plate. What do you see between where the volcano is and the plate? In other words, is this volcano here . . .
Keith:	Cuz they're on the edge of the uh . . .
Cristobal:	They are located on the edges of the . . . of the plates. Now so what we want you to be able to do, excuse me. This is the skill we want you to have. Can you look at something and get pieces of information and write it down. What do I see? All the volcanoes are located pretty much on the edges of the plates. Now, Ms. Beers said, "wait a minute wait a minute wait a minute. What about that one?" . . .
Jen:	So you guys were talking about volcanoes under the ocean. Do you remember the word *hot spot?* Did we cover– did we cover that? Can anyone tell me what a hot spot is?
Students:	Yeah.
Cristobal:	What's a hot spot?

It is important to note that when we started this process, the coteaching was jagged and disjointed instead of seamless and continuous. Instead of stepping forward and stepping back in a fluid motion, we maintained specific roles during classroom instruction. Initially, teaching in this manner was difficult because I needed to develop a certain amount of confidence regarding my role as an educator. I also needed to become comfortable with coteaching and build a dynamic relationship with the other teachers in the classroom. It was not until we were able to read each other—in the way Chris and Cristobal are doing in chapter 2 of this book—and appreciate the schema and practices that each person brought to the classroom that we were able to negotiate our positions at any given moment in a class period. Once this was in place, teaching at the elbows of the other teacher became easier to negotiate. For example, if I were using the didactic method of teaching, Cristobal would regularly raise his hand if he had something to add to the lesson. This would be my signal to take a step back and allow

Cristobal to further explain an idea, add an example or pose a question for the students to answer. In other instances, I would pose a question to Cristobal and this would signal that I wanted him to step forward and help clarify an issue.

In enacting coteaching in the classroom, our participation varied and evolved over time. This evolution in our roles was not limited to content and clarification; rather, it also pertained to issues regarding classroom management. Cristobal would regularly step into the discussion in the event of classroom management issues or assist us when we struggled with particular students. As a result of the coteaching, we were more readily able to adhere to the classroom rules because we worked as a team to construct and enact them. Although Cristobal had the ultimate authority in the classroom and was held accountable in the larger macro structure of the school, there was a sense that he "had my back" at any given time. As a result of this type of trust, we were able to share collective responsibility for developing effective lessons and assisting the students in learning science.

My coteaching experiences with Jared and Cristobal also created the space for me to make important connections between theory and practice. As I moved between the university and the high school, I was inundated with theoretical approaches to teaching, pedagogical methodologies and general social theory, which was supposed to assist me with understanding how to teach in an urban high school. The theory that I studied as part of my teacher education would not have been as useful had I not been able to experience learning to teach through coteaching with others. In many cases, it is often difficult to answer questions such as, "Why did you do that during your lesson?" or "How did you know how to present this today?" Applications of theory are often accomplished without conscious decisions on the part of the teacher. Thus, coteaching allowed the co-participants to witness the unconscious acts of teaching and then more meaningfully reflect on the shared experience.

Finally, coteaching provided the opportunity for others to help fill in the gaps with regard to my content knowledge and the more practical aspects of teaching science. In many respects, my knowledge of physical science was limited by my experiences as a classically trained biologist. Creating a space where the other teachers in the classroom could participate in my lessons provided me with the opportunity to learn how another would present the same content. If I struggled or stumbled over how to handle a particular event in the classroom, Jared and Cristobal were always there to provide me with the support necessary to become a successful teacher. Furthermore, in the in situ experience that coteaching offered, I was not able to hide behind a desk or escape into the role of passive observer; rather, I was asked to make decisions and participate as a stakeholder in the shared experiences of the classroom community. My interactions with the students and other teachers forced me to rethink how I would approach teaching in an urban classroom. These interactions enriched my cultural toolkit and strengthened my pedagogical approach to teaching science.

Egos, power, and unsuccessful coteaching moments

During my year at CHS, other participants in coteaching activities lamented over some cooperating teachers' inability to relinquish control of the classroom to more inexperienced new teachers. Through conversations with other new teachers, it seemed that the cooperating teacher made sense of their roles as teachers in terms of having control of what happens in the classroom and did not see learning as a sociocultural activity with numerous resources to mediate learning—of which teachers are one valued human resource. In many of these situations, the cooperating teachers appeared to have a very clear idea of how a class should be managed or how content should be presented. Other unsuccessful coteaching activities were the result of strained relationships between the two new teachers. In both instances, it seemed that the unbalanced power relationships between teachers in the classroom prevented collaboration and closed the door to the possibility of effective coteaching experiences.

While my coteaching experiences with Cristobal and Jared were characterized by patterns of thin coherence that involved collegiality and collaboration, there were instances of contradictions that did involve power and ego. These contradictions typically occurred during the initial period of coteaching, which was jagged and disjointed when we were still learning about the others' schema and practices and those of the students. As is the case with any new teacher, both Jared and I struggled with issues of classroom management and relied on Cristobal to help us set up the structures needed for effective teaching and learning. Although I was committed to coteaching, I also I believed I would not learn how to teach if I was not given the opportunity to stumble and fall. In many respects, I felt as if my identity as a teacher depended on getting things right and teaching autonomously. In this first semester of coteaching, there was one specific episode when I became aware of how power and ego can serve to complicate the collaborative relationship that is afforded by coteaching with others.

October 31, 2000: The class started off with the normal routine of getting the students to their seating and asking them to take out a notebook and pen. During this time, there was the typical rustling of papers and "cross-talk" between students. Typically, I try to ignore this because the students police themselves and they are fairly attentive when I am trying to speak. When they became more restless, I decide it was time to switch to a new activity which involved filling out a review sheet on static electricity. I briefly explained what to do: "What I want you guys to do is read through the worksheet and answer the questions." I paused for a second and the students began to moan and display their disgust at the activity. I then asked one student, Brandon, if he wanted me to do the first question with them. At this point, Cristobal walked to the front of the class and said, "May I?" I nodded, "Yes," because I was feeling a sense of pressure. He then said, "Okay, I'll do the first one with you and then you do the rest, okay?" I stepped off to the side, feeling some way dejected and allowed Cristobal to take over the class. I really wanted to ask him why he did this, but I didn't. I left him to finish modeling the activity and started helping the students answer the questions.

Coteaching works when there are no egos involved. Control of the class and style of teaching must be a cooperative effort. In most cases, this works well for our group. Today, my ego was "front and center." For the first time, I felt like I almost had it all under control. I just wanted to "sink or swim" to see if I could handle my responsibilities and myself. I'm the kind of person who needs to feel "in control"/"in the driver's seat" in order to gauge my progress and my abilities. When Cristobal stepped in, my ego was bruised and I thought to myself, "I almost had it today. Am I not doing the right things? Am I doing all right?" This second-guessing left me angry with Cristobal and myself. But rather than confront him, I let it go.

In reflecting back on this experience, I remember thinking that I should pay attention to what Cristobal was saying to the students and how he was interacting with them instead of silently stepping back and allowing my ego to be bruised. At that point, I realized that I could learn more than just how to teach in an urban school; rather, I could learn how to approach teaching in any educational setting. It was the first time I consciously recognized that coteaching opened the possibility of becoming an effective teacher. Throughout my experience with coteaching with Cristobal, I felt that we approached the situation as both teachers and learners. This allowed us to develop a relationship in which I began to feel comfortable making decisions in the heat of the moment. Toward the end of my coteaching experience, we worked together as a unit or one entity. There was a tangible sense of continuity and the process of teaching became seamless in the way it is described in chapters 1 and 2. We shared collective responsibility for developing effective lessons and assisting the students in learning science. More importantly, coteaching with Cristobal was, at most times effective because we worked in the absence of a power differential.

Creating a space for agency

In many urban high schools, student academic performance is associated with coping strategies and realms of interaction that frame experiences of the African-American student. The African-American academic dilemma must be understood in terms of the incongruence between the motivation and values of the teacher and those of the students (Boykin, 1986). Thus, students' unwillingness to participate in classroom activities, in part, stem from such disparities. In gaining legitimacy through cultural and social reproduction, the school marginalizes the students who resist their values. The coping strategies employed by the students may reflect the fact that African Americans must negotiate three realms of experience: "the main stream, the African-rooted Black culture and the status of an oppressed minority" (p. 59). For many students, the contradiction between superficially believing in the dominant culture's achievement ideology and marginally achieving in school is indicative of the complexities associated with negotiating these different experiences.

Another concern for students involves creating the space for the development of their agency both as learners and members of our society. In light of the challenges presented by the triple quandary for African-American students, agency is related to the students' ability to code-switch between the dominant system of meaning and that of their own localized subculture (Anderson, 1999). In the classroom, it is difficult, if not impossible, to change the current structural distribution of social and cultural capital; however, by understanding and utilizing the students' interests, values and motivations, I believed it was possible to begin giving some of them access to the schema and practices of the mainstream culture. This may have not only empowered them to work within the dominant culture; rather, it may have also provided them with the tools necessary to critically address the historical and systemic patterns of marginalization and oppression.

Cogenerative dialogues

One way to address some of these bigger issues and, more locally, the problems associated with the structure of the classroom, is through the use of cogenerative dialogue. As part of our coteaching experience, Jared and I were required to hold cogenerative dialogues (Eldon & Levin, 1991) with selected stakeholders in the classroom experience. Ideally, participants discuss a particular classroom event or activity in an attempt to cogenerate an understanding of both the conscious and unconscious practices of the teachers and students. More importantly, and what makes these different from a typical discussion, is that the participants should co-construct a specific outcome or action that may help transform the structures of the classroom to afford the agency of all of the stakeholders. In this regard, cogenerative dialogues can also be considered a field where culture can be enacted and which is nested within the larger field of the classroom (Seiler,

2001). Since fields have porous boundaries, schema and practices of the participants can be transferred from one field to another; then the schema and practices
that are shared within cogenerative dialogues can be used to help change the
structures in the classroom. Moreover, these dialogues are also powerful tools
for helping participants build symbolic, social or cultural capital that can be used
in the classroom.

For me, cogenerative discussions with students provided some very powerful, shared experiences with respect to learning about the students, their lives
and their goals for the future. In these dialogues, I tried to be diligent about creating an open and safe environment for discussions about what was also occurring in the classroom; however, a lot of the discussion involved sharing life experiences that occurred outside of school. I tried to impress upon the students
that we share responsibility for what occurs in the classroom and improvements
can only be made if we work together. In these discussions, I viewed my students as teachers and myself as a learner. I sat down at the table ready to learn
and I think this gave the students a sense of power that they do not normally
have in their experiences in the school.

This type of shared experience with students became an integral part of my
practice as a teacher. I started to see how students and teachers in the classroom
bring with them a wide variety of cultural resources and notions about science.
Moreover, I recognized that these could serve as a starting point for learning on
a number of different levels. During this first year of teaching, the difficulty
rested in actually harnessing these aspects of the classroom dynamic; however,
the kind of conversation that one has during a cogenerative dialogue showed me
how it could be possible to learn science *and* learn about each other. I am not
sure if I informed the students' identities in any real or tangible way; however, I
do believe I helped them tackle issues surrounding how science can marginalize
those who are disenfranchised. I would also hope that I was able to help them
challenge how science is positioned in their lives (Barton, 1998a, 1998b) and
work toward creating a curriculum that centered on science as a means for dealing with issues of social justice. In turn, I know that the students informed my
identity and my practice as a teacher. In sharing their life experiences and their
ideas about science, I was definitely a different person as compared with the
young woman who walked through the door of City High in September.

Learning from contradictions

During my year at City High, the practice of using cogenerative dialogues was
still in its infancy and the importance and power of these discussions was not
well understood by my team of teachers. In some cases, Jared and I conducted

cogenerative dialogues because it was a requirement rather than because we viewed it as a useful tool in developing our curriculum and our practices as teachers. The rigors of our degree program, in addition to our responsibilities as classroom teachers, constrained our ability carry out these discussions with the students. Moreover, these dialogues were not used to cogenerate understandings; rather, we used them for fact-finding about particular classroom structures or to get to know our students. My naïve conception of cogenerative dialogues also did not afford me opportunities to see the importance of following through with suggestions made by the students. My ability to follow through was also constrained by my schema and practices as a White, suburban young woman who held a very mainstream notion of what a teacher should and should not do in the classroom. In this regard, when the dialogues centered on classroom structures and my practice, I spent more time justifying myself to my students rather than simply listening and working toward a specific outcome that would improve the quality of the teaching and learning in the classroom.

While these more formalized dialogues between teachers and students were sometimes ineffective because of timing and the lack of attendance by all three teachers, it is important to point out that there were other instances of cogenerative dialogues that were less formal and did not involve our students. For instance, our coplanning efforts could also be considered a form of cogenerative dialogue because these discussions not only led to curricular change, but also they helped draw out the conscious and unconscious practices of all three teachers. In addition, there was also a cogenerated outcome and a division of labor with regard to the lesson plans and activities for the classroom. There were also several occasions when the three teachers in the classroom would employ a huddling technique. This technique is analogous to the type of activity used by football players on the playing field and could also be considered a form of cogenerative dialogue that took place in the heat of the moment (for a detailed study of huddles as cogenerative dialogues, see Wassell, chapter 6). During several lessons, we formed a huddle either off to the side or in the front of the room. This gave us the space to make collective decisions dealing with immediate concerns relating to the lesson or classroom management.

While huddling was an effective way of hearing other opinions during certain lessons, it may have also signified to the students that we were unsure about what we were teaching or trying to accomplish in the classroom. This may have contributed to the initial problems that Jared and I faced concerning how the students perceived our roles as teachers in the classroom. Through an interview with a student, Jared and I both learned that huddling in the front of the class may undermine what students perceived to be the traditional role of the teacher in the classroom.

Jen: Kia, what's it like to have three teachers in the classroom?

Kia: It can be confusin'. Like, I don't know who is the real teacher. Sometimes you be in the front of the class. Sometimes it's Mr. Headley ((Jared)). And, sometimes Mr. Carambo ((Cristobal)) comes in and take it all over. You should just decide who it be and one of you teach the class.

Jen: But, we are all teachers. Each one of us. What do we do that is most confusing?

Kia: Like... like when you are up there and you be having trouble with Derrek or Jamal. I be like...let her teach. Then Rumbo ((Cristobal)) comes up and wants to talk to you. Then, Mr. Headley comes. It's like you don't know what you be doin' half the time. They should just let you teach. Just let the lady teach. It would just make it easier.

Many other students in the classroom also shared the sentiment expressed by Kia. In setting up an effective coteaching arrangement, we learned that it was necessary to make our roles more transparent to the students because it was difficult for Jared and me to build the necessary symbolic capital as teachers in the classroom. This interview points out that, as major stakeholders in classroom activities, students were initially confused by the coteaching arrangement. Who should they listen to for direction? Whose opinion mattered? Who would be evaluating and assessing their learning? Cristobal's initial role as the manager who relinquished the classroom instruction to the new teachers created a situation in which the students did not appear to respect our roles as teachers. Instead, students seemed to view the arrangement as a point of confusion rather than from the perspective of added resources in the classroom. It became apparent that it was important to be as explicit as possible about the roles of each of the actors involved.

In reflecting back on this experience, cogenerative dialogues would have been an important way of addressing this type of problem. If the students had been involved in a discussion about the roles of the three teachers and the structures of the classroom had been made more explicit, then we could have worked together to transform the structure so that all of the students could have been made aware of the benefits of having three teachers in the classroom. Moreover, the infrequent cogenerative dialogues did not allow us to build the interaction ritual chains and associated solidarity needed (Collins, 2004) to build community and the assent to learn.

Life after City High

After my year of coteaching at CHS, I left the school to begin a new job in an urban charter school. The mission of this school is to boost the achievement of urban high school students and provide them with a quality college preparatory experience. The student population is drawn from the same pool of students as other schools in the school district. Thus, many of the students would have attended a neighborhood or comprehensive high school in the city if they had not been enrolled in this charter school. Moreover, many of these students come from similar backgrounds and life histories as those students at CHS.

Learning to teach by coteaching also instilled the importance of encouraging even the most reluctant observer to participate in the class. If an individual, such as an administrator or other teachers, enters my classroom, then I would expect them to participate and share the experience of learning and doing science. Understanding one's practice of teaching and the decisions that one makes in the classroom depends on taking part in the shared experiences of all the stakeholders in the class. One cannot evaluate one's teaching while sitting on the side and passively observing the events in the class (Tobin & Roth, 2002). Moreover, sharing expertise and actively participating in the classroom activities provides students with a rich and diverse experience. This not only enhances their education, but also it provides them with the opportunity to develop more meaningful relationships with individuals other than their teacher.

Despite this element of collaboration among the team of teachers and administrators in this high school, there was now a feeling of isolation in the classroom. Thus, in this first year there was an important contradiction that has occurred between learning to teach through coteaching and being placed in a classroom alone. I was no longer a member of a coteaching team in the classroom; rather, I was now left to make many of the key curricular and pedagogical decisions on my own. While coteaching affords the opportunity to collaborate with other teachers even in the heat of the moment, as a first-year certified teacher, I was still making mistakes and still in need of the dialogue that results from the shared experiences in the classroom.

Throughout that first year of teaching on my own, I constantly felt like there were aspects of my praxis that needed to be refined and reworked; however, it was not until my second year when I started work on a collaborative research project that I recognized how my teaching practices were culturally incongruent with respect to my students. Moreover, it provided a space for me to be reflective in the presence of other stakeholders in the classroom and brought to light how my praxis created a structure that truncated the agency of my students and prevented all of us from being successful. In contrast to my experiences at City High, where cogenerative dialogues were largely ineffective and coteaching only occurred between the teachers in the classroom, this new context opened a window into connecting with my students and recognizing them as valuable resources that I had in my classroom. In this regard, it afforded me an opportunity to see that I am never alone in my classroom; rather, I am in the presence of other participants who have a valuable stake in the how the classroom is structured and how that structure impacts the teaching and learning that occurs daily.

Coda

My experiences with coteaching at City High made me aware of the importance of giving new teachers the space to create lessons, try new things, and make mistakes. Accordingly, when in my second year of teaching I was given the opportunity to collaborate with two new teachers I was well prepared for coteaching. Immediately I suggested to Alan and Keisha that they pick a class in the first week where they would take the lead role in terms of grading, preparing the daily lesson plans, and so forth. In these classes, I took a more peripheral role and raised my hand to step in and out of the lessons. Also, I worked more one-on-one with students and helped the lead teacher with classroom management.

Coplanning was also an integral part of the experience for Alan and Keisha. We spent a lot of time working together to develop the lessons and general flow of the curriculum. We tried to ritualize these coplanning sessions, which I found to be important to the whole experience for all of the stakeholders involved. It created a space for me to be reflective about what I do in the classroom. At the same time, it also set up a structure for Alan and Keisha to share their ideas and gain feedback from me and, sometimes, other teachers who were teaching the same course. This was also a time to debrief about the lessons and the students and all of our experiences each week.

I approached the coteaching experience with Alan and Keisha as a peer or colleague rather than as a cooperating teacher or mentor. Although I was held accountable to the school and administrators for what happened in the classroom, I wanted to help structure the new teachers' experiences with me in ways that afforded all of us opportunities to learn from each other and the students. As a second-year teacher, I was still learning how to teach and I approached my year with the new teachers with the attitude that I am not an expert in the classroom.

Huddling was an important technique in the very beginning because we didn't know how to read each other. I would often check in with the new teachers about how to present a concept or direct the students for a particular activity. As the first term went on and Alan and Keisha became more comfortable with their role as lead teacher, I tried to intervene less and less often. Instead, there was more fluidity in our interactions with each other, and we trusted each other to just take a step up or back when needed.

I also asked them for help when I was teaching a lesson. If I saw that they had a particularly effective way of explaining a concept or used a particularly interesting example while teaching their own classes, I often took a step back and asked them to come forward to teach the class. So, as I became less and less present in their classes, I also tried to allow them to be increasingly present in my own.

This experience made me more reflective. As I watched Alan and Keisha teach, I often thought about how to change the way I presented a concept or structured an activity. Also, they brought with them ideas about how to structure the class physically and create rituals that would help students keep track of their grades in the class. Alan and Keisha also designed some really creative activities for students that were used by all of the teachers teaching the course.

I also benefited from coteaching because I was able to think through ideas about curriculum with them, especially since I was teaching out of field. Alan and I were at a slight disadvantage in that we were teaching earth science rather than biology. Therefore, we had to learn the material and attempt to keep ahead of the students. I think I also became more comfortable sharing with the students that I was not an expert in the classroom because there were two other teachers in the room working with us.

Personality issues were always resolved through open communication. If one or more students had difficulties, I suggested that we sit down and talk with them. Often, I was merely a facilitator in these conversations and then debriefed with Alan and Keisha after the conversation. I also tried to model the importance of following through with the students and reaching out to the most difficult ones to attempt to create a cohesive classroom community. Alan seemed to be much more open-minded with regard to cogenerative dialogues; however, the whole-class cogenerative dialogues did not work very well for him. This was probably due to Alan's classroom management style and the fact that we did not set up the rules and roles for this dialogue form.

Sarah-Kate was the university supervisor for the two new teachers. We had a good relationship and she was a coresearcher in my classroom, undertaking research on the teaching and learning of urban science. I only asked Sarah-Kate to intervene as a last-ditched effort. Often she intervened when she perceived contradictions; however, she always consulted me first. Sarah-Kate met with the

94 BEERS

student teachers at the same time I was teaching and, therefore, I was unable to participate in those conversations. She helped Alan and Keisha by making suggestions about activities and classroom management and coparticipated in cogenerative dialogues with the new teachers and several students from my class.

Sarah-Kate saw me struggling to teach my students and worked with me to research my own practice. She participated by coteaching in my class as well as working with the student teachers in their classes. She really saw the big picture and worked with all of us to improve our practice. I think she saw the transformative potential of the entire experience with regard to improving the quality of teaching and learning in the classroom. She never positioned herself as "expert" and worked together with us as a stakeholder in the classroom community. She fostered positive relationships with the students and worked with them one on one. In this regard, she never appeared like an authority; rather, she positioned herself as an equal.

Reflecting on the experience reported here reveals how important all participants were to the learning of individuals. Alan's and Keisha's learning was mediated by working with one another, Sarah-Kate, and me; my learning was mediated by working with the interns and Sarah-Kate; and, though not reported here, Sarah-Kate certainly learned by working with the three of us. These experiences definitely speak in favor of coteaching and cogenerative dialoguing as modes of praxis that also produce learning.

References

Anderson, E. (1999). *Code of the street: Decency, violence and the moral life of the inner city.* New York: W.W. Norton.

Bourdieu, P. (1977). Cultural reproduction and social reproduction. In J. Karabel & A. H. Halsey (Eds.), *Power and ideology in education* (pp. 487–511). New York: Oxford University Press.

Barton, A. C. (1998a). *Feminist science education.* New York: Teachers College Press.

Barton, A. C. (1998b). Reframing "science for all" through the politics of poverty. *Educational Policy, 12,* 525–541.

Boykin, A.W. (1986). The triple quandary and the schooling of Afro-American children. In U. Neisser (Ed.), *The school achievement of minority children* (pp. 57–92). Hillsdale, NJ: Lawrence Erlbaum Associates.

Collins, R. (2004). *Interaction ritual chains.* Princeton, NJ: Princeton University Press.

Eldon, M., & Levin, M. (1991). Cogenerative learning: Bringing participation into action research. In W. F. Whyte (Ed.), *Participative action research* (pp. 127–142). Newbury Park, CA: Sage.

Roth, W.-M., & Tobin, K. (2002). *At the elbows of another: Learning to teach through coteaching.* New York: Peter Lang.

Sewell, W. H. (1992). A theory of structure: Duality, agency and transformation. *American Journal of Sociology, 98*, 1–29.

Seiler, G. (2001). *A critical look at teaching and learning science in an inner city neighborhood high school.* Unpublished doctoral dissertation, University of Pennsylvania, Philadelphia.

Tobin, K., Roth, W.-M., & Zimmermann, A. (2001). Learning to teach science in urban schools. *Journal of Research in Science Teaching, 38*, 941–964.

5 Cogenerating culturally and socially adaptive practices

Sarah-Kate LaVan

I hated her in the beginning. She was boring and I thought she disrespected me every opportunity she got. Instead of asking me what was wrong she yelled at me, was very disrespectful which made me mad a lot of times so I resisted, didn't do work in class, talked to my friends and tried to just slide by. (Ace, student electronic journal, reflection of his teacher, 2003)

Well I thought Ace and I were cool on a personal level. I knew he didn't like me as a teacher but whatever. I was like whatever he doesn't have to like me he just has to take my class. That was my mentality you don't have to like me you just have to do what I say. I mean that's essentially what you're taught in teacher education. . . . I can vividly remember Ace my first year. Ace was the kid that sat in front of the class and fought me about everything, about a binder, about copying notes, about doing work. Everyday, I mean, he sat right in front of me, proximity rule. I could not get him to do a damn thing . . . . I absolutely couldn't figure him out. (Jen Beers, teacher, cogenerative dialogue, 2004)

As illustrated in the opening narratives, students and teachers can have strongly divergent perspectives about their classroom relationships and this disconnect can have a profound impact on their mutual success. While one might conclude that the above passage represents an isolated case, where the adverse interactions are attributable to a disinterested teacher and an unmotivated student, interactions are much more complex, being mediated by social, cultural, and historical factors that participants bring to the learning environment. Lisa Delpit (1995) states that "one of the most difficult tasks we face as human beings is communicating across our individual differences, trying to make sure what we say to someone is interpreted the way we intend" (p. 135).

Teachers and students communicate through a number of channels and practices over a class period and what may seem like innocuous practices by one participant may be easily construed as being disrespectful or threatening to another. These misunderstandings can often stimulate feelings of anger and frustration and can serve to undermine positive relationships and productive future interactions. Over time, disconnections between teachers and students can work to widen borders (Davidson, 1999) between the participants. Further, cycles of symbolic violence, resistance, and domination break down successful learning communities, and perpetuate school failure for certain students (Bourdieu, 1986). Although misinterpretations between students and teachers occur to some degree in all classrooms, the frequency and pervasiveness of these unsuccessful patterned interactions (Collins, 2004) in urban high schools, and specifically the classroom in which this study takes place drives the exigency of this research.

Specifically, this chapter examines a ninth-grade science classroom that was characterized by an ineffective learning environment and failed interaction rituals (Collins, 2004) between Jennifer Beers (see her chapter 4, this volume), a white, middle-class teacher, and her black students. In this chapter I explore how practices and schema (Sewell, 1999) developed in the field of cogenerative dialogue (Roth & Tobin, 2001) informed the structures of the science classroom and facilitate positive and productive interactions and communication among the classroom participants. Thus, allowing differing stakeholders to develop cultural and social congruence and a more effective learning community.

Context of the study

Charter High School

The research reflected in this chapter takes place in a small urban Charter High School (UCHS) located in Philadelphia. At the time of the research the school was in its second year of operation and enrolled approximately 200 students in what is the equivalent of the ninth- and tenth-grade levels. As with most other charter schools in the school district, students in this school were selected from the same general pool of applicants as the comprehensive schools, and thus were comprised mainly of black students from a wide range of educational, social, cultural, economic, and geographical backgrounds.

Unlike traditional high schools in the United States, UCHS operates on an extended school-year cycle, utilizes a nontraditional grading system, and employs block scheduling. Thus, students focus on three courses per quarter and are advanced through the course sequence based on their ability to show that they have mastered specific content and skills as laid out in the school's academic standards—with mastery being defined as achieving an 80 percent or better on the assignments and activities defined by the curriculum. As a consequence of this type of structure, only students who master the material can move onto the next course in the sequence and rotate teachers at the end of each trimester. Therefore, it is possible for students who do not show competency in the specific course to remain in the same class for a number of semesters.

The earth science classroom

The course in which this study took place was an introductory earth science class. One of the first courses in the science sequence, it focused on providing students with foundational knowledge and skills necessary to move on to more advanced science courses. Since students came to the class with a wide range of home and school science experiences, they differed greatly in the social and symbolic capital (Bourdieu, 1986) and resources (human, material, and symbolic) that they could access to support their learning of science. For example, some students had experiences in their homes and middle schools that were a foundation for learning science, while others had experiences that did not so obviously support their learning of science.

When our research began fourteen out of the fifteen students in this class were repeating the course because of their failure to reach mastery on a previous attempt. From a sociocultural standpoint, ideological and physical structures (Sewell, 1999) found within the school, such as the nontraditional grading system, student resistance to being in school, home lives that impede the completion of homework assignments, and poor relationships with teachers, were possible explanations for the students' academic struggles. For these reasons among many others, a majority of the students not only resented the fact that they were enrolled in this course again, but also felt that since they had been exposed to the course content, just showing up for class everyday would allow them to master the material needed to move on to the next course in the sequence.

In this context, the structures of the school field also presented contradictions for Jen as she endeavored to reflect on possible pedagogical strategies that would build from what she could do, connect to the cultural capital of students, and be compatible with the rule structure that was set in place by the school. Jen had to account for a range of student educational and personal experiences, consider how to engage students who had negative emotional energy (Collins, 2004) associated with science and meet the needs of students who had already taken the course at least once.

Unsuccessful interactions and truncated agency in the classroom

Compounding the negative emotions students associated with science and the class were negative histories that some students brought with them regarding their teacher and her teaching practices. In the past, many students had come to know Jen as an "interfering, authoritarian teacher," who did not value the culture that the students brought to the classroom. Additionally, the students perceived that Jen did not understand how their experiences outside of science class and school impinged on their learning while in her classroom. Throughout our research, the students often pointed out that the porous nature of the classroom field allowed culture from external fields to enter, yet when they enacted practices and dispositions (Boykin, 1986) from external fields, Jen shut down these strategies in order to settle students and regain control of the class. These feelings are illustrated in the following excerpt of a conversation I had with Ace, a student-researcher.

Ace: Ms. Beers was mean. Nobody really liked her.
SK: Why not? What did she do?
Ace: A lot of things. She would just yell at us or bark orders at us. She would
            tell us that we needed to sit down and listen to her. She didn't let us ask
            lots of questions or challenge her, like her ideas or what we were doing or
            that we didn't really get it. . . . And she didn't get that some of us had stuff
            outside of the science to do so we couldn't do every homework that she
            gave. But when we tried to explain it to her she just told us to get it done.
            When we started doing cogenerative dialogues she started to listen and
            figure out what we could all do to get our work done.

The enactment of unconscious shutdown strategies, such as the ones described above, caused symbolic violence (Bourdieu, 1992) for many students and over time, furthered students' animosity toward Jen and frustration toward the class. As a result, students engaged in practices that did not afford the collective goals of teaching and learning science and stimulated anger and dissatisfaction from Jen toward the class as a whole. Thus, Jen's unconscious use of shutdown strategies, in conjunction with a culturally incongruent style of teaching, created a division between her and her students that involved issues of power, resistance and domination. Further, it served to truncate the students' agency in the classroom, break down the potential for community and prevent opportunities for the students' success with regard to learning science.

    A second example of the cultural incongruence that was cultivated and maintained is illustrated through Jen's interactions with students during whole-class activity. One pattern that emerged through video analysis was that a great deal of class time required students to complete tasks individually and interact mainly with Jen. While students occasionally worked in pairs or groups of three, this was not typical. In a conversation about this practice, Jen proposed many reasons for this, including her lack of social and symbolic capital with the students, her lack of confidence and knowledge regarding earth science, and the importance of students developing note taking, organizational, and writing skills for subsequent science courses. Furthermore, difficulties students historically encountered (regarding the sharing of resources, helping one another, and discussing ideas) when provided with group work or inquiry-related activities reinforced this structure and perpetuated the beliefs of all participants—that the students were not capable of learning in ways other than this fashion. Consequently, the classroom was structured to support an interactive lecture as the main pedagogical practice, rather than to encourage the group's engagement in inquiry together.

The following transcription is drawn upon to illustrate how these structures helped to shape participants' roles and generally depict classroom activity and interactions. During this particular day, Jen was positioned at the front of the room near the dry erase board lecturing about various types of land formations. Students, seated at their respective tables facing the front of the classroom, were taking notes.[1]

Time	Speaker	Discourse	Gestures
00:00:00	Jen:		Standing at the front left of the room. Hands down at her sides.
00:00:03		What does that mean?*	*Turns head to the left to look at a student.
00:00:06	Fran:	It just naturally appears.	Looking at the front of the classroom and then down at her notebook.
00:00:07	Jen:	It just naturally *appears As *opposed to what?	*Raises right hand upward *Shifts weight and takes one step to her left. Touches her hair with right hand and puts hand on cheek.
00:00:10	Marc:	Being man made	Looking down at his notebook.
00:00:11	Jen:	Being man made okay. Right so it's so. . . so. . . .	Takes three steps toward board.

Although the above transcription spanned only eleven seconds, this was none-theless representative of the both the pedagogical styles and relationships which occurred in this classroom at the beginning of the research. During interactive lectures, which encompassed much of classroom activity, Jen generally posi-tioned herself at the front center of classroom, removed from the students. Jen's movement and position did not generally vary over the course of these interac-tive lectures. In this particular instance, Jen was, as one student described, "stiff standin'." In this regard, she moved no more than four steps in either direction from her original spot. Additionally, as reflected in the transcript, Jen's hand and body pose changed in a very limited manner (e.g., hands raising and lowering from her face and the shifting of her weight). Although this transcript repre-sented only a brief moment in the class period, Jen sustained this interaction style for nineteen of the remaining thirty-five class minutes.

Furthermore, Jen's attempts to involve students in lectures were frequently unsuccessful, as noted microscopically in the above transcription by the long pauses between speakers and consistent teacher-initiated talk (e.g., students speaking only when asked a question). In describing the rhythm of successful conversations, Collins (2004) noted that the human ability to perceive interac-tions and occurrences is quite attuned. Therefore, pauses of 1.0 second or more appear as a gap in the interaction, and thus a break in the flow. In essence, the rather long gaps in conversation in the above transcript were quite disruptive to the rhythm of the interaction and indicative of unsuccessful interactions and un-healthy social relationships among classroom participants. These unsuccessful interactions, in turn, often frustrated Jen and served to maintain the teacher-directed style of teaching and the teacher-student-teacher interaction dynamic. As a result, reinforcement of the notion that the teacher is keeper of knowledge (noted in videotape through statements such as "eyes up here" and "you need to be quiet so I can explain this") prevented students from developing ways of in-teracting with their peers.

Although not noted in this transcription, another pattern of coherence emerged as a contradiction to the long pauses between speakers and the teacher directed talk—student questions and talk overpowering the teacher. At times when student talk, questions, and high-energy interactions (e.g., yelling across the room, not listening to one another) overpowered Jen, she often structured the classroom in ways similar when students were reluctant to interact during whole class instruction that promoted her control and authority.

As cycles of unsuccessful interactions continued, Jen's low emotional en-ergy (as noted microscopically by her limited voice inflection, monotone pitch and restricted movement [see Roth, this volume, for this form of analysis] and her desire to remedy the situation often furthered instances of teacher-controlled talk and activities. Although there were only occasions where emotional energy increased during this type of activity (as noted by cross-talk, overlapping speech patterns, sustained mutual focus, greater movement), this pattern was generally sustained throughout the first quarter of the research.

Early in the research, while Terrell and I were analyzing videotape of classroom activity from January 16, Terrell's reflection on Jen's teaching during one particular day captured the essence of the patterns describe above.

The way Ms. Beers was teaching was appalling. She just stood in the corner or sat on the table and lectured the students. In most clips you can see the students are very uninterested and are not listening. Students' heads are down; others are looking around the room. . . . Ms. Beers was also lacking power. I say this because earlier in the clip the students were out of control and very rambunctious and when she said stop they ignored her. Only some students who were actually paying attention. . . . Most clips she started yelling and shouting commands and instructions at the class. Yelling to your class isn't effective because it will just be an invitation for that student to be impertinent to you and to be resistant towards you. A student may also sense that the teacher doesn't care if she/he yells at the student like she did here. (Terrell, January 30, 2003)

Terrell's analysis captured two extremely critical points about the recursive relationship between Jen's dispositions and schemas and those of the students. As the borders widened and frustration and fear rose, Jen resorted to increasing amounts of activities that she could actively control such as note-taking, worksheets, and lectures. She became reactive to the students by yelling. Consequently, as students tried to enact and transform science culture through structures that emphasized and valued the dispositions of the teacher, students' agency was consciously and unconsciously truncated.

Methodology

Cogenerative dialogues and collaborative research

In this study, cogenerative dialogue was an integral theoretical and methodological frame for which to think about enacting structural change within classrooms in general, and specifically this classroom which participants have not been successful in the past. Evolved from debriefing sessions used by Tobin, Seiler, and Walls (1999), cogenerative dialogue is based on the understanding and ideology that one needs to articulate and explain personal experiences through collective understanding and activity. These conversations between stakeholders allowed all participants to share in the responsibility of thinking about and making sense of events and activities and identify and review practices that are unintended and unconscious, while discussing the power relationships and roles of participants. Since all participants are represented, their perspectives are used to inform the "emerging understanding of the factors that mediate the activity of the different members of the community and how those patterns of activity contribute to collective activity and accomplishment" (Seiler, 2001). Furthermore, because of a redistribution of power (vertically and horizontally) all stakeholders could discuss future actions and activities as well as aid in planning for improving the quality of teaching.

In addition to the cogenerative dialogues, the interpretive nature (Guba & Lincoln, 1989) of the research also challenged us to change power relationships and the division of labor not only within the research but within the classroom as well. In order to do this, a research team comprised of Jen (the classroom teacher), four student researchers (Ace, Terrell, Shania, and Derek), ten student participants, and myself (a university researcher), was initially formed to inform our research and class activities.

Cultural sociology and hermeneutic phenomenology (Ricœur, 1991) informed the selection of student researchers and various other participants in the research. Since the class in which this research took place was one of the first science courses taken by students at UCHS, students enacted a wide range of cultural practices (habitual and intentional) and schema (beliefs, values and ideas). For some students these cultural practices and schema were incongruent with those expected by Jen and the school as a whole. In this regard, the agency of these students was truncated because they were prevented from participating in class and became frustrated in their endeavors to learn science. On the other hand, those students who were successful in learning science seemed to be able to adjust their practices so that they more closely matched with Jen's expectations. Accordingly, in an attempt to bring varying voices and perspectives into the research it was imperative for us to choose students from a wide range of cultural, social, economic, and science backgrounds.

As the study progressed and more students from the class became interested in the research and changing the classroom structures, additional students became student researchers or attended cogenerative dialogues in which we used video resources to examine and analyze classroom activities. By the end of the study, all but two students regularly attended cogenerative dialogues, examined videotape of classroom activity, and openly discussed the practices used by Jen and the students.

Use of video analysis

The rationale for our use of video in our methodological framework derives from the work of a growing number of researchers and teachers in science education who have begun to understand the benefits of capturing and evaluating classroom activity through the use of videotape (e.g., Elmesky, 2003). One of the many advantages of using videotape as a data resource is that it allows researchers and teachers to review activities that are often missed due to the unfolding nature of social life and participants being unaware of practices that are habitual. However, for us, the use of video as methodological, theoretical, and analytic frameworks held even greater importance. By replaying videotape, participants were able to discern patterns in practices and associated contradictions that occurred in the classroom. Videotape has become a powerful tool in that it provided a springboard for discussion during cogenerative dialogues and as a source of reference for changing classroom activities and structures.

In our research, classes were generally recorded two to three times a week (an hour per class). When necessary, taping increased to four or five times a week, as was the case when students were working on projects, laboratory activities or when Jen needed another adult present in the classroom. Classes were recorded from varying positions within the classroom, and due to the collaborative nature of the research, which required me to coteach, students often took charge of videotaping daily activities. Occasionally, there was a need for all stakeholders to be involved in the classroom activities, and therefore the camera was placed either in the back or front corner of the room on a tripod and left to record.

Once video data were captured, analyses began with mesoscopic level explorations using field notes, journal entries, comments by the teacher and students from interviews and reviewing tapes on normal and fast forward, in order to gain a general perspective of teaching practices and activities occurring in the classroom. Given the nature of our collaborative project, student researchers played an integral part of our mesoscopic analyses by viewing the video data and selecting salient video clips that would later be discussed in cogenerative dialogues. The video analysis then moved to a microscopic level that allowed for descriptions of teacher and student practices. Specifically, body movement, verbal interactions, physical spacing among the participants, on/off task behavior and discussion were all analyzed in order to examine teacher practices and students interactions.

Findings

Over the course of this research, I observed countless ways in which Jen's class-room had been transformed. However, rather than cursorily reflecting on each pattern of transformation (as well as the associated contradictions), I instead chose to consider the transformed classroom in terms of the participants' dispositions. In this section I present how these dispositions served as resources to create resonances for participants and to afford them with opportunities for developing additional dispositions and fluency with one another.

One particular aspect that colored the structures of the classroom and thus interactions, was the mismatch that occurred between Jen's mainstream Eurocentric curricula and teaching practices and black cultural ethos (BCE) which characterized the students in her class (Boykin, 1986; Nobles, 1980). Both Boykin and Nobles describe BCE as a derivation of West-African culture (including beliefs, values, and traditions) that characterizes the way blacks perceive, interpret, and interact with the world. Although noting the great variability among blacks as a group, Boykin conceptualizes BCE through the articulation of nine dimensions or dispositions. As reflected in our data resources, five of the nine dispositions (verve, movement, communalism, orality, and affect) became salient to the participants' interactions and the teaching and learning in this classroom. Marked by emotion and prior experiences, the mismatch among individuals' cultural dispositions often furthered the already apparent cultural incongruence, miscommunication, and discord by perpetuating negative feelings, and by sustaining moments of asynchrony and individual focus of attention.

After the formation of the collaborative research team and the regular use of cogenerative dialogues, both in small groups and as a whole class, a pattern of coherence emerged in which all of the participants (teacher and student) began to reshape the classroom structure by affording opportunities to draw on these dispositions as resources rather than shutting them down. Within this trans-formed classroom structure, positive emotional energy, solidarity and collective responsibility for the teaching and learning of science emerged. As evidence for this transformation I offer two vignettes which demonstrate Jen's use of three of the dispositions (verve, movement, and communalism), and highlight how these can be used as resources to support student engagement in more meaningful learning of science.

Stiff standin' no more—verve and movement

One of the ways that the classroom structure was transformed was related to a change in Jen's practices to include an increased use of verve and movement during classroom lectures. Boykin defines movement as integration of rhythm, music, and dance that is vital to an individual's psychological health. According to his definition, movement is more than just the need to move, as it encompasses an orientation toward life that is pervasive throughout one's ways of being and self-presentation. Verve, which is an element of movement, is defined as the proclivity for high physical stimulation, in which intensity and variability are greatly welcomed (Boykin & Allen, 1987). An environment encompassing verve is likely to sustain a high level of noise (intensity dimension) and a dynamic quality (high variability) that is marked by participation in several activities and events.

The transcription below illustrates a typical interactive lecture, and the increased verve and movement Jen came to employ as the trimester ensued. In this vignette, Jen was positioned at the front of the classroom lecturing to the students about the movement of the continental and oceanic plates. Students were seated at their tables with their notebooks open, facing the front of the room.

Time	Speaker	Discourse	Gestures
00:00:00	Jen:	NOW your sayin, HERE'S ↑*	With notes in hand and her back to the students, Jen *draws diagram on the board.
00:00:01		Where the plate *stuff comes in okay?↑	*She takes three steps away from the board and faces the students.
00:00:04		So as this *ROCK↑	Extends left arm toward board and *points to the diagram.
		Is moving in a *circle↑ in a circular motion	*Makes circular motion with finger on the board and then drops hand.
00:00:08		And the *ROCK↑ could be	Moves back toward the board. Takes marker in right hand, *points to board and looks back at students
		*And in some cases it could be goin' this way right? ↑ Okay it	*Draws arrows on the board representing direc-

could be goin' that way, at which   tion of movement
point the plates would be moving
in the opposite direction okay?

Although Jen's increasing verve and movement were demonstrated in a number of ways, one important manner in which this was reflected was through the modulation of her voice and her corresponding body movement. In comparing this transcript with its videotape, Jen's inflection (noted by the upward arrows in the transcription) and raised volume (indicated by the capitalization) were generally modulated when she sought to draw the students' attention to emphasize a specific point. As demonstrated in the beginning part of the transcription, Jen's variation in voice occurred when she was drawing on the board, pointing to drawings, or making hand gestures to illustrate ideas. Additionally, students often raised their heads to look at Jen and the board directly following Jen's changing voice inflection and pitch. Even more noticeable in the following section of the transcript (noted by students' heads following Jen as she points and moves around the room), Jen's voice and coordinated hand movements served as resources for students, as they afforded students with signals regarding which concepts were being emphasized and where to focus their attention (a skill that is important for note-taking). By doing so, this structure afforded the students and Jen with a mutual rhythm in which they could share the focus of attention and engage in the lecture.

00:00:21	Jen:	It's like a <u>conveyer</u> belt↑ did you ever, you've been to the airport right? ↑	Steps away from the board. Walks up the aisle of students toward the back of the room. One hand up by her mouth. Many students' heads follow Jen.
00:00:24	Terrell:	Yeah	
00:00:25	Ace:	The where?	Head follows Jen's movement.
00:00:26	Jen:	You've been to the AIRPORT↑	Continues walking up the aisle toward the back of the room. Puts one hand up by her mouth.
00:00:26	Ace:	No I↑ never been	Head continues to follow Jen.
00:00:27	Jen:	Awww.	Turns around and walks quickly back toward the

			board.
00:00:28	Wayan:	No I never been on a plane	Head down looking at his notes. Lifts head to look at Jen after finishes speaking.
00:00:29	Jen	Damn↑	Moves back to the front of the classroom. Releases hand from mouth. Opens and raises both hands signifying uncertainty and looks around at students.
00:00:29	Tanya:	I never been on a <u>plane</u>!	Looking at Jen.
00:00:30	Class:	Inaudible chatter	Rise in energy level— noted by students' rapidly changing head positions and Jen's increased movement around the room.
00:00:31	Ace:	I never been outta Philly!	
00:00:33	Ken-	[I saw it on the movies though…	

00:00:33	Class:	*[Inaudible chatter*
00:00:33	Wayan:	[I <u>have</u> been there

By changing the inflection and pitch of her voice and increasing her movement in the classroom, Jen was able to invoke student attention and encourage mutual focus. For example, in the section of the transcript shown above, Jen's upward inflection and corresponding movement toward the back of the classroom served as a resource to invite them to interject, share comments, and pose questions. In responding to Jen's questions, the students used this opportunity to create a discussion that included both their peers and Jen. In so doing, this structure provided students a forum in which to be social and share their experiences with each other. This in turn afforded students opportunities to become more relaxed and lively, to change the acceptability of the classroom noise in level, and to increase their movement (as noted by their shifting body and head positions).

This structure also served as a resource for Jen in that it provided her time and space to listen to the students' experiences. As Jen realized the ineffectiveness in using an analogy of a conveyer belt to illustrate the movement of plates, her movement throughout the classroom increased. This increased movement in turn served as an additional resource, allowing Jen the opportunity to ponder an alternative approach to explain the concept. Furthermore, since students were relaxed and talking to one another, the students' attention was not focused on Jen, which provided her the opportunity to devise a new approach. Nonetheless, in an effort to assist Jen with an example to explain the concept of the movement of plates, I interjected that the students had "been on escalators."

00:00:35	SK:	They've been on escalators.	Speaking from behind the camera. Jen shakes her head up and down and picks up marker from table and puts notes down.
00:00:36	Jen:	Okay that'll work. Alright I was [was thinking of the airport	Moves away from front table towards students. Shakes her right hand around in a circle.
00:00:38	Wayan:	[*inaudible*	Making a circular motion with his pencil in the air.
00:00:42	Jen:	and the airport has these really cool [like like they ( ) move they're called the people movers↑ right?	Continues shaking her marker. Takes both arms from chest and pushes them straight out in front of her signifying something going forward.
00:00:42	Wayan:	[those black rounds things that go around	Shows a circular motion with his right hand.
00:00:46	Ace:	Oh:h	Leaning back, head turned to left to watch Jen.
00:00:47	Jen:	=And they↑ move you stand on it and you move and it's really kinda cool especially when you're like lugged down with luggage or you can *walk and you can walk faster than the people that you're next to …	Walks forward. Repeats gesture of moving—taking both arms from chest and pushing them straight out in front. *Walks back and forth moving hands.
00:00:57	Anyon:	Baggage claim* goes around	*Making the circular motion with his arm.
00:00:58	Jen:	Ah:h baggage claim exactly too. Same thing a conveyer belt and a baggage claim the *bag sits there and the conveyer belt moves. [Same or an escalator. *Same* principle.	Points to gesturing student. Shifts weight back and forth, moving side to side. *Raises right arm, makes sliding movement downward. Moves toward board to point but then moves away and walks up the aisle toward back of room.

Both consciously and unconsciously, deciding that she could explain her initial example effectively to the students, Jen began to describe the motion of a conveyer belt and how it related to the movement of the crust. In articulating the concepts, Jen employed extensive gesticulations. The students' comments (e.g., oh:h) not only reflected the success of Jen's communication method but also their understanding of the chosen analogy. In this way, verve and movement served as a resource for Jen to explain the concept of a conveyer belt even though most students had never seen one. Additionally, Jen's verve and movement helped structure a dynamic environment that resonated with the students and sustained their interest in the topic (noted microscopically through eye gaze, common rhythm sustained in the interaction, and synchrony of interaction). It is important to recognize that verve and movement were not necessarily the only factors that contributed to sustaining these positive interactions. Jen's increased social and symbolic capital from being in cogenerative dialogues with the students provided her the confidence to attempt to explain the concepts. In addition, the students had developed assurance in Jen's ability and concern for their learning.

The title of this section, as well as the decision to use this vignette to illustrate Jen's transformation was conceived by one of the student researchers, Terrell. In analyzing the video vignette and explaining his ideas surrounding the dispositions of verve and movement, Terrell insisted that these two factors would seem insignificant to most and therefore, not contribute much to the teaching process. Nonetheless, for Terrell as well as many other students, incorporating these dispositions into daily activities sustained his interest in topics that were not understood or identified with, and "allow[ed him] to have fun." For example, another student, who was extremely tall and had difficulty staying still, confessed that Jen's use of verve and movement, reduced his level of self-consciousness when he was required to move about the classroom. For Jen, her increased verve and movement were accompanied by amplified gestures and reduced lecture time. As she and the students began to access and appropriate other resources, Jen began to move away from traditional teacher-student-teacher discourse interactions typically noted in science classrooms. This forged a pathway for greater student input and student-student interactions.

Students as resources and coteachers

The second transformation that occurred involved the transition toward students as coteachers. In several cogenerative dialogues students often complained about taking notes and indicated that they would like to take a more active role in the classroom community. As Jen gained social and symbolic capital with students and began to understand the importance of communalism (particularly the aspect of collective responsibility) in learning situations, Jen and the students began to restructure her practice to more effectively utilize students as resources. In the process, teacher focused lecture time became shorter, students came to be involved as coteachers, and peer interactions became more complex. The following vignette illustrates the complex and varied interactions that took place during one activity in which various students were asked to come to the board and explain their understandings of "how convection currents move the plates."

After observing many students struggle with an assignment to write their understandings of the how energy and particle movement were related to convection currents, Jen requested that those who thought they understood the concepts come to the board to help the class pull together a collective understanding. The following transcript depicts events in which one student, Wayan, was piecing together his own ideas as well as those of his peers in order to help develop the "big picture" understanding.

00:00:1	Jen:	Okay. Alright um what's <u>moving</u>?↑	Walks so that she is next to Ace at the board. Jen looks at Ace and then to the class. Ace looks down at his marker.
00:00:1		What do those <u>arrows</u> ↑represent?* Because there aren't <u>little arrows</u>↑ running around in the asthenosphere right?	*Ace looks at the board. Jen smiles.
00:00:1	Wayan:	Rock.	
00:00:1	Kenyon:	=Rock.	
00:00:2	Jen:	Right ↑okay *so↑.	Jen moves closer to the board and Ace. *Reaches to board to pick up a marker.
00:00:2	Wayan:	Hot rock.	
00:00:2	Jen:	What did you say?	Turns around to the students and moves away from the board.
00:00:2	Wayan:	Hot rock.	
00:00:2	Jen:	Okay so let's first, first thing's	Starts walking up the aisle

		first. Wayan? Right?	toward Wayan until she is about a foot away.
00:00:3		So there aren't little <u>arrows</u> running *around in the asthenosphere.	Smiling. Turns her body and points toward the board. *Turns back around and looks directly at Wayan. Body slightly leaning toward Wayan.

As Jen's views surrounding the importance of dispositions and capital for teaching and learning evolved, her perception of the roles and rules guiding legitimate participation (Lave & Wenger, 1991) in the classroom transformed as well. As a result, during these types of activities Jen often acted as facilitator (as noted in the transcription by her location within the classroom, silence during student presentations, and allowance of student answers to be incomplete or incorrect), deciding which student would come to the board to present and guiding the discussion that occurred in between presenters. Jen's reflection on this transcript as well as other vignettes revealed that she too began to recognize and appreciate her role as "more like a facilitator than a 'teacher' teacher." Although not represented in this vignette, it is important to note that specific instances occurred when more guidance was required (e.g., when presenters did not clearly articulate the concepts). During these occasions, Jen was more active in assisting students to develop their understandings and in guiding them through their explanations.

While this structure promoted the student as teacher (one with knowledge and authority) and the teacher as guide and listener, it also extended to the students in the audience an active role in co-constructing knowledge and shared understandings. The students in the audience responded to the rise in pitch and intensity in Jen's voice (denoted by upward arrows in the transcription) by interjecting their thoughts. This, in turn, afforded Jen the opportunity to select the appropriate next student teacher.

00:00:32	Jen:	So it's hot <u>rock</u> so you wanna explain it now? ↑	Holding marker out toward Wayan, Jen backs away toward the board. Ace who had been at the board the entire time, walks back to his seat.
00:00:38	SK:	Go on Wayan you can do it!	From behind the camera.
00:00:38	Jen:	Come on Wayan!	Walks to the board and ges-

			tures with the marker for him to come. Looks back at Will and then goes to erase the board.
00:00:39	Terrell:	Go Wayan!
00:00:40	Kenyon:	[Come on Wayan!
00:00:41	Class:	[Go Wayan ((other cheers for Wayan))

By encouraging student input and creating an engaging environment for students to share their knowledge, the students learned to value and view one another as resources. This was illustrated by the respect of the class toward the presenters (noted microscopically by silence in the classroom during presentations, and mutual focus) and by the many positive reinforcements that the students shared to encourage Wayan's participation at the board. At the microlevel of analysis, it was intriguing to note that the students who were prompting others to the board were often the same students who in the past shared particular difficulties interacting with Jen and many other teachers (e.g., Terrell). These students were drawing on communalism, verve, movement, and orality for the betterment of the class in order to meet the collective goals of teaching and learning. As Jen would say to the students, they were using their dispositions and capital for "good and not evil." Thus, this structure created resonances for students like Terrell to draw on their strengths (some of which represent dispositions not previously valued), in order to benefit the structure of the class.

Although not reflected in the transcript, cheers from the students were sustained for approximately ten seconds before Wayan accepted the responsibility with positive emotional energy (noted by his smile, the quick tempo at which he approached the board, and his synchrony in taking the marker from Jen's hand) as the next student teacher.

00:01:20	Wayan	There's rock up here.	Pointing to a diagram he created.
00:01:21	Ace:	Right right.	
00:01:21	Wayan:	The rock down here is more denser than the rock *up here. At the top.	Pointing to his diagram with his marker. *Looks back at the class and then back to the board.
00:01:24		*So when this get heated up it rises to the top.	*Lowers head and raises hand to head in thinking position. Then shows movement with marker.

00:01:26		As *this moves, the plates that movin with the rock is less dense to go down here	*Moves marker up and down on board.
00:01:30		And *when the rock moves down the plates stop movin	Looks away from board and toward class. Smiles.
00:01:31	Jen:	Right.	
00:01:31	Wayan:	=Right.	Smiles.
00:01:32	Terrell:	[Okay Mr Bammer.	
00:01:33	Jen:	[I have a question, Mr. Bammer why did the rock change, what's my question? Why is the rock on top less dense than the rock on the. . .	Seated in a chair at the back room.
00:01:37	Wayan:	=Because the rock on the top is more cooler than the rock on the bottom.	Smiling.
00:01:39	Terrell:	=Mr. Bammer does this cause the sea floor spreading?	

As illustrated in this transcript, it was not enough for students to explain their understanding. In order for the students to begin to formulate a big picture understanding of the concepts and relate them to the details, they as a community had to organize the ideas, link specific facts and ideas, and come to a shared understanding about the concepts. Jen stated that this was a crucial stage in the learning process because it was not only another way to validate that the students brought valuable understanding and knowledge to the discussion, but in that it was also a key way to illustrate that it takes many people's understandings to build knowledge. This was reflected by Terrell's question at the end of the vignette about sea floor spreading. In the past, Terrell's questions would often serve to disrupt the mutual focus of the activity by interrupting and attempting to get Jen off topic. However within this structure, Terrell's question served to further his own knowledge, advance the class discussion, and for Wayan to gain social capital (as he answered the question correctly, without hesitation).

The significance of activity became clear when this vignette was contextualized within the students' individual and collective histories. In the beginning of the term, students often had great difficulty listening to and providing one another with respect. Students would often feel disrespected during the course of interactions. During this vignette, although not reflected in the sections of transcription provided, there were frequent occasions in which students could have been disrespected. However, by placing greater emphasis on the collective, Jen and the students proactively and communally removed some of the contradictions that occurred. For example, in getting ready to explain his understanding, Wayan erased Ace's diagram; however, comments made by Jen and myself about each person needing a diagram and the reinforcement of Ace's explanation being correct, but limited, enabled Ace to sit back down and accept his role as learner. Furthermore, this series of interactions also provided Jen with several opportunities to build capital with the entire class and at the same time build bridges with individual students. First, by changing the roles of students, positioning herself at various locations within the room as they explained the concepts (e.g., seated at the back of the room with other students), addressing students by Mr. and Ms., and reaffirming that all students contributed to the greater understanding, Jen demonstrated that she trusted and believed that all students were capable teachers and learners.

The social nature of science learning is one of the most important aspects of the interactions required for the development of scientific dispositions and fluency. The use of students as resources is one way to validate student knowledge and foster a community of practice. Often times, this is especially difficult given that different individuals and groups of students will approach the same tasks in different ways by applying different resources, culture, and dispositions in the solving of the same problem. Jen's use of students as coteachers is important because it provides a venue in which these differing dispositions and science understandings can be appreciated and where students can begin to collectively take responsibility for their learning.

Conclusions and implications

For several reasons, an individual's pedagogical and ideological commitment to teaching for diversity and transformation may not be enough to produce success. A teacher's actions, which are often influenced by structures in multiple fields, may not in fact, match her beliefs. In addition, other stakeholders are involved in the teaching and learning process and their beliefs contribute to the structure of the learning community. Therefore, it is also not enough for a teacher to simply examine her beliefs outside of the teaching practice. Doing this prevents the teacher from examining and asking the difficult questions surrounding the social location (e.g., in terms of ethnic and cultural background, socioeconomic status, gender), ideological location (e.g., values and beliefs), and academic location (e.g., education and skill level) that affect the stakeholders' perceptions of teaching and learning.

In order for classrooms to become discourse communities where transformative learning occurs, teachers also need to change the power structure that they have in their classrooms and get rid of the archaic notion that they are the sole holders of knowledge (that is salient to the learning of science). We have found that one important way in which this can be accomplished is through the use of collaborative research, which employs cogenerative dialogue as a means to focus on reflection and pedagogical change through the eyes of all stakeholders. In our research, cogenerative dialogues served as a field for participants to collectively review classroom unconscious and conscious schema and practices in an effort to talk across age, race, gender, and economic borders. These focused discussions between participants promoted a shared sense of responsibility as stakeholders because they actively worked toward making structures more conducive individual and collective goals. In this regard, it helped to inform both Jen's and the students' schema and practices as well as allow participants to develop practices and schemas that serve to facilitate positive and productive interactions and communication.

Our use of collaborative research and cogenerative dialogue also created opportunities for Jen and her students to change their roles in the classroom. The role of teacher-as-learner and student-as-teacher can have a powerful impact on teacher praxis. It enabled a new division of labor in the classroom where there develops an ethos of collective responsibility toward learning. By privileging student voice with regard to the system of practices and structures in place in the classroom, Jen and the students created solidarity among the stakeholders and enabled them to buy-in to learning activities. For Jen, it also created a window into the schema and practices of the students that she could access to improve their learning.

Finally, our research suggests that the use of collaborative research with cogenerative dialogue can have a long-range impact on how we currently view the process of new teacher education and the continuing education of experienced teachers. Our research suggests that those in charge of university methods courses and professional development should keep in mind the possibility that exploring teacher beliefs and identities through traditional discussion alone may not be an effective means to analyze and transform praxis. Since much of teaching is an unconscious act that occurs in the presence of other stakeholders, new teachers and experienced teachers alike should be given the space to engage in this type of professional development. It will not only allow teachers to become aware of the impact of the unconscious acts associated with their practice; rather, it also will also give them the opportunity to gain perspective and strategies that will lead toward a type of learning community envisioned in current educational reform.

Notes

1. In this chapter, the following transcription conventions are used:

↑	Rising intonation
↓	Falling intonation
___	(Underline) Emphasis on word
ROCK	(Upper case lettering) Yelling
*	Coordination of language and gestures
[	Simultaneous talk by two speakers, with one utterance represented on top of the other in the moment of overlap marked by left brackets
,	Pause or breath without marked intonation and laughter breaking into words without speaking
=	Interruptions or next utterance following immediately, or continuous talk represented on separate lines because of the need to represent overlapping comment on intervening line
[...]	Transcriber's comments

References

Bourdieu, P. (1986). The forms of capital. In J. Richardson (Ed.), *Handbook of theory and research for the sociology of education* (pp. 241–258). New York: Greenwood.

Bourdieu, P. (1992). The practice of reflexive sociology (The Paris workshop). In P. Bourdieu & L.J.D. Wacquant (Eds.), *An invitation to reflexive sociology* (pp. 216–260). Chicago: University of Chicago Press.

Boykin, A. W. (1986). The triple quandary and the schooling of Afro-American Children. In U. Neisser (Ed.), *The school achievement of minority children: New perspectives* (pp. 57–92). Hillsdale, NJ: Lawrence Erlbaum Associates.

Boykin, A. W., & Allen, B. (1987). Rhythmic–movement facilitation of learning in working-class Afro-American children. *Journal of Genetic Psychology, 149*, 335–348.

Collins, R. (2004). *Interaction ritual chains*. Princeton, NJ: Princeton University Press.

Davidson, A. (1999). Negotiating social differences: Youths' assessments of educators' strategies. *Urban Education, 34*, 338–369.

Delpit, L. (1995). *Other people's children: Cultural conflict in the classroom*. New York: New Press.

Elmesky, R. (2003). Crossfire on the streets and into the classroom: Meso|micro understandings of weak cultural boundaries, strategies of action and a sense of the game in an inner-city chemistry classroom. *Cybernetics and Human Knowing, 10*(2), 29–50.

Guba, E. G., & Lincoln, Y. S. (1989). *Fourth generation evaluation.* Newbury Park, CA: Sage.

Lave, J., & Wenger, E. (1991). *Situated learning: Legitimate peripheral participation.* Cambridge, UK: Cambridge University Press.

Nobles, W. (1980). African philosophy: Foundations of Black psychology. In R. Jones (Ed.), *Black psychology* (pp. 23–36). New York: Harper and Row.

Ricœur, P. (1991). *From text to action: Essays in hermeneutics, II.* Evanston, IL: Northwestern University Press.

Roth, W.-M., & Tobin, K. (2001). Learning to teach science as practice. *Teaching and Teacher Education, 17,* 741–762.

Seiler, G. (2001). *A critical look at teaching and learning science in an inner city, neighborhood high school.* Unpublished doctoral dissertation, University of Pennsylvania, Philadelphia.

Sewell, W. H. (1992). A theory of structure: Duality, agency and transformation. *American Journal of Sociology, 98,* 1–29.

Sewell, W. H. (1999). The concept(s) of culture. In V. E. Bonell & L. Hunt (Eds.), *Beyond the cultural turn* (pp. 35–61). Berkeley: University of California Press.

Tobin, K., Seiler, G., & Walls, E. (1999). Reproduction of social class in the teaching and learning of science in urban high schools. *Research in Science Education, 29,* 171–187.

6   Coteaching as a site for collaborative research

Beth A. Wassell

Numerous studies have examined the benefits of using the coteaching model to prepare urban science teachers (e.g., Roth, Masciotra, & Boyd, 1999; Roth & Tobin, 2002; Tobin, Zurbano, Ford, & Carambo, 2003). In this chapter, I expound upon two important aspects of the model in the context of two preservice teachers' experiences: the division of labor that was constructed between the two neophyte teachers and the opportunities for collaborative research that ensued from their arrangement. Ian and Scott, the participants who serve as the focus for this chapter, both entered a teacher preparation program with bachelor's degrees in engineering and sought certification in physics and math. Their case was particularly significant because of their backgrounds in an applied field of science and their similar interest in working in urban schools with diverse student bodies. In addition, the cooperating teacher who worked with Ian and Scott was certified in vocational education and thus knew little about physics or science education.

Exploring this particular arrangement offers an account of a nontraditional, yet innovative means for individuals to transition into teaching. However, Ian and Scott's case offers other points of interest that will be analyzed in this chapter. First, the division of labor established in their coteaching experience fostered a particular structural arrangement, which has specific implications for the practices that Ian and Scott acquired as beginning teachers. Second, their practices as student teachers included several opportunities for collaborative teacher research, which has innumerable implications for classroom inquiry. Even though several studies have cited the reflective nature of coteaching, I outline four particular sites that were evidenced by this case as the participants employed the coteaching model. Using the dialectical relationship between structure and agency (Sewell, 1992) as an analytic tool, I explore these two ideas in an effort to gain broader insights into the benefits of coteaching as an alternative

teacher preparation experience that provides enhanced opportunities for reflection. Two questions drive this chapter: (a) How did Ian and Scott's involvement
in coteaching shape their teaching practices? and (b) How did Ian and Scott use
coteaching as a site for collaborative research?

The context for study and sources of data

In keeping with the organization of their teacher education program at the University of Pennsylvania, Ian and Scott began their student teaching during the
first semester, which ran from September until January. Both experienced varied
teaching scenarios with several cooperating teachers during the first semester;
for instance, Ian cotaught both physics and mathematics with veteran teachers at
City High School (CHS), an urban school that largely serves students from
working-class and impoverished families. Starting in January of 2003, Ian and
Scott began their coteaching experience in a second semester physics of engineering class at CHS. According to the school's organization, students switch
courses halfway through the year in a manner consistent with a traditional college schedule. Thus, Ian and Scott began teaching the engineering physics
course at its inception with a new group of students. Mr. Prince, a vocational
education teacher who specialized in automotive repair, was scheduled to work
with them. Needless to say, the absence of a cooperating teacher certified in
physics was one factor in creating an unusual structure for their experience.

Of the twenty students in the engineering physics class, most were juniors
in the SEM^2 (Science, Engineering, Math, and Motivation) charter, one of the
school's "small learning communities," or schools within a school. In order to
take the engineering physics course, students should have taken a basic physics
course beforehand, but in reality there was no prerequisite to be placed in the
class.

Approximately twenty hours of video data were collected in Ian and Scott's
fifth-period engineering physics class. This particular class met daily from approximately 1:00 P.M. until 2:35 P.M. Classes were taped one to two times per
week during a period from February until April of 2003. Since the classes were
96 minutes long, usually two (one-hour) digital videotapes were used to capture
the entire instructional time. The camera was positioned on either the right or
left side of the classroom so that all aspects of the classroom could be seen (i.e.,
the front board, each of lab tables, etc.). The room actually consisted of two
laboratory classrooms that could be divided by a folding wall-type structure. The
students worked at the small lab stations; student desks were not present in the
room.

The division of labor

In studies that have examined coteaching (e.g., Tobin et al., 2003), a division of labor, which stems theoretically from cultural, historical activity theory (Engström, 1999), is typically constructed among the participants. In this, participants enact practices that become patterned and can be described as succinct roles in the classroom. Other requirements that structure the organization and actions of coteachers include a set of rules (both implicit and explicit), which govern participants' involvement and focus on shared outcomes. The division of labor in coteaching can be described as:

In whole class activities it is customary for one coteacher to assume central roles while others have peripheral roles and an understanding of when and how to step forward to assume a central role as the unfolding events of the classroom present opportunities for them to afford the collective learning of the community. (Tobin et al., 2003, p. 52)

Tobin et al.'s description easily translates into the discourse used to describe Sewell's (1992) structure|agency dialectic; coteachers employ agency when they "step forward to assume a central role" because of the constantly unfolding structure (or "events of the classroom"). The unfolding structure offers opportunities for the collective agency of the participants (the coteachers as well as the students) as all individuals in the community have enhanced learning opportunities.

As Ian and Scott grew increasingly comfortable in their new arrangement, patterns suggesting an accepted division of labor became apparent. Although both teachers were involved in teaching activities during the entire period, each had preferred roles that became apparent: Ian concerned himself more with circulating around the room and talking to students individually or in small groups, while Scott often took control at the board in the role of lecturer. Contradictions to these patterns were indeed evident, for instance, when Scott would circulate or Ian would deliver part of a lesson at the board; however, the roles in which each seemed more comfortable (either on a conscious or unconscious level) were increasingly noticeable as the video data were analyzed at the meso level.

Ian's role: building capital and creativity

Many of the video data suggest that Ian attempted to build both social and symbolic capital (Bourdieu, 1986) with the students. Ian claimed that building capital with students was stressed in his science methods course and he saw it as one of the most important goals to be pursued to establish a productive learning environment. In viewing the classroom tapes longitudinally, it was evident that the students began to recognize Ian as their teacher and seemed increasingly comfortable asking him physics-related questions; thus, he managed to effectively build symbolic capital with them, or status as a capable physics teacher who they could use as a resource in the classroom. On a more personal level, the students also seemed to get along well with Ian; he would often talk to them informally about topics unrelated to class. The students trusted him with important and highly personal information; for example, Ian told the story of a student that came to him because another student wanted to fight with him after school. Ian was able to mediate in the situation and talk to the vice-principal, an action that assisted the young man to avoid the fight. Scenarios such as this suggest that Ian had built social networks with the students, or social capital.

According to Ian, getting to know the students was one of his top priorities and because of the structure provided by Scott's teaching practices and his coteaching arrangement, he was able to employ agency to do so.

Ian: It was like, I wanted to do certain things, and Scott wanted to do certain things, but since we were both there, it was easier for us to do those because the other person was always handling the other things. You know what I mean?
Beth: What do you mean you wanted to do other things, like an activity?
Ian: Yeah, or even like more specific like, let's say that Scott's doing something at the board, and then I want to, I want to talk to some of the kids, I want to try and get personal relationships with the kids, right, that's one of my goals, so I have that time to talk to all the kids while he's doing something. And the rest of them are all doing it with him, and I can [talk] specifically to someone, whatever. So, he's affording me time to do that. (Interview with Ian, 1/21/04)

Ian's attempt to forge personal relationships with the students was evident in the video data; at one point during a lesson in which the students worked in collaborative groups, he spent eleven minutes chatting with a particular group. During another lesson, Ian spent several minutes helping a student work through a problem at the board. Rather than inviting the entire class to get involved in this teaching moment, Ian focused solely on this particular individual and helped her work through the problem. As Ian mentioned in an interview, building relationships with students was a specific goal, one that he consciously hoped to incorporate into class time. Thus, the structure of the class, which according to Sewell's definition consists of "sets of mutually sustaining schemas and resources that empower and constrain social action and that tend to be reproduced by social action" (1992, p. 13), incorporated Ian's beliefs about the importance of building social and symbolic capital. This structure was directly related to the agency of the collective, or their power to access resources; as the structure of the class unfolded, which included Ian's schemas and practices, the participants' abilities to access resources were affected.

Another role that Ian expressed in several interviews was that of the creative force behind many of the hands-on activities.

Ian:	Really, eighty percent of the activities we did, or maybe more, I came up with.
Beth:	Okay. The stuff where the kids are working and it's not up at the board.
Ian:	Yeah. And then like, the technology stuff, or the like movies or whatever, that was always Scott.
Beth:	Like movies to show the kids?
Ian:	Yeah. Or like, yeah, he would find physics stuff on the Internet and show that. He'd always have that stuff. I don't know it just worked well because we were better at different things. (Interview with Ian, 1/21/03)

Scott also attested to Ian's creativity in crafting mini-lab activities that they used often; "He had more an intuitive sense to write up these 'fifteen-minute mini-labs' we called them, so he wrote up more of those than me" (Interview with Scott, 2/12/04).

One of the arguments for coteaching is the enhanced ability for teachers to transition into the teacher role—sharing the teaching responsibility with another individual allows for added "wiggle room" and allows someone else to step in and help out if needed. This change in structure from the traditional teaching arrangement afforded Ian's agency to become effective with the practices that were especially important to him:

We were able to do what we wanted because we always had someone there. It was like, I wanted to do certain things, and Scott wanted to do certain things, but since we were both there, it was easier for us to do those because the other person was always handling the other things. (Interview with Ian, 1/21/04)

Because Scott was there to lend a helping hand, Ian was able to comfortably get involved in authentic teaching experiences, such as working with a student one-on-one or fine-tuning the problems with a creative mini-lab as it was being enacted. At times, Scott cleared the path so that Ian could explore his new terrain in the classroom, and vice versa. Scott explained this as a great opportunity to build routines that enabled the class to run smoothly; elements of the class such as checking homework and transitioning between activities were easier to accomplish with the presence of Ian.

Scott's role: the lecturer and organizer

Two patterns in Scott's practices were evident in the data: first, his sense of comfort with being in front of the class and delivering the lesson, and second, his concern with accomplishing varied activities during the class period and structuring class time efficiently. I observed many instances in the data in which Scott raised his voice, walked up to the board and began to directly instruct a given concept to the students. This was particularly evident during one class period early in the semester when Scott clarified the instructions for the "do now" activity that had been written on the board. In the exchange that follows, Scott led the class in trying to reach a consensus on the weight of the students' participation grade.

Scott:	To the participation and the group work grading scale. Any, any changes to that sheet that you were graded on?
James:	((Looks to Ian who is standing closer to him in the back of the room.)) What's he talkin' about?
Ian:	((Loudly.)) We're talkin' about number two, on the do now, anyone want to vocalize [what (inaudible).
Scott:	[Are there any changes, deletions, additions to that group work grading scale. (Video transcription, 2/23/03)

During these moments, Scott took the lead in motivating the students to give input on one of the class structures—the weight of participation on a rubric for group work. Prior to Scott taking the initiative at the front of the room, the students were talking amongst themselves; it was not clear whether they were actually working on the "do now" activity. Scott took advantage of the opportunity to refocus the class and in effect, restructure the class events through his practices. This action also affected the collective agency of the class; as Scott stepped forward he became a central resource for the students to access in order to accomplish the do-now task. Even as Ian rephrased the directions, Scott drowned out Ian's utterance (probably unconsciously) with his own clarification of the assignment.

During another class period, the students worked on equations to find the velocity of an egg as it drops to the ground. At one point during the lesson, two students were at the board, working on one of the equations. After negotiating the problem by themselves for a few minutes, Scott addressed the students at the board about the problem.

Scott: Um, alright, yeah, you need uh, well, what happened to the seconds, when you multiplied ten meters per second square times one second.

Student: The seconds crossed off.

Scott: What's that? How did, how did you get—the answer you originally wrote, how did you get that?

Student at board: ((Second student at the board moves away to watch.)) Oh, 'cause I did ten meters per second squared times one second.

Scott: And what happened to the seconds?

Student at board: One crossed off.

Scott: One crosses off. In the first one two crossed off. In the first one two crossed off because T was squared, right? ((Walks up to board and points to part of the first equation with a marker.)) ((During Scott's explanation, the student at the board anxiously moves around, yet continues to stay close to the board.)) T squared, so seconds squared crosses out with this seconds squared. This is a different equation though. T isn't squared here so he's only got seconds to the first power, one second numerator crosses off with second squared in the denominator so he's left with one. It looks like this in terms of fractions—ten—I would write your units so that the sec—the units are in the denominator as well, so that you can see how they cross off. ((Ian walks up and stands to the left of the board where Scott is teaching.)) Right, this, multiplying these two together is the same thing as saying seconds over seconds squared, and that's equal to one over seconds. Okay. So we're left with v f equals ten meters per second. ((Student moves away from the board.)) How does that compare to yesterday's solution.

Ian: Bill?

Bill: I didn't hear the question.

Scott: How does that compare to yester—thank you.

Bill: Same answer.

Scott: Same answer. Did we use anything in terms of energy here?

Student: No.

Scott: None.

Ian: Did we need the mass? We need the mass?

Scott: ((Louder than Ian)) What happened to the mass in yesterday's equation?

Student: They cancelled out.

Scott: They cancelled out. Is it any surprise then ((Ian walks away from the board, his arms folded across his chest.)) that mass is not even in these equations and we can still get the answer.

Student: No, (inaudible).

Scott: All right, very nice. Now did anyone else get a different answer? (Video transcription, 2/23/03)

In this vignette, Scott took the lead to show the students how to solve the equation successfully. Ian, on the other hand, walked up to the board, but did not give any direct instruction until he asked whether the mass was needed. Even though Ian made the attempt to pose a question to the class, Scott rephrased the question louder than Ian.

As the students worked on the problem at the board, Scott employed agency to change the structure of the lesson; instead of watching the students work independently, he jumped in to offer a clear, direct explanation. When Ian attempted to change the structure of Scott lecturing by himself by posing a question to the class, Scott quickly reframed the question. An important note is that these actions were most likely unconscious; it is doubtful that Ian thought about changing the structure of the lesson while he was in the moment. However, this vignette shows evidence that Scott seemed comfortable taking a traditional, teacher-centered role during the lesson. An interview with Ian confirmed Scott's tendency to lean toward the role of lecturer:

Beth: Did you see yourself falling into particular roles? Like you would do the same things and he would do the same things?
Ian: Yeah.
Beth: Because I notice that on the tape, but I'm just interested to hear what you thought.
Ian: I think so, because he's more of a lecturer and I'm not. So, he usually did that. And he felt more comfortable doing that, so it just naturally would occur. And I noticed—I mean, I noticed that stuff—and I was like, Scott always does this part. (Interview with Ian, 1/21/04)

Scott also mentioned that he felt comfortable "launching the theory" behind some of the concepts discussed during labs and other hands-on activities. Because Scott had had the same students in his Physics I class the previous semester, he felt comfortable assessing which topics he needed to clarify for the students:

I had already had them in Physics I, so I had an idea what they knew theoretically in physics class. So that's why I felt comfortable launching a lot of the theory myself that was related to what they just did. (Interview with Scott, 2/12/04)

Scott's tendency towards an organized, time-efficient class was also noticeable in the video data. During one class period approximately ten minutes into class time, Scott walked quickly around the room glancing at student work. After a few seconds he looked at his watch and said, "Whoa! We need the do now; I don't see anybody's do now. We're way past time!" In contrast, during most class periods, Ian walked around slowly to observe students working and often stopped to talk to individuals for several minutes. Scott generally walked around quickly and spoke to students to answer a specific question. Ian explained this as a difference in personality between he and Scott:

But its like, our personalities are just different. He would just get very tense about things sometimes. So then I would sort of [say] "alright." And it wasn't like he was mad—it wasn't anything between him and I, but you know class is starting and he wants to—it's just these little give and takes, you know. But, definitely, he usually did the stuff at the board I guess. (Interview with Ian, 1/21/04)

Whereas Ian seemed passive in allowing the class to unfold naturally, Scott had a particular idea of how the class should be consciously structured, which would often include positioning himself in a more central position. This contrasts with Ian's practices; he often performed the "behind the scenes" creative role and concerned himself more with building social capital, or relationships, with the students.

Both coteachers clearly acknowledged each other's strengths; their arrangement may have been an ideal pairing because of their different strong points and their willingness to work collaboratively throughout the coteaching process. Initially, however, I framed questions regarding the division of labor between Scott and Ian using a deficit lens: I questioned whether Ian's success was at the expense of Scott's or vice versa. In further exploring their arrangement and the agency afforded to each of them (both individually and collectively) by the structures that unfolded during each class period, I recognized that the division of labor for this particular pairing allowed much more flexibility than I had initially expected. Even though Ian and Scott appeared to be more comfortable in certain roles, there were ample opportunities for each to participate in all aspects of teaching. Thus, contradictions existed in the role patterns I described in this section.

Coteaching as a site for collaborative research

One of the most important benefits of coteaching cited by Ian was the opportunity to reflect on and discuss classroom events immediately after or during their enactment. When I interviewed Ian about coteaching after he had begun his first year as an autonomous teacher, he was quick to describe the value of having someone else with whom to discuss the class:

[Scott and I] were always talking. That's what I miss. Because I don't have anyone. You don't have anyone saying, "Well, what could we have done better?" Whereas Scott and I were like, we want to get [the students] to do such and such and then we would say, hold on, maybe we need to change that. That's the issue, really. (Interview with Ian, 1/21/04)

While coteaching, Scott and Ian had opportunities to negotiate ideas for the class. In the sections that follow, I describe four specific sites for collaborative research that took place between them: coplanning that transpired regularly before class, "huddles" between coparticipants that occurred during class time, informal debriefing sessions after the lesson and both formal and informal cogenerative dialogues. Each of these events can be described as *fields* (Bourdieu, 1977), which served as contexts for the pair to do collaborative research on their own teaching practices. In addition to the fact that the construct of field offers an analytic convenience for organizing events by space, time and the participants involved, an important characteristic of fields is their porous boundaries. Thus, practices in one particular field can traverse boundaries and become useful in another.

Coplanning

Ian and Scott's engineering physics class did not begin until early afternoon, after most students in their class had a lunch period. Even though Ian taught a math class at a nearby K–8 school during the early morning hours, he was able to get together with Scott daily to talk about their plans for the class. The twosome also took part in postclass discussions to plan for upcoming lessons.

Several researchers who have studied the enactment of coteaching have cited the efficacy of coplanning (Tobin et al., 2003; Roth, 1998; Eick et al., 2003). In this, coteachers have the opportunity to reflect on their classroom practices as they negotiate the use of activities that are appropriate to a particular group of students. McVay (2003) explains the benefits of coplanning as an important aspect of student teaching:

While engaging in a joint effort to prepare for the daily activities of the classroom, teachers actively engage in discussion of student learning and evaluation of their own practices. In ideal situations, these reflective coplanning discussions would serve as conduits to the development of local theories and strategies of action to improve learning but also the development of teachers' pedagogical content knowledge. Teachers would gain insight into the curriculum through the eyes of others engaged in the same context, have their approaches critiqued in supportive communities, and continue along a path of life-long learning. (McVay, 2003, pp. 23–24)

Ian and Scott's use of coplanning was a means to fine tune aspects of a lesson that one of them had created individually. The following dialogue took place during one of their coplanning sessions and began with an exchange about the logistics of the "egg-drop activity," a mini-lab that Ian had created:

Scott: We can add on or have the whole class performance [In adapting the group work rubric].

Ian: Oh yeah. Okay, you can write on there if you want to.

Scott: What do you see is the physics behind this [the egg drop activity]?

Ian: Free fall, kinetic energy . . .

Scott: What about momentum?

Ian: We can talk about momentum but I don't think . . .

Scott: I think we need to make it very crystal clear as far as what it means [the criteria for a successful egg drop project]. What if the shell cracks but it doesn't come out?

Ian: Okay. No damage. No hairline fractures.

Scott: That kinda limits the uh . . .

Ian: I don't know how you want to do it.

Scott: It limits reps of trials because if it hairline cracks the first trial . . .

Scott: They could do frequency with this ((Holds up the bicycle tire)). Are we going to do [science in the news] presentations today?

Ian: I say just have them do it [science in the news] individually today.

Scott: Trade with someone else. Answer five [questions]; create five [questions of your own for your article].

Ian: How will they answer five?

Scott: Trade with someone else.

Ian: So they read four?

Scott: Just start today reading. (Video transcription, 2/20/03)

In this discussion, the coteachers had the opportunity to negotiate the activities and assessments for the lesson. Interestingly, traces of the division of labor discussed previously emerge; Scott took the role of organizer when he stated that they should "make it very crystal clear as far as what it means [the criteria for a successful egg-drop project]." Ian was the creative force behind the egg-drop activity, however Scott asked for clarification of the physics concepts to be targeted ("What do you see is the physics behind this [the egg-drop activity]?").

Through coplanning the two were able to discuss the lab activity and negotiate an additional activity to be used in the lesson, such as the students' creation of science questions using relevant articles from the newspaper. This was also an opportunity for them to consider the conscious structure of the class: Which practices would facilitate the students' agency and thus learning of the targeted concepts?

Huddles for on-site collaboration

According to Tobin et al. (2003), coteachers regularly participate in "huddles," which serve the purpose of "touching base and fine tuning a lesson, reaching agreement on what to do next and identifying and securing the resources needed to meet agreed upon goals" (p. 53). The objectives behind a huddle strongly resemble those of cogenerative dialogues; in a sense they can be viewed as miniature, informal cogenerative dialogues. In the case of Ian and Scott's coteaching experience, huddles involved various arrangements of the stakeholders in the class: Ian, Scott, Mr. Prince (the cooperating teacher), a graduate student studying coteaching, the student teaching supervisor and their science teaching methods instructor, among other participants. During an average class period, the co-participants huddled approximately ten times; each huddle lasted between fifteen seconds and three minutes.

Frequently Ian and Scott would huddle to talk about the practical aspects of the class when the students were working on individual or group activities. The following summary gives an example of the huddles (designated H1 through H10) that occurred during one period in which the students were working on the egg drop activity:

H1:   Ian mentions to Scott that he is standing in front of the board, blocking the view of some of the students.
H2:   Mr. Price approaches Scott to discuss with him the necessary procedures that must be followed in order to obtain the license for the Lego Robotic Kit software.
H3:   Scott checks in with Ian, deciding what to do next.
H4:   Scott asks Ian if they are going to assign groups for today's work. Ian responds, "No." and then instructs the students to divide themselves into groups of four for the class.
H5:   While Scott was presenting concepts in the lecture portion of the class, the resource room teacher entered the room wishing to talk with the teacher about a specific student. Mr. Prince fields her questions and then in this huddle, describes the conversation to Scott and suggests that he follow up with the resource teacher.

H6:   Scott approaches Ian to ask about the groups he has been observing. He asks who has been doing the most of the work. He then asks Ian how long he thinks the students should have to work on the lab activity.

H7:   Ian tells Scott, "I can go between these two groups if you want to stay with that one over there." Scott says, " I like how the group work thing worked out." Ian replies, "Yeah, it was good."

H8:   Scott addresses Ian, "We're not gonna have time to finish. Should we work on it tomorrow?" Ian says, "Yeah, I guess what about stage 3—finish that tomorrow too?"

H9:   Ian talks with Scott and then goes over to check how Scott's group is doing on the lab.

H10:   End of class huddle, "What are we doing with these worksheets? Homework. Questions tonight for HW?"
(Huddle summary, 3/6/03)

The data contained in these descriptions show that over the course of one ninety-six-minute class period, numerous negotiations occurred between the coparticipants, each of which had the power to affect the structure of the classroom either explicitly or implicitly. Specifically, Scott, Ian, and Mr. Prince were able to discuss the class procedures (H3), ways of grouping students (H4), particular issues with a special education student (H5), the amount of time needed for an activity (H6), the evaluation of an activity (H7), and an appropriate time frame for continuing the activity (H8 and H10). Each of the actions discussed would have implicitly occurred in a classroom taught by a solo teacher, albeit in an unconscious, individual manner; however, in the coteaching arrangement, Scott, Ian and Mr. Prince had the opportunity to actively negotiate decisions to be made while the lesson was being enacted and thus positively affect the unfolding structure of the class.

Debriefing sessions

According to Roth (1998), debriefing sessions that take place informally between coteachers or other coparticipants after the close of a lesson can lead to greater understandings about classroom events and possibilities for future change. He argues that these moments can be used to make explicit events and practices that often go unarticulated. Eick and Ware (this volume) also confirm the importance of "dialogue on practice afterwards with their coteaching partner and teacher." In this professional discourse, teachers co-construct their own interpretations of classroom events. Debriefing sessions took place regularly between Ian and Scott. After one lesson in which the coteachers split the class into two groups, they had the opportunity to discuss one particular student's comprehension of a concept:

Scott:	I think they got it, theory vs. actuality.
Ian:	Yeah, they had problems with that too. Derek said the numbers weren't working out [for the lesson's lab].
Scott:	The scale isn't that accurate. I don't think I did a good enough job of pointing out sources of error. Was he [Derek] frustrated today?
Ian:	No, it was my fault—I wasn't explaining it well. It was my fault. (Video transcription, 2/28/03)

In this short debriefing discussion, the coteachers were able to confer on the concepts that the students may not have comprehended fully. In addition, Ian and Scott discussed their own practices, which may have contributed to the students' frustration or created a structure that inadvertently truncated the students' agency. The session was an opportunity for the coteachers to reflect on the events of the class and elucidate issues, such as their explanation of "sources of error," that could be changed in future lessons. In essence, they were able to make less conscious aspects of the structure more explicit, which enabled them to consider ways to restructure the environment more effectively in future lessons.

Cogenerative dialogues

Throughout their science methods course, Scott and Ian were encouraged to use cogenerative dialogues. The concept is grounded in Ricœur's (1991) claim that individuals enter a field of activity with their own experiences and perspectives; they also experience and interact with structures within the field in unique manners. In an effort to maximize the efficacy of varied perspectives, cogenerative dialogues were designed as a means to "promote the emergence of cogenerated understandings and collective responsibilities for agreed upon decisions about roles and insights into possible ways to distribute power and accountability" in a given field (LaVan & Beers, 2004, p. 177). Ian and Scott saw cogenerative dialogues as a means of both initiating collaborative research and fostering a community of learners in which all participants held responsibility for action.

About a month into the semester, Scott and Ian invited their engineering physics class to participate in a cogenerative dialogue during their lunch period, which took place immediately before the engineering physics class. Often, cogenerative dialogues are effectively used after a lesson is enacted so the group has an impetus for discussion. However, this cogenerative dialogue took place before the day's lesson was enacted, so Scott and Ian took the opportunity to discuss some of the general class structures. Afterward, Ian described the session as follows:

The purpose of this discussion was to include the students in the design of the class, give Scott and me a chance to explain some reasons for the way the class was run, allow the students to voice their opinions about the class, to give us a chance to hear what the students thought about physics in general, and finally to allow the class to form an atmosphere of shared responsibility. This discussion was reviewed by Scott and me, and as a result of it, and ones like it, certain aspects of our class were altered and we too altered our own teaching methods to some degree. The discussion was full of insights that I would not have been aware of otherwise. For example many of the students realized that physics is needed for their everyday life and for their potential college future. (Ian's Master's Portfolio, 2003)

During the dialogue, Ian and Scott inquired about numerous aspects of the class, including the students' conceptions of a science class, Scott and Ian's roles as teachers, the purpose and efficacy of group work and class discussions, the relevance of physics in the students' daily lives and the importance of the students' suggestions for the class. Even though the group involved in the cogenerative dialogue was larger than expected, making it difficult for each student's voice to be heard, several important issues were brought to the table, some of which became motivations for change in the course structure. One outcome from the dialogue was a student's suggestion for an innovative, yet nontraditional, class activity:

Sierra:	With the suggestions, whatever, I think y'all put into mind our concerns and stuff like that, but it just takes time for y'all to get to them. Cause I still have my concerns up there ((She points to the "concerns" section of the board.)) and I know it takes time, and um, and that's what I think. It takes time.
Student:	Which one you wrote?
Sierra:	To have skits.
Student:	Oh that say skits?
Sierra:	((Everyone laughs.)) What say—oh you thought it said something else?
Boy:	I thought it said shirts.
Scott:	I like that one
Ian:	What does everyone else think about that?
Girl:	Yeah I would love that. ((Everyone talks.))
Boy:	Make our own plays up about physics. That'd be hot. ((Everyone talks.))
Sierra:	If we put our minds together we could come up with something powerful.

Scott: I think, I think I, I've never done it before in a science class, so I've, I've
                kind of, I'd have to have a lot of time to think about it, but maybe our ap-
                proach should be, let you guys—let's brainstorm with you guys about this
                activity. [Let's structure it together.
Student: [I think that would be interesting. (Video transcription, 2/27/03)

This particular vignette within the cogenerative dialogue gave several members of the class community an impetus for responsibility; with Sierra's suggestion and positive responses from other members of the group, Scott and Ian decided to incorporate skits into the class and use the students' help to structure the activity. Even though Sierra had written her suggestion on the "concerns" board that Ian and Scott had created specifically to elicit student comments, the cogenerative dialogue became an important field for the participants to talk about the students' concerns and their incorporation into class activities. It also gave other students the opportunity to voice their comments and to collectively negotiate the implementation of the activity. Through this collective negotiation, the participants discovered a means of changing the structure of the class (creating skits) that would allow for the students' agency as they took part in enhanced, creative learning experiences.

At another point during the cogenerative dialogue, the coteachers asked questions that indexed the relevance of the class content in the students' everyday lives. This served not only as a means for Ian and Scott to gauge the students' perceptions about the value of physics, it also showed that the students could comfortably and appropriately apply the concepts they were learning to other fields of activity. Earlier in this vignette, Scott posed a question regarding physics' relevance in their daily lives. Brad answered the question during the following dialogue:

Brad: I feel as though, cause, I caught myself starting to relate uh, physics to
                like, stuff I do.
Scott: ((Smiles and stands up.)) Oh my gosh. ((Walks toward Brad.))
Brad: I was on the trolley, right, and I was goin' downtown, right, and the trolley
                was packed so I had to stand up. So, my mom came down from the bus,
                but we all had to stand up, so uh, so uh, I was like mom, watch, watch we
                all gonna jerk back cause, uh, cause the inertia. And she was like, "What's
                that?" ((Many laughs.)) And then I start tellin' her what it was, and she
                was like, "Oh."
Ian: Well that's good, Brad.
Scott: ((Smiling.)) Warms our hearts.
Ian: I can sleep at night. (Video transcription, 2/27/03)

The excitement shared by the two teachers is obvious in their reactions to Brad's story. Thus, cogenerative dialogue was also a way for the coteachers to assess student learning. This episode helped Ian and Scott to realize that the traditional types of student assessment—through the use of tests, quizzes, homework assignment or typical question-answer sessions, are not the only means of evaluation in the classroom. The coteachers' schemas regarding the assessment of student learning in physics were transformed when they realized that cogenerative dialogue could be another arena for students to talk about physics concepts in terms of their everyday lives.

Overall, cogenerative dialogue was an effective way for Ian and Scott to investigate the classroom dynamics. As they cogenerated understandings about the class with students and actively sought to restructure the environment to promote student engagement and learning, the group's collective agency was fostered. Cogenerative dialogue easily became a site in which the coteachers could access the students as resources to inform their practices. Even if the practices of coplanning, huddles, and debriefing sessions are difficult for Ian and Scott to maintain as autonomous teachers, cogenerative dialogue will be an effective way for them to continue to research and improve classroom structures.

Conclusion

From the contents of this chapter, it is clear that Ian and Scott's student teaching experience offered several valuable experiences unique to the coteaching model; central to their experiences were the numerous opportunities they had to develop particular practices through their establishment of a division of labor and to become researchers of their own teaching. Ian offers a summative reflection on the value of these opportunities in the following written narrative:

As student teachers we need to be brought into the job in a practical experiential manner. Teaching is something you can read about your whole life and still have little clue how you will feel the first time you stand up to talk to the class. Coteaching has worked very well for me and has led me to reevaluate the role of the teacher in the classroom to some degree. Coteaching allowed me to observe more of the classroom environment and understand better why some students perform poorly. Coteaching also made me aware of how much I might miss if I were the only teacher, therefore it has helped me not only in the sense of preparing me for traditional single teaching but also has made me aware of aspects I would have missed otherwise. (Ian's Master's Portfolio Essay, 2003)

After finishing their intern teaching experience, Ian and Scott were able to critically evaluate their own teaching goals in an effort to better align them with student goals; they emerged from the teacher education program with a commitment to continually improving as teachers by incorporating several reflective, research-oriented activities into their repertoires of practice. In addition, the arrangement gave Ian and Scott the opportunity to develop teaching practices that aligned with their own schemas about the necessary roles of a teacher specific to the classroom in which they cotaught. Thus, rather than framing the act of coteaching as a possible risk for their futures as autonomous teachers, the experience allowed Ian and Scott to become more comfortable and competent with practices that would support a successful classroom structure in the engineering physics class. However, extensive inquiry into coteachers' experiences as they become autonomous teachers is a priority.

Two specific implications for the field of teacher education can be drawn from the issues discussed in this chapter. First, the division of labor established between the participants in the coteaching arrangement allows each the opportunity to focus on particular practices that he or she believes to be integral to the act of teaching. Thus, Ian was able to align his practices with the belief that building meaningful relationships with students was highly important. Because of the division of labor that had been established, Ian was often able to solidify the practices that were important for him to reach his goal. As Ian was helping students individually, Scott was able to accomplish goals he felt to be pertinent, such as conveying particular physics concepts through lecture.

Second, because the two were together throughout the experience, they constantly had the opportunity to reflect on their practices and other structures in the classroom that directly affected their personal and collective agency. The sites that fostered an ethos of collaborative inquiry in their situation could also be forged in non-coteaching scenarios; preservice as well as in-service teachers could also efficiently incorporate such spaces into their classrooms in an effort to become competent researchers of their own practices. Clearly, coteaching offers a structure for beginning teachers to access the resources that foster enhanced opportunities for them to become reflective, proficient teachers.

References

Bourdieu, P. (1977). *Outline of a theory of practice.* Cambridge, UK: Cambridge University Press.
Bourdieu, P. (1986). The forms of capital. In J. Richardson (Ed.), *Handbook of theory and research for the sociology of education* (pp. 241–258). New York: Greenwood.
Eick, C., Ware, F., & Williams, P. (2003). Coteaching in a science methods course. *Journal of Teacher Education, 54,* 74–85.

Engeström, Y. (1999). Activity theory and individual and social transformation. In Y. Engeström, R. Miettinen, & R.-L. Punamäki (Eds.), *Perspectives on activity theory* (pp. 19–38). Cambridge, UK: Cambridge University Press.

LaVan, S. K., & Beers, J. (2004). The role of cogenerative dialogue in learning to teach and transforming learning environments. In K. Tobin, R. Elmesky, & G. Seiler (Eds.), *The world waitin': Reforming urban science education* (pp. 141–163). Lanham, MD: Rowman & Littlefield.

McVay, S. (2003). *Effective professional development: Does coteaching align with the standards?* Unpublished Master's Thesis, University of Pennsylvania, Philadelphia, PA.

Ricœur, P. (1991). *From text to action: Essays in hermeneutics, II.* Evanston, IL: Northwestern University Press.

Roth, W. (1998b). *Designing communities.* Dordrecht, The Netherlands: Kluwer Academic Publishers.

Roth, W., Masciotra, D., & Boyd, N. (1999). Becoming-in-the-classroom: A case study of teacher development through coteaching. *Teaching and Teacher Education, 15,* 771–784.

Roth, W.-M., & Tobin, K. (2002). *At the elbow of another: Learning to teach by coteaching.* New York: Peter Lang.

Sewell, W. (1992). A theory of structure: Duality, agency and transformation. *American Journal of Sociology, 98,* 1–29.

Tobin, K., Zurbano, R., Ford, A., & Carambo, C. (2003). Learning to teach through coteaching and cogenerative dialogue. *Cybernetics & Human Knowing, 10*(1), 51–73.

7   Exchanging the baton: exploring the *co* in coteaching

Kenneth Tobin

Our ongoing research in urban schools has persuasively shown that coteaching allows science teachers to improve their teaching by teaching and planning with others, thereby deepening their understandings of science, and creating social networks with students (Roth & Tobin, 2002). Using microanalyses of video-tapes, we explored how coteachers learn to teach like one another in ways that involve the uses of space and time, physical resources such as charts and equipment, voice and body movements, including walk patterns, sways, wiggles, and gestures (Roth, Tobin, Carambo, & Dalland, 2004). However, we have not yet studied in detail the quality of the interactions between coteachers, especially those that do not turn out as well as expected. Since it cannot be assumed that all interactions in coteaching are successful, the identification of types of unsuccessful interactions is regarded as a central next step in our research that seeks to understand learning to teach. The dynamic nature of the structure of a classroom makes it virtually impossible to plan interactions in advance and it is assumed that well-intentioned teachers learn to teach together in anticipatory ways by coteaching together. However, in a study by Tobin, Zurbano, Ford, and Carambo (2003) two coteachers experienced great difficulty with moving in an out of the lead teacher position, a process we denote by "exchanging the baton" (Roth & Tobin, 2002). The senior coteacher wanted to use pauses so that the high school students could figure out solutions to problems he posed. His coteacher, a new teacher seeking certification in chemistry, wanted students to have a basic toolkit of science facts. When the senior teacher paused, providing time as a resource for his students' thinking, the coteacher stepped in and provided the answers. Also, when she was teaching, she frequently did not relinquish control when the senior teacher wanted to contribute to the lesson.

Quickly frustration built among the coteachers until it reached a point that mutual respect had diminished to such an extent that the teachers avoided coteaching. As a complement to the research in this volume, the investigations presented in this chapter explore empirically the ways in which coteachers enact teaching to reflect the centrality of the prefix *co*, meaning together, with, and joint.

In this chapter I first describe the context of my research and then present what I learned from an ethnography of coteaching and associated microanalyses of selected videotapes. I describe the division of labor employed in different coteaching arrangements. This is followed by an analysis of the interactions between Brian and Judith, whose teaching was characterized by high levels of synchrony and successful interactions. Microanalyses explore the prosody of the verbal interactions among coteachers and students. The next three sections involve analyses of Victoria and Jessica, who enacted less successful coteaching, and provide examples of smooth baton changes, withholding the baton, and seizing the baton. The conclusion explores what I learned about coteaching in terms of future research and associated implications for enacting coteaching in professional development and teacher preparation programs.

Research design

Site and participants

This research is part of a research program consisting of critical ethnographies of the teaching and learning of science in urban schools. Explorations of the manner in which control is exchanged between coteachers were based on a database that is extensive and includes videotapes of coteaching that occurred over a six-year period. These studies involved teachers whose experiences and qualifications to teach science varied, ranging from new teachers seeking certification to teach science, to veterans like me who had to relearn to teach science in urban schools (Tobin, 2000). For the past seven years coteaching has been used at the University of Pennsylvania in its graduate program leading to certification in science. In each of those years City High was a site for coteaching and associated research on learning to teach. The research presented in this chapter is situated at City High.

City High is an urban high school that caters to students from Philadelphia. As a comprehensive neighborhood school, City High has about 2,000 students and, during the time in which these studies were undertaken, the school was organized into ten small learning communities, or schools within a school. Most students who attend are African American and more than 90 percent of them experience home circumstances of economic hardship.

My roles

My roles included researcher, methods instructor, and university adviser for the coteachers involved in this research. I have undertaken research at City High on a continuous basis for seven years and have been no stranger to the teachers and students at the school. Generally I did not participate in coplanning of the activities and my involvement in the lessons was as a legitimate peripheral participant. I was in the classroom several times a week and when I came in I usually interacted with individuals or small groups of students. Only occasionally did I contribute to teaching the whole class.

Since I was not involved in planning the details of the lessons in which I was a participant observer I brought to the class an outsider perspective and frequently made suggestions to teachers or students that related to the unfolding aspects of a lesson. My role was not to judge the teaching of others, but to suggest how teaching and learning roles, and resources to support them, might be changed to improve the quality of learning. For example, I suggested in one lesson that Darnell, a student who had completed his assigned tasks, assist Esther, a peer who was struggling and becoming frustrated. I knew Darnell would willingly agree to participate in this way because he had indicated in a cogenerative dialogue (Roth & Tobin, 2002) that he enjoyed teaching his peers. The coteachers adopted my suggestion: Darnell took his role as peer teacher seriously and assisted Esther in ways that were substantive and clearly went beyond what I might have accomplished. At the end of the lesson I encouraged the coteachers to incorporate more peer tutoring into the planning of subsequent lessons.

As an instructor I focused on connecting what new teachers were experiencing during a yearlong field experience to the curriculum of the science education methods classes that I taught at the University of Pennsylvania (one in the fall and one in the spring). To meet the requirements of the field experience, new teachers taught each morning in the fall and each day in the spring. In the spring semester, where the study is situated, at least one ninety-six-minute class was cotaught. Since all new teachers were coteaching I requested that at any given time all teachers in a classroom should be teaching together and I explained that a central part of successful coteaching was to step back when a coteacher wanted to step forward. Also, new teachers were required to conduct one or two cogenerative dialogues per week with their students, thereby providing a forum for analyzing the quality of teaching and learning and cogenerating resolutions for change.

Procedures

I reviewed the research memoranda on each of the coteachers from a large data-base associated with our ongoing research on learning to teach in urban schools. I used the principles described by Guba and Lincoln (1989) to select as foci for this study two pairs of coteachers that were as different from one another as pos-sible. The first pair I selected (Victoria and Jessica) comprised two females who were frustrated throughout the field experience and experienced emotional melt-downs frequently (e.g., outbursts of anger and tears). Even so, both teachers worked hard to succeed and expressed strong commitments to the youth in their classes. They identified the senior resident teacher in their small learning com-munity as a primary source of frustration, especially because he was often too busy for coplanning, coteaching, and cogenerative dialogues. The second pair of coteachers (Brian and Judith) taught in the same small learning community at the same time. In contrast to Victoria and Jessica, they had a more settled field experience. They scheduled daily coplanning sessions and regularly participated in cogenerative dialogues. The emotional states projected by Brian and Judith were positive, stable, and energetic.

In this study I employed a variety of data resources to explore coteaching (e.g., field notes, analytic memoranda, interview transcripts, videotapes). Coteachers arranged for their classes to be videotaped and later they analyzed them, identified and clipped significant episodes, and created video vignettes about their learning to teach. Another source of videotapes of coteaching was university researchers, such as me. I brought a small digital video camera with me to class and used it to record what was happening as I moved around, inter-acting with students and coteachers. If necessary I placed the continuously re-cording camera on a nearby desk, which allowed me to assist students with their learning. On such occasions it was common for students or coteachers to take the camera and record events they considered salient. After initial review, video-tapes were labeled and archived, allowing access for university researchers and teacher and student researchers.

This study consisted of two parts. In the first part I reviewed the videotapes and associated research artifacts available for twelve new teachers from the co-hort in which the two pairs of coteachers were situated. Each of these new teachers was assigned to City High for field experiences in the same learning community. The amount of videotape resources (i.e., raw footage and video vi-gnettes) varied for each teacher from several hours to more than twenty hours for Victoria and Jessica. I analyzed all of these resources to identify categories associated with the exchange of control as coteaching occurred in a variety of settings. These categories were based on the metaphor of a baton exchange in a relay race and many of them were associated with unsuccessful interactions. The emergent categories were smooth handoffs, withholding the baton, and seizing the baton. Another category, not dealt with in this chapter, was refusing the baton. In this case a new teacher, when called on to step forward, declined because he felt he had nothing of value to contribute. Roth, Tobin, Carambo, and Dalland (2004) address this example of an interaction that mediates successful coteaching. The second part of the study consisted of microanalyses of selected excerpts from coteaching segments for Victoria and Jessica set against a background of similar microanalyses of Brian and Judith's coteaching.

Divisions of labor

Teaching individuals

The roles of coteachers reflected the arrangement of students and the goals of the activity. One of the most common roles was to assist students in one-on-one situations, which coteachers enacted in much the same ways across all examples of coteaching and in different arrangements of students (i.e., as they engaged in individualized, small and whole-class groups). Because of the presence of multiple teachers it was possible for coteachers to focus on effectively communicating with students who had requested assistance, listen to them, and attend to their needs. It was typical for a coteacher to either sit, crouch, or bend down to bring her head to the same level as the student, thereby making interactions relatively private. Also, because of the presence of multiple teachers it was possible for one-on-one interactions to be prolonged. Not surprisingly students regarded one-on-one assistance as one of the key features of coteaching.

Teaching small groups

When students were arranged in small groups, as occurred in labs and discussions, the coteachers frequently taught in different parts of the classroom, interacting with one or multiple groups. These interactions were more public than one-on-one interactions; accordingly, teaching was a resource for the learning of all or most all participants in the class even though it was directed toward one or more groups of students. Consequently, the coteachers, students and other stakeholders present at the time (e.g., science educators from the university, researchers, school administrators) experienced and could potentially access and appropriate interactions throughout the room, even though the coteachers might not have intended to afford the learning of more than those students to whom their teaching was directed. The manner of experiencing unintended interactions was frequently conscious and there were numerous examples of individuals intently focused on interactions that were not intended for them but were nonetheless affordances for their learning. On other occasions the interactions involving a coteacher and one or more groups of students were part of a background that was experienced by all participants as they engaged in the ongoing activity of the classroom. In this case the ways in which participants experienced, accessed, and appropriated the interactions as resources, were unconscious. Even so, the opportunity to experience those interactions may have shaped the ongoing learning of all participants (e.g., the learning of science and the learning of how to teach science).

Teaching from the front

Whole class interactive settings are most likely to involve situations in which coteachers need to step forward and step back. Accordingly, these were central to the research in this chapter. I chose a vignette compiled by Judith and Brian, two coteachers seeking certification in chemistry, to feature interactions among coteachers in a whole class organization. I identified segments for analysis in which both teachers taught from the front of the room, using the whiteboard as a primary resource. As they taught the coteachers moved throughout the space in a complementary fashion so as to achieve what appeared to be a balance in the use of space.

The coteachers were conscientious in their coplanning and embraced the spirit of coteaching in the ways in which they seamlessly collaborated to create resources that afforded their students to participate and learn. During coplanning for this lesson it was decided that Judith would be lead teacher. After the initial set up of the lesson Brian and Judith coordinated their teaching with student learning as the key focus. Brian proactively ensured that the whiteboard at the front of the room was cleaned for Judith to make notes on (as they had planned). As Judith wrote the notes, based on contributions from students to her initial question, Brian maintained the momentum of the lesson by calling on students to respond, reacting to their responses, and at times providing more structure through questions and explanations. As Judith moved away from the whiteboard Brian stepped back and allowed her to teach, successively monitoring the students and Judith, moving his body to maintain an active presence as a back-up coteacher. His actions showed that he was involved in the lesson and prepared at any moment to step forward, if called upon to provide resources to afford learning.

At one time in the lesson Judith moved over to the left-hand side of the teaching space and began to teach to a group on that side of the room. Brian then moved toward the right side of the classroom and began to teach to the remainder of the class. For the next few minutes both coteachers taught from the front of the room simultaneously, thereby providing continuing opportunities for all students to learn from their teaching.

Very little time was associated with management and control. As part of what we referred to as "the grade-nine experiment" (see Tobin & Roth, chapter 3), Brian and Judith taught at one end of a classroom while another coteaching pair taught at the other end. Their class consisted of sixteen African-American youth, arranged in three rows. Throughout the lesson it was quite noisy, mainly because of students participating at the other end of the room and the other teachers' voices. However, the teachers and the students maintained a focus on the lesson, which was brisk and, with few exceptions, the students were attentive, participatory, and focused on learning. Both Brian and Judith taught in an animated way, using wide gestures and brisk movements across the space between the first row and the whiteboard. They spoke expressively and exhibited verve in the coordination of voice, gesture and body motion. Through leaning forward, facial expressions, and hand orientations both teachers communicated their interest in hearing what students were saying and in this regard they clearly demonstrated their respect for students and a keen interest in their learning.

In the segments I analyzed there was only one instance of either teacher attending to a student who was off task. A male student, in the front row was struggling to stay awake for the entire lesson. At one stage he seemed to succumb to tiredness and his head slumped onto the desk. In a short interaction Judith called his name, moved quickly toward him, placed her finger on a piece of paper in front of his head, and moved the paper back and forth vigorously. As the student raised his head Judith quickly backed off and recommenced teaching. The entire episode took less than three seconds from the moment the student's head hit the desk to when Judith resumed teaching. Hence her effort to refocus the student was quick and the momentum of the lesson was maintained.

Synchrony among coteachers

Prosody is an important resource in face-to-face interactions, including coteaching (see Roth, chapter 2). In terms of the speech intensity, for example, neither Brian nor Judith spoke over one another or the students. Furthermore, their talk "fit" one another's talk in terms of rhythm and intonation, especially timing, amplitude, and frequency. Similar patterns were observed when the coteachers followed one another in talk turns and when verbal interaction involved coteachers and students. The most significant changes in amplitude and pitch occurred in a transition from a whole class interactive setting to a small group setting. As Judith gave instructions for the change in organization she raised both pitch frequency and amplitude of her talk (to a peak of 73 decibels [dB], 325 Hertz [Hz]), which made her voice stand clearly above the background noise.

Judith seemed to speak louder than Brian. Her utterances typically varied in whole-class interactive settings from 65 dB to 70 dB (i.e., almost quadrupling loudness), the louder utterances being reserved for assigning instructions prior to a transition. When Judith asked a question, which required her to project her voice, she seemed to intentionally keep the amplitude relatively low. Typically Judith's questions began at approximately 70 dB, 285 Hz, and her reactions to responses, usually acceptances, were lower in amplitude and frequency (e.g., 69 dB, 264 Hz). Brian gave the impression of being softly spoken. However, the amplitude of his talk varied through approximately the same range as Judith's, although his pitch was lower on average (approximately 289 Hz with a high of 333 Hz).

The only occasions in which students raised their voices were when they were asked to repeat a phrase and especially if they felt defensive. For example, when Judith inquired of a student, "What were you saying?" the amplitude of her initial utterance was 67 dB and the frequency was 314 Hz. When the student responded he commenced at a much higher amplitude and frequency, "I ain't sayin' . . ." (75 dB, 497 Hz). However, it is noticeable that as his turn at talk was established and the emotional content died down, so too did the amplitude, which finished at 71 dB.

The talk patterns I observed in Judith and Brian's teaching appeared to be adaptive to the ways in which African-American youth interact orally (Boykin, 1986). In work we have done elsewhere, Michael Roth and I have found that when students argue (i.e., there is disagreement), successive speakers will raise the amplitude and the frequency of their voices. However, when students are speaking with friends and are in agreement, successive speakers tend to use amplitudes and pitches that fit with the end points of the speaker he or she is following. Also, if a person is trying to show respect to another it is common to speak with lowered amplitude and pitch. These patterns are consistent with those we observed in the whole class interactive settings in this cotaught ninth-grade class. Judith and Brian interacted with one another and the students in ways that suggested they respected what students had to say. They did not speak over them and oriented their bodies, eyes, and ears to see the students and hear what they had to say.

Smooth handoffs

As lessons unfolded and coteachers and students accessed the resources available to them, baton exchanges were enacted, often such that the coteachers were without awareness of their occurrence. Given all that happens as teaching and learning occur it is probable that the fine structure of interactions involving coteachers with the structure of the classroom are beyond the awareness of the coteachers—unless of course events do not unfold as intended. This appears to be the case with the distribution of control among coteachers. Smooth handoffs were common in all of the coteaching analyzed in this study. These were typified by one person being willing to step back or step aside (i.e., relinquishing a teaching turn) and then handing-off to the coteacher with a verbal acknowledgment, a gesture, a head nod, or orientation of the body. Verbal signals that an exchange was imminent took many forms, including a statement of the intent, posing a question, decreasing the amplitude of speech, lowering the frequency of talk, and calling the name of the coteacher. Especially when coteachers have taught together for several lessons the interactions between them appeared seamless as they focused on the learning of students and taught accordingly. However, the resources available for teachers to work with in a classroom are dynamic, and as they are accessed and appropriated by coteachers, the associated practices also become resources for subsequent learning.

Jessica and Victoria taught chemistry to a class containing mainly juniors and a few seniors. The room was spacious since the resident teacher had refurbished two adjacent classrooms by pushing back the dividing wall, affording the creation of a new front to the room, consisting of what were previously the side walls of two rooms. A brick pillar, where the dividing wall had been, marked the center of a new front and a whiteboard was mounted on either side of the pillar. On the right of one whiteboard was a large periodic table (similar in size to each of the whiteboards). For whole-class lessons the students were seated in three rows, facing the whiteboards and the periodic table. In this arrangement no front bench separated the teachers from the students.

The vignette I used for this microanalysis involved Victoria and Jessica teaching a review lesson on limiting reagents. The segments I selected were whole-class interactive settings with both coteachers at the front of the room. That is, the division of labor involved both coteachers interacting with the whole class using the whiteboard as a primary resource to augment their uses of voice and body. The following transcript[1] provides an example of a smooth baton exchange between the coteachers.

#	Time	Speaker	Utterance	Notes
1	0.0	Jessica	How do we know which one is the limiting reagent and which one is in excess? (8.4)	Jessica is teaching from the edge of the whiteboard, adjacent to the periodic table. After asking the questions she stands motionless, gazing across the classroom. After a silence of 8.4s Victoria strides to the whiteboard from the side of the classroom.
2	11.6	Victoria	Yo! What . . . What's the difference between (1.3)	Victoria starts to speak some distance from the whiteboard and the lengthy pause is to allow her to reach the whiteboard and point to text written on it.
3	15.3	Darnel	It's less than. (0.3)	Darnel uses the period of silence as a resource to answer a question that has not yet been posed.
4	16.2	Victoria	What's the number? The difference between this number and this number?	Victoria points to the numbers as she speaks and Jessica also points.

Jessica commenced this segment in a loud and confident manner (75 dB, 286 Hz). Having asked a question she stepped to the side of the whiteboard and did not look at the students, or Victoria, who was to her left and rear. After more than eight seconds of silence Victoria strode toward the front of the room, using the silence, the students' failure to respond in a reasonable time, and Jessica's lack of movement as resources to begin teaching. Victoria started to speak with the same loudness as that characterizing Jessica's question and a characteristically lower frequency (75 dB, 261 Hz). Through the use of gestures and the whiteboard Jessica endeavored to support Victoria's question, one that was more focused than the original, even though it was less clear. Salient features of this baton exchange are that Victoria was decisive in her use of voice and body movement including verve and energetic gestures. Similarly, although Jessica did not speak again in this short segment, her efforts to support Victoria's teach-

ing were physically energetic and evidence of active efforts to teach collaboratively.

Later in the same lesson another smooth baton exchange occurred as Jessica
and Victoria discussed how to decide which compound was the limiting reagent
in a reaction involving the oxidation of magnesium. In this instance both teachers fluently answered questions and gestured to parts of the equation and associated calculations. As students asked questions the coteachers stood together at
the whiteboard, Jessica on the left-hand side and Victoria on the right. Using the
students' questions as resources the coteachers collaborated to clarify understandings and emphasize rules about how to solve problems such as these when
they appeared in tests. The coteaching was conversation-like as students and the
coteachers clarified the rules for determining from a balanced chemical equation
and information about reactants and products, how to determine which substance was limiting.

The following transcript provides insights into the coordination of talk,
pauses, gestures and body orientation during coteaching. Smooth handoffs occurred at turn 7 as Jessica began to teach and episode 14 when Victoria resumed
teaching.

#	Time	Speaker	Utterance	Notes
5	86.6	Victoria	=This is excessive. (0.8) So, either one I do. I don't have to do both. (1.3) Either one I do will tell me the an- swer. (2.3) If one is excess the other one has to be limiting. If one is limiting the other has to be excess. You guys see that? (1.2) This one now tells me here (1.7) between the two that this one is excess (1.6). Don't have to do both steps (2.0)	
6	113.8	Student	Why would you do that? (2.1)	This is an off-task remark by a female.
7	117.1	Jessica	So are we clear about that equation? (0.2)	
8	119.0	Student	Y# (0.3)	
9	119.7	Jessica	Of what we're doing and	

			why we're doing it?
10	121.3	Student	=Can you have one where both u:m excess or limiting?
11	127.1	Jessica	=You can't have them all one way. One has to be limiting and one has to be excess.
12	131.6	Student	=It wouldn't go all the way.
13	133.2	Jessica	But there are several different things
14	134.4	Victoria	=There were different tubes. (0.6) Each tube has one excess and one limiting. Yeah. That's different. The trend may be different but in each separate tube there is one limiting and one excess always. (3.1)

For the most part the amplitude of the coteachers' talk was between 68 dB and 71 dB in the above vignette, with each teacher maintaining her characteristic frequency of approximately 280 Hz and 240 Hz for Jessica and Victoria, respectively. The exception was that Victoria increased amplitude and frequency on occasions when she sought to emphasize particular rules. For example, on one occasion she emphasized "the trend ((79 dB, 283 Hz)) may be different but in each separate tube there is one limiting one excess always."

Victoria's teaching turn continued for almost two minutes without any verbal input from Jessica (between turns 4 and 5 and during turn 5). During this time Victoria filled relatively long pauses by writing on the whiteboard and gesturing to text that was already inscribed. Even though Jessica was at the front and supported the unfolding teaching with her gestures and body movements, the responsibility for developing and completing the review on limiting reagents remained with Victoria. In other parts of this lesson pauses of more than 0.5 seconds were resources for coteachers to wrest control from one another. However, in this sequence Jessica made no move to request or seize the baton.

Jessica resumed teaching in turn 7. The catalyst for her stepping forward was an off task remark in the form of a student question that followed a lengthy pause that may have signaled that Victoria had finished teaching. Following Jessica's question about clarity a student asked a specific question, to which Jessica responded. When it was apparent that Jessica had completed her response to the question Victoria once again stepped forward (turn 14) to reinforce a generalization about limiting reagents.

Withholding the baton

There were instances where one of the coteachers stepped forward, to take a turn at teaching a whole class, and the baton was not exchanged, leaving the coteacher who had stepped forward looking and perhaps feeling a little awkward. Withholding of the baton (when it might have been relinquished) is illustrated in the following vignette. In a revision lesson on molarity Jessica was teaching at the front whiteboard with Victoria standing off to her right (as she faced the class). In a series of turns, Jessica developed ideas on molarity and resisted Victoria's effort to contribute to the teaching.

#	Time	Speaker	Utterance	Notes
1	0.0	Jessica	So, for molarity it's very important to remember that molarity is moles per liter. (0.5)	Jessica stands with her back to the board, using her right hand to point to text she has written on the board previously. Victoria is watching the class and is positioned close to the periodic table.
2	6.3	Jessica	So, if I give you something in grams, what do you have to do? (0.6)	Jessica moves to her left, in front of the pillar between the two whiteboards. She still gestures to the written text on the whiteboard to her right.
3	9.9	Darnel	Convert it to moles.	
4	10.5	Jessica	=Convert it to moles. (0.2s)	
5	11.6	Victoria	If I could just[	Victoria steps forward as Jessica continues to talk and gesture.
6	11.6	Jessica	=If I [give you something in milliliters what do you have to do? Convert it to liters.	Victoria stops talking as Jessica increases the pitch and amplitude of her utterance.

As Jessica said moles she paused for just 0.2 seconds as if to emphasize the point. Victoria used this short time interval as a resource to take the baton as she stepped forward, and began to speak. However, the pause time was too short to disrupt Jessica's flow of utterances, gestures and body movements. Jessica continued to speak at the same time as Victoria, in fact they uttered the same two words (combined signal was 73 dB, 322 Hz) and at 12.2 seconds, as Jessica said "give," she significantly raised both the amplitude and the pitch (76 dB, 450 Hz) to retain control of the teaching turn and to hold on to the baton. Victoria ceased speaking, stepped back, and raised her left hand to her hair as she looked intently at Jessica and the board. Jessica did not step back, signaling her resolve to continue by speaking louder and gesturing emphatically, using a chopping motion with her right arm and hand. The relatively loud talk and associated emphatic gestures, punctuated by the use of her right hand to point to text on the whiteboard, were part of a fluent discourse that continued to the end of turn 7 (see next section).

Seizing the baton

Smooth baton exchanges were frequent occurrences in most coteaching in whole class interactive settings. Handovers usually occurred at moments signaled by lengthy pauses between speakers and teacher and student actions of many types. However, some baton exchanges involved high energy whereas in others, the changeovers were characterized by different agendas that the coteachers appeared to pursue.

High-energy takeover

The following transcript shows that as Jessica continued her revision of molarity it is evident that Victoria was seeking a turn at teaching. She observed Jessica intently and through her eye gaze, gestures, and body movement she communicated to the class her intention to get involved. When Victoria was cut short while attempting to teach she stepped back, scratched her head with her left hand and then folded her arms while observing Jessica teach. She then took four steps forward to the center of the right hand whiteboard and leaned forward to better view what Jessica was referring to on the left-hand whiteboard. Victoria was clearly preparing for a turn to teach. She took four steps backward, all the while watching Jessica. Victoria reached the edge of the whiteboard at exactly the time Jessica finished speaking. At that moment Victoria began a gesture that would eventually point to text she had previously written on the whiteboard. The gesture occupied 0.9 seconds of silence between Jessica finishing her utterance ("liters") and Victoria beginning hers ("Or"). In a sense the gesture filled the pause and staked a claim to a turn of teaching. As Victoria began to speak loudly Jessica's head turned sharply to look at her. As is evident from the transcript below, Victoria seized the baton (turn 8) and her turn at teaching was soon in full flow.

#	Time	Speaker	Utterance	Notes
7	17.5	Jessica	So, *in order to use this do you want to divide liters into moles? You've got to make sure you've got moles and you've got liters. (0.9)	*Victoria begins to walk across to the brick column that divides the two white-boards. She examines what Jessica has written and then moves back to where she had been standing at the edge of the second white-board, adjacent to the peri-odic table.
8	25.0	Victoria	Or you can do (0.6) Remember Mr. R. showed us two ways. (0.2)	Victoria begins to write on the white board as she speaks. Jessica, with her back against the brick col-umn, watches intently. At the end of this utterance, just as Victoria said ways, Jessica swung her right leg forward and began to move rhythmically for the next five seconds.
9	29.1	Victoria	Moles per liter is the same as moles* per 1,000 milliliters (0.3)	*Jessica completes her rhythmic body movement and watches Victoria. As she completes the utterance Jessica gestures toward what she has written.
10	36.4	Victoria	Right (0.4)	Affirmation by both Jessica and Victoria. As Victoria says right, Jessica gestures and also makes a comment that appears to be "right."
11	37.2	Victoria	He showed us both ways (0.3)	Victoria gestures at what she has written on the whiteboard. Jessica watches intently.
12	39.0	Victoria	We only care about this.	For emphasis Victoria cir-cles part of what she has

| 13 | 40.7 | Victoria | And we give you milliliters of solution. (1.0) Use this (0.3) it's just the same thing. | written on the whiteboard. Victoria gestures for emphasis and then points back to the whiteboard, making eye contact with the students. As Victoria says solution Jessica repeats her rhythmic movement and as Victoria finishes the utterance Jessica folds her arms and looks Victoria's way. |

Victoria began her teaching turn with a gesture to the board at precisely the moment that Jessica completed her final utterance ("liters"). It was as if the gesture claimed the turn to talk next, in so doing wresting the baton from Jessica. Victoria then spoke for a little over twenty-one seconds (at approximately 70 dB, 235 Hz) while Jessica observed what she did, paced rhythmically back and forth, and occasionally gestured with her arms to reinforce what Victoria was saying. Jessica's participation was evidence of verve, maintaining a beat that would enable her to resume her turn of teaching whenever it was appropriate. For example, at turn 10, Jessica gestured vigorously and appeared to say right at the same time as Victoria. She was tuned into the lesson and it is likely that if Victoria had paused for longer Jessica was ready to recommence. In fact, it is possible that at turn 10 Jessica attempted to resume teaching. However, Victoria's teaching was fluent and there were insufficient resources to support Jessica recommencing teaching at that time. Jessica's folding of her arms in turn 13 is ironic since Victoria often acted in this way when she felt she was prevented from teaching.

Pursuing different agendas

The following vignette is a review of limiting reagents that occurred one day prior to the one used in the previous section. In the first segment Jessica set up and balanced an equation for the reaction of magnesium and oxygen gas.

#	Time	Speaker	Utterance	Notes
1	0.0	Jessica	I'm giving you . . . this is your equation you're starting off with. Solid magnesium . . . oxygen gas. Remember this? We went through this	

			again and again but, if we write down words oxygen gas you should know immediately that since oxygen's a diatomic molecule you won't find it by itself. It's gonna be O_2. Right↑? (0.2)	
2	21.8	Darnell	It's always going to be two of them? (0.4)	
3	23.4	Jessica	Right↓. You won't ever find oxygen by itself. (0.7)	
4	26.1	Victoria	I'm going to give you the list of the seven diatomics.	Victoria steps forward with arms folded and begins to speak, unfolds her arms and begins to write as she continues to speak.
6	28.8	Darnell	=I have them in my notebook.	Jessica begins to take one step back but she continues her hand motion as if she is not aware of Victoria's teaching. As she moves her right hand and felt pen she appears ready to resume her central role.
7	30.2	Victoria	=O_2 Br_2 *F_2 Cl_2 I_2 N_2. What else am I forgetting? (2.4)	*Jessica writes MgO on the board, thereby completing the equation.
8	40.4	Jessica	=And this is what? What's the name of this?	
9	42.8	Students	Magnesium oxide	Low-level buzz.
10	44.0	Jessica	Magnesium oxide. Perfect. (0.5) Now is this equation balanced? (0.9)	Victoria writes the missing diatomic element H_2, on the whiteboard. 2:44

Jessica's initial comment of more than 21 seconds duration lay out a context for completing the equation. Her first querying right (66dB, 219 Hz) provided Darnell with an opportunity to test his knowledge of the diatomic nature of oxygen. He began to speak (65 dB, 157 Hz) and when he finished Jessica provided only a short pause of 0.4 seconds before providing an affirming right (66dB, 202 Hz). Her confirming comment that "You won't ever find oxygen by itself" and a longer pause of 0.7 seconds was a resource for the students to consider what she had said in relation to the equation and a resource for Victoria to step forward and seize the baton. Victoria began to list the seven diatomic molecules (61 dB, 189 Hz) and her delivery had a slightly lower pitch than Jessica's and much the same amplitude profile. As Jessica's voice trailed off she turned toward Victoria and looked intently at her as she wrote the diatomic molecules on the board. At the same time that Victoria said and wrote "F_2," Jessica turned back toward the board, completed the equation on the whiteboard, and stepped toward the class. For a moment both coteachers spoke simultaneously, Victoria to the whole class and Jessica to a student who was in front of her and close by. Jessica used the pause following Victoria's query "What else am I forgetting?" to refocus the class on the equation. She reclaimed center stage and resumed her teaching of the whole class. Jessica provided no time for further talk about diatomic molecules. Just as Jessica had done before in continuing to balance the equation, Victoria stepped back from the whiteboard, reviewed the list of molecules for 6.5 seconds, and then added the missing molecule to the list.

This example of coteachers stepping forward and stepping back was not seamless. When Victoria seized the baton Jessica was midway through the writing of an equation. She mentioned oxygen as a diatomic molecule and this utterance was a resource for Victoria who wanted students to know that there are seven diatomic molecules and where they are positioned on the periodic table. The pause between Victoria beginning to speak and Jessica completing her previous sentence was a little more than half a second and it is no surprise that Jessica was focused on completing the writing of a balanced equation. Her body orientation, while away from the board, positioned her to review what she had written so far and she did not attend to what Victoria was teaching the class. Almost with impatience Jessica wrote magnesium oxide as the product and informed a student who had eye contact with her that it was magnesium oxide. Then, when Victoria paused for a little over a half a second, Jessica continued her teaching to the whole class. Victoria had not completed her segment on diatomic molecules and eventually she wrote "H_2" in her list on the whiteboard as Jessica taught. In the analysis Jessica appeared to continue to teach in the fourteen seconds in which Victoria dealt with diatomic molecules with the whole class. Her gestures and body movements show her continued engagement in writing and balancing the equation and while Victoria spoke to the whole class, Jessica addressed one or a few students in her immediate vicinity, resuming whole class teaching as soon as Victoria provided a sufficient pause.

In both instances in which the baton was seized, once each by Victoria and Jessica, the pause of about a half a second appears to have been a sufficient resource for stepping forward. It seems reasonable to claim that the quality of the teaching and learning was scarcely afforded by either intervention. If Victoria had held off her teaching of diatomic molecules it might have allowed the students to ask substantive questions about electronic configuration, bonding, and stability. Whereas it seems desirable for students to know there are seven diatomic molecules and to remember what they are, the discussion and associated inscriptions produced by Victoria were resources for learning that were not as fully appropriated as might otherwise have been the case. That this occurred was due to Jessica's failure to be an attentive listener to what Victoria was saying and to use her question as a resource for mediating the learning of her students. Instead it appears as if her focus on completing a review of limiting reactions led her to allow Victoria to speak without interruption but then ignoring what she had contributed and resuming her own coverage as if she had been uninterrupted.

Conclusions

When the practices of coteachers are complementary and aligned there is a likelihood that interactions among coteachers will be successful. That is, when there is synchrony between coteachers and entrainment in the sense that the coteachers' actions are coordinated, coherent, and focused on collective goals, then the presence of coteachers can have a synergistic effect on opportunities for students to learn from teaching. Synchrony and entrainment between coteachers led to smooth handoffs and a continuous flow of teaching, not just in teacher talk, but also in the use of gestures, body movement, and material resources. Hence, relatively long periods of silence were often filled nonverbally during a teaching turn and were not opportunities for disrupting teaching fluency. During smooth baton exchanges coteachers coordinated prosody with gestures and body movements to produce fluent teaching that connected with (i.e., resonated with) the practices and other resources available to support learning.

During coteaching we observed that teachers continued their teaching even when their coteacher was interacting with a whole class. This was done relatively unobtrusively in one-on-one interactions and when coteachers interacted with small groups of students. However, when coteachers interacted with a whole class of students some contradictions emerged. In most instances forms of practice evolved in which coteachers coparticipated in teaching with the practices of one (peripheral) coteacher supporting those of the other (lead) coteacher. When the peripheral participant used gestures and other body movements there were fewer examples of one coteacher breaching the practices of the other.

However, when both coteachers talked the structure was such that the baton either would be withheld or seized. Such occasions often led to unsuccessful interactions in that teaching moves did not appear to impact learning to the extent they might have, and at least one of the coteachers became frustrated.

Prosody was a key to both withholding and seizing turns at teaching. If the rhythm and intonation of a coteacher was high energy then the teaching usually had sufficient fluency to continue through silent pauses, even if a coteacher endeavored to initiate a teaching turn. To successfully seize a turn at teaching it appears that a coteacher would have to employ an action that was at a higher-energy level (i.e., incorporated more verve) than that being used by the other coteacher. Hence, successful efforts to breach the teaching of a coteacher usually were associated with a pause of more than a half a second and an utterance of greater amplitude and pitch than those being enacted by the coteacher. From the perspective of the person blocked from a central teaching role the interactions associated with her failure to teach would most likely be seen as unsuccessful and may be accompanied by feelings of disappointment, frustration, and even resentment, all of which are expressed in and made available to others through prosody. Based on the recent work on emotional energy by Collins (2004), extended in our research on the teaching and learning of science in urban settings, it is as well to identify and minimize interactions that are unsuccessful and associated with negative emotional energy. There are implications for teacher education for new and more experienced teachers. I see considerable benefits in providing teachers with software tools, such as QuickTime Pro and PRAAT, to enhance their roles as researchers of their own practices. Micro-analyses of videotapes in which coteachers teach together can identify segments that show a lack of coordination, cooperation, collaboration, co-responsibility, and co-respect. A topic for ongoing analysis in cogenerative dialogues can be the extent to which coteachers embrace the meanings of *co* in all of the contexts in which participants in a community of learners are together, with, and jointly involved.

Notes

1. In this chapter, the following transcription conventions are used:

↑	Rising intonation
↓	Falling intonation
*	Coordination of talk and gestures
[	Simultaneous talk by two speakers, with one utterance represented on top of the other in the moment of overlap marked by left brackets
=	Interruptions or next utterance following immediately, or continuous talk

	represented on separate lines because of the need to represent overlapping comment on intervening line
(3.4)	Time in seconds is shown in round brackets.

Acknowledgments

Wolff-Michael Roth introduced me to PRAAT (Boersma & Weenink, 2004), a tool for analyzing the prosody of digital audio files. As is often the case the availability of a new tool can greatly expand the questions addressed in research. This has been the case for this study. The tool has allowed me to conveniently address burning questions that were the focus of my research in the 1970s, notably the centrality of time as a resource for teaching and learning and the salience of the quality of teacher talk. Being able to operationalize prosody and measure such variables as amplitude and frequency of talk is a powerful step forward. Also, although I fully accept responsibility for what is written in this paper I am grateful for Michael's critical reviews of earlier versions of this chapter.

References

Boersma, P., & Weenink, D. (2004). PRAAT: Doing phonetics by computer. Amsterdam: Institute of Phonetic Sciences. [Software available free at http://www.fon.hum. uva.nl/praat/]

Boykin, A. W. (1986). The triple quandary and the schooling of Afro-American Children. In U. Neisser (Ed.), *The school achievement of minority children: New perspectives* (pp. 57–92). Hillsdale, NJ: Lawrence Erlbaum Associates.

Collins, R. (2004). *Interaction ritual chains.* Princeton, NJ: Princeton University Press.

Guba, E., & Lincoln, Y. (1989). *Fourth generation evaluation.* Thousand Oaks, CA: Sage.

Roth, W.-M., & Tobin, K. (2002). *At the elbow of another: Learning to teach by coteaching.* New York: Peter Lang.

Roth, W.-M., Tobin, K., Carambo, C., & Dalland, C. (2004). Becoming like the other: Learning to teach through coteaching. *Journal of Research in Science Teaching, 41,* 882–904.

Tobin, K. (2000). Becoming an urban science educator. *Research in Science Education, 30,* 89–106.

Tobin, K., Zurbano, R., Ford, A., & Carambo, C. (2003). Learning to teach through coteaching and cogenerative dialogue. *Cybernetics & Human Knowing, 10*(2), 51–73.

Part III

COTEACHING:
ADDRESSING GLOBAL PERSPECTIVES

Introduction: part III

The four chapters in part III examine coteaching and cogenerative dialogues in sites away from where we started these practices, the University of Pennsylvania and Philadelphia, on the one hand, and British Columbia, on the other. These new sites include two states in the United States (Alabama and Delaware) and two countries (Australia and Ireland). Different forms of inquiry are used at each site to explore the extent to which coteaching and cogenerative dialogues are associated with learning to teach science and improvements in the quality of learning opportunities for students in elementary through high school grades. For us, the importance of these studies includes their role as confirmatory evidence for the feasibility to organize coteaching in sites other than where they were originally developed. More so, these studies constitute evidence that coteaching is possible in other countries as well, though at present the mainstream ideology that shapes education in all countries is saturated by Anglo-Saxon culture. In the research that is situated in inner-city schools (principally in the USA and Ireland) we have explored how coteaching has produced forms of practice that are adaptive to the students' culture. It remains to be seen what forms coteaching will assume in other mainstream cultures such as Asia.

In chapter 8 Donna Rigano, Stephen Ritchie, and Trish Bell present an ethnography of their coteaching in a grade 1/2 classroom in a suburban school in Australia. The three coauthors of the chapter are also the coteachers and their insider perspectives afford deep insights into the ways in which the different forms of expertise of each of the coteachers contribute to coteaching and the quality of the enacted science curricula. The research addresses different forms of knowing about teaching and shows how different stakeholders collaborate and how ways of enacting coteaching evolve over time. The research addresses a number of substantive issues in science education, including a focus on inquiry, the role of student interests in designing science curricula, getting parents involved and corespecting different forms of expertise. Convincingly the study shows how new teachers can contribute to the quality of science education and catalyze reform within a school in ways that the school seeks to sustain.

Organizing coteaching in one configuration requires substantial rethinking of existing practices. The organization of coteaching as a vehicle for the development of new teachers currently in training is associated with organizational issues at a new level. Chapters 9 through 11 provide ethnographic descriptions of how coteaching was implemented as the context in which precertification teachers participate and develop in the practice of science teaching. Charles Eick and Frank Ware (chapter 9) explore coteaching as a preinternship experience for new teachers enrolled in a science methods course for prospective high school teachers. The study is an ethnography that involves coteachers assigned to high school science classes in Alabama. The research focuses on the transitions from the initial parts of the coteaching assignment, when they observed the resident teacher and provided assistance, to later parts of the preinternship when they assumed more central lead roles in planning and teaching. Subject matter knowledge and practical knowledge are investigated and so too are issues of personality in building professional relationships. A central data resource in this study is entries posted on an electronic bulletin board used in the course.

From the very beginning Colette Murphy, Jim Beggs, and the principal of a local primary school regarded science student teachers as resources for the improvement of professional development and curricula in elementary schools. In chapter 10 Colette and Jim describe the results of a comprehensive study of coteaching in a range of primary schools in Ireland that range from inner city to rural. They employ mixed research methods to identify the positive outcomes of coteaching for student and regular teachers. Their studies include the roles and power relations among coteachers and whether or not harmonious interactions among participants occur during coteaching.

Eick and Ware make salient the possibilities that reside in coteaching for building professional relationships. Such relationships are also the focus of the last chapter. In chapter 11 Kathryn (Kate) Scantlebury investigates coteaching and cogenerative dialogues in the science teacher education program at the University of Delaware. Kate describes how coteaching and cogenerative dialogues are infused into the teacher education program and how critical matters are addressed, such as coteachers teaching without the presence of a resident teacher. In this, her chapter describes the same configuration that was one of the starting points for the studies in Philadelphia—precertification teachers take responsibility for a science class without the presence of a cooperating teacher. Here again, the new teachers participate in legitimate ways and are formally recognized as a tremendous resource to the school community. The chapter also addresses the salience of socialization practices between new and resident teachers and the manner in which gender roles are associated with the creation of social networks, corespect and coresponsibility. Kate investigates the importance of cogenerative dialogues in establishing effective coteaching that focuses on the creation of improved learning environments for high school science students.

As a set the studies in this section address the manner in which coteaching and cogenerative dialogues can be adapted and enacted to create improved science teacher education practices and to catalyze changes in K–12 schools situated in different parts of the world. What we learn from these studies complement what we learned from the studies in part II of the book and in earlier studies of coteaching and cogenerative dialogue (Roth & Tobin, 2002).

References

Roth, W.-M., & Tobin, K. G. (2002). *At the elbow of another: Learning to teach by coteaching.* New York: Peter Lang.

8   Developing wisdom-in-practice through coteaching: a narrative account

Donna Rigano, Stephen Ritchie, and Trish Bell

Donna begins: Scanning the grade 1/2 classroom, twenty eager faces of six- and seven-year-old students looked expectantly back at me. I was talking to the students about what it was like to work as a research scientist. As I described how I worked with different chemicals and tested new drugs on animals their faces appeared to be alive with interest. "What color were the chemicals?" "What kinds of animals did you use?" "Tell us about the poisons you used." At last I was able to put my ideas about science teaching into practice. I had dabbled around the edges of science teaching for so long, first as a university tutor in biochemistry and later as an education researcher in science classrooms—building up an extensive knowledge base about other people's school teaching. But I had never been in a classroom where I bore the responsibility of teaching young children in science.

There were many reasons for my career shift from biochemistry research to science education research, a significant one being the desire to move away from the solitary aspects of laboratory research to the more social and interactive culture of school teaching and learning. This shift mirrored my beliefs about learning in general; that is, learning involves social interaction as well as individual development. As I worked in education research my interest in the theoretical aspects of learning motivated me to reenroll as an education student (I had completed one year of an education degree before changing to a science degree as an undergraduate). I was unable to complete the practicum component of this course due to family and business commitments, and I abandoned the notion of ever teaching in a school classroom. However, my understanding of the nature of learning and the various knowledge bases required for teaching continued to grow with my ongoing involvement in qualitative educational research projects. Eventually I found myself in the unique situation of being able to experience teaching in a practicum setting.

My colleague Steve invited me to participate in a research study that involved coteaching. The initial focus of this study was to document whether the coteaching model described by Roth and Tobin (2002) could be used to assist the professional development of a teacher attempting to incorporate inquiry teaching into her science lessons. We were interested in science inquiry instruction because the new Queensland science syllabus in Australia promoted the use of inquiry teaching as part of the Working Scientifically Framework. Goodrum, Hackling, and Rennie (2001) argued that inquiry approaches were essential to any science curriculum because they not only exposed children to the nature of science and the scientific enterprise, but also they had the potential of facilitating meaningful student learning. Yet scientific inquiry is a complex process that requires specific teaching practices and supportive curriculum.

Initially my role in the yearlong study was to bring my expertise in scientific practices (e.g., research skills) into the classroom. However as the study commenced we realized that I could also add another dimension to the study. It became apparent that we were presented with the opportunity to investigate whether we could apply the coteaching model to preservice science teacher education. In other words, I was now able to finish my once-abandoned practicum, and intriguingly I was able to report on the outcomes as an experienced education researcher who had once been a professional scientist.

In an earlier study of learning to teach, Steve and I demonstrated that student teachers could begin to access more experienced teachers' wisdom through questioning strategies (Ritchie, Rigano, & Lowry, 2000). We further argued that there was a special type of wisdom that could be tapped only through being in the classroom and practicing as a teacher: wisdom-in-practice. So the broad question that guided our writing of this chapter was: "How did I develop my understanding of classroom science teaching through the application of a coteaching model?" In other words, "How did I develop my wisdom-in-practice?"

Towards a wisdom-in-practice view

Teacher knowledge is generally described in terms of either procedural or propositional knowledge. Procedural knowledge is the practical knowledge of how to do things while propositional knowledge is higher-order knowledge involving sense making and reasoning. Shulman's (1987) efforts to understand the nature of knowledge required for the enterprise of teaching led to the description of seven sorts of teaching knowledge which were primarily propositional; however, he did fashion the term *wisdom of practice* to refer to teachers' practical knowledge. This knowledge is related to other constructs such as personal practical knowledge, craft knowledge, and practical theories, which have in common the notion that teachers develop a type of knowledge that is distinct from formal research knowledge. In a different vein, Schön's (1983) work on reflective practice emphasized teacher reasoning where teachers stand back from their practice to reflect on their experience. The wisdom generated from such reflection-on-practice was termed *deliberative wisdom* by Feldman (1997). But Feldman also declared that there was more to becoming a good teacher than the possession of knowledge (wisdom of practice) and then reasoning about one's practice (deliberative wisdom). What was missing was an understanding of being a teacher and what it meant to teach; that is, *wisdom-in-practice*.

Russell and Hrycenko (2004) elaborated on the distinction between *episteme*: our familiar experiences of schooling involving principles, rules, theorems, and conceptual knowledge; and *phronesis*: how our experiences influence our perception, our ability to perceive and discriminate the relevant details. They further posited that learning to teach involves going beyond deliberate, intentional, and sequential processing to a more dynamic processing that is rapid, spontaneous and simultaneous, and pays attention to information that is sensorial and interesting. Russell and Hrycenko (2004) argued that this dynamic processing leads to the conceptual changes that teacher educators seek to develop through practicum experiences.

In describing the difficulties faced by student teachers learning to teach science, Asoko (2000) described how a student teacher became aware of the need to "see the science" and "talk the science" during her interactions with students in order to promote conceptual understanding. She argued that success for student teachers depends on his or her ability to capitalize on the planned and unplanned opportunities for promoting learning that arise in the classroom, their ability to develop wisdom-in-practice. Teaching, however, is not an individual enterprise, but rather teachers work within a community of practice. Leont'ev's (cited in Knight, 2002) description of interactions distinguishes between operations, which become nonconscious with practice; actions, which are more mindful; and activities, which are suites of actions. A change to operations or actions can be achieved by changing routines but a change to activities involves reappraisal of assumptions, beliefs and values and requires much more of learners than instruction and technical learning. What is missing here is how teachers bring their wisdom-of-practice and deliberative wisdom into operations, actions and activities and how they operate in a community of practice. This is wisdom-in-practice.

Traditional approaches to teacher preparation and professional development have generally involved single event, isolated workshops which deliver new strategies to teachers (new procedural knowledge) in the hope that teachers will develop better teaching through the use of new routines and procedures; that is, new operations (Knight, 2002). Teacher learning from this approach is at best additive; that is, it involves the addition of new skills to teachers' existing repertoires but their practice is unlikely to be transformed. Transformative learning, or changes to activities, on the other hand requires wholesale changes in deeply held beliefs, knowledge, and habits of practice. This type of learning is not based solely on the psychology of the individual but also incorporates social and organizational factors.

Teacher preparation and professional development require learning experiences that acknowledge there are aspects of teaching that are intimately tied to the lifeworld of the classroom (Roth, 2001). Roth proposed coteaching as a model of teacher preparation and professional development that "allows teachers to experience the classroom at the elbows of another practitioner and thereby develop a sense of practice through the eyes of the other" (p. 15). Furthermore, he argued: "through coteaching, teachers develop a sense of practice they share, a common sense" (p. 15). It seems that coteaching might provide a means for developing wisdom-in-practice because it provides practitioners with opportunities for reflection-in-action and the appropriation of practices. This chapter serves to provide a detailed view of how a preservice teacher developed wisdom-in-practice through coteaching.

Context

The study was undertaken in a composite grade 1/2 class with twenty (twelve girls, eight boys) children, thirteen of whom were in first grade and the remainder in second grade, at a small primary school in a large city in Queensland, Australia. The school was chosen because a mutual trust had previously been established between the researchers and the principal and teachers. As this study commenced the school also introduced a science program that involved hands-on activities for fourth through seventh grades as the teachers had identified science instruction as an area for improvement in the previous year's annual review of curriculum needs.

Donna, Trish, and Steve were the coteachers during the study. Trish had accumulated twenty years experience as an elementary school teacher, but this was her first foray into formal research. Steve and Donna were university-based researchers who had been working collaboratively in the field of science education for ten years. Steve had been a high school science teacher for twelve years prior to his university appointment. As mentioned earlier, Donna was a biochemist who had undertaken partial studies in education. During the initial stage of the study we, as coteachers, met to discuss the details of the science lessons we co-planned. In coteaching whole-class activities:

It is customary for one coteacher to assume central roles while others have peripheral roles and an understanding of when and how to step forward to assume a central role as the unfolding events of the classroom present opportunities for them to afford the collective learning of the community. Just as the passing of the baton in a relay race needs coordinated effort, in coteaching moves from peripheral to central participation and back must be coordinated with coteachers trusting and respecting one another's practices, including those that are dispositional and which are enacted without conscious awareness. (Tobin, Zurbano, Ford, & Carambo, 2003, p. 52)

Steve and Donna took up central roles when they each delivered early lessons, while Trish undertook peripheral roles to assist and maintain classroom routines. Lessons were typically sixty to ninety minutes long at an interval of approximately every two weeks. At the end of each lesson we would briefly discuss how Trish could further reinforce and extend the activities of the lesson throughout the week, for example through story telling, show and share sessions, or simple drawing activities. In second term the lessons were planned to correspond with themes Trish had already intended for the class. In third term Donna helped Trish modify her own science lessons to incorporate formal hands-on experimentation. As the year progressed Trish assumed more and more responsibility for the teaching while Steve and Donna took on peripheral roles as assistants and sometimes as consultants in the classroom.

As we worked and talked together we became colearners and coresearchers as we shared the lived experience of coteaching in an elementary classroom. Most of the text of this chapter represents a collective narrative of our experiences, unifying our three voices. Interspersed within this narrative we foreground individual voices to enrich the telling of our story. Where we need to make the distinction between the university-based researchers and the teacher-researcher we use the shorthand version of researchers and teacher, respectively.

The data for this study were constructed from classroom observations, discussions between coresearchers and coteachers, interviews with teachers, students and parents, as well as the personal narratives from the coresearchers. The university-based researchers made journal notes of classroom observations as well as coteacher and student discourse. Donna also kept a detailed journal throughout the course of the study that recorded observations, reflections, and personal interpretations. In addition to these storied forms of data, artifacts created throughout the duration of the study became part of the data corpus. (We borrow the term "storied data" from Abell [2000] and refer to data constructed from interviews, discussions, observations, and journals as opposed to numerical or primary sources of data, and distinct from interpretive understandings of these data.) These artifacts consisted of student science notebooks, poster presentations, drawings, and models. Gergen and Gergen (1983) recommended the employment of self-narrative to establish the "coherent connections among life events" (p. 255). We too used our own lived experience of coteaching to construct phenomenological understanding and employed narrative to communicate these understandings.

Developing wisdom-in-practice

The findings are organized around three critical incidents identified in the data and deemed to provide insight into the development of wisdom-in-practice.

Getting started

The following extract from Donna's journal is an example of a critical incident that related to initiating the coteaching model in the classroom.

When I first began to plan for the science activities I meticulously outlined a teaching schedule that included the date, duration, and content of all activities, as well as a research schedule, along with detailed information handouts for Trish and for parents. I thought I was being thorough and organized. When I showed this to Steve he advised me to be cautious about presenting my planning to Trish. He was concerned that she might be overwhelmed by the demands of such strict schedules. After some reflection I realized that my planning was at odds with a collaborative approach. I took a step back and pared down the planning to include only the essential elements, which I took to Trish at our first formal meeting. Here we discussed timetables, scheduling, content, formats, and all the other details for our first teaching session in a far more collaborative, cooperative fashion. Hearing Trish's input and willingness to support the inquiry approach made me realize that I did not need to control every minor detail of the project, and that the whole nature of the project could evolve through cycles of collaboration, action, and reflection.

A great deal of attention is given to lesson planning in preservice teacher preparation courses. Preservice teachers are expected to plan lessons regularly. Anecdotal reports of beginning teachers staying awake past midnight every night of the week going over lesson plans are abundant. University educators view detailed lesson plans as a path to good teaching which would eventually enable preservice and beginning teachers to establish the repertoire of teaching strategies and approaches that experienced teachers have developed. It is little wonder then that Donna too became preoccupied with planning. However in terms of collaboration with other teachers, individual planning is not conducive to the sharing and open conditions required for collaborative partnerships. As Tobin et al. (2003) noted, "collaboration in coplanning is essential, and as lessons are enacted, and after they have been completed, it is desirable for coteachers to participate in cogenerative dialogues, a collective endeavor to make sense of and generate theory about the praxis of teaching, focused on building collective responsibilities for learning" (p. 52). After Steve provided some guidance Donna was able to see that attempting to implement a rigid schedule was not likely to lead to a successful collaboration with Trish on at least two levels. First, ownership of the process and activities must be shared among participants if the collaboration is to succeed. Second, any teacher would feel somewhat threatened at the prospect of university researchers coming into his or her classroom for observations and coteaching. Steve and Donna deliberately tried to address this possibility by positioning themselves as less experienced in the context of the grade 1/2 classroom. For example when an activity required students to work in groups, they relied on Trish's expertise to decide on the structure and direction of those groups. Trish routinely stepped in when students needed to be settled down or reminded of routines. Particularly in the early stages Steve and Donna always deferred to Trish's judgment on such issues as literacy, attention spans, and possible follow-up activities. In these ways the researchers were able to initiate and sustain a collaborative relationship with Trish that was flexible and sensitive to the needs of all participants.

Collaboration between teachers is widely advocated as a means of enhancing both teaching and learning. Yet teacher education programs rarely focus on this aspect of teaching, instead choosing to focus on the individual performance of student teachers. While it is doubtful that there exists a single blueprint for a successful collaboration, collaborative partnerships probably involve a shared vision, interconnectivity, and support within the system. The nature of initial discussions between coteachers is crucial in setting the tone for the collaboration. If Donna had presented her rigid schedule to Trish as a fait accompli tensions may have arisen that could have tainted the future collaboration. Instead, adopting a flexible and cooperative approach gave us opportunities to discuss, amend, revise, reflect and refine the project as it evolved—learning with and from each other. In particular, Donna learned through the coteaching model what was required for a successful collaborative partnership with another teacher.

Posing questions

An important aspect of science inquiry is the ability to develop investigable questions. At the end of the first term Steve asked students to pose questions about making shadows, like: "Does my hat make a shadow?" and "Does a pencil make a shadow?" Even after several questions and explorations were modeled for the class and answered collectively, the first response to posing a question came in the form of the statement: "my hand" (instead of: "Does my hand make a shadow?"). This was not so surprising in light of Fleer's (e.g., 1994) work with investigable questions. We do not consider that children of this age are reticent inquirers. Rather, we suggest that formalizing inquiry in terms of posing a question that is then addressed in the form of a scientific investigation is alien to children's out-of-school experiences. They inquire by checking out the shadows formed by their hands but are not used to declaring that such an activity is in direct response to a formal question. The statement of a formal question is a communication style or genre constructed artificially in the alien context of a science classroom. Yet it is arguably a very useful communication strategy to develop because it features so prominently in the discursive practices of scientists.

Extra exploratory activities were incorporated into our teaching schedule to allow the students to engage further in the practice of generating questions. Eventually each student was encouraged to generate an inquiry-style question by making his or her particular interest known during a dialogue with Donna or Steve, who then interpreted the students' intentions and re-presented them to each student for affirmation. The crucial step in this process was using the students' initial ideas as the starting point. This technique is similar to the interactive process of transformative communication described by Polman and Pea (2001), which they used as a cultural tool for guiding science inquiry. They identified a common pattern in the dialogue between teacher and students who had successfully undertaken independent inquiry in the classroom. In this four-step process student and teacher work together to create meanings that neither participant alone brings to the interaction. The dialogue sequence between student and teacher involves the student making the first move, verbal or written, which the teacher recognizes as a potential situation to advance students' development and learning. The teacher reinterprets the student's move and together student and teacher reach mutual insights. As the student appropriates the teachers' reinterpretation the meaning of the original action is transformed and learning takes place. This interactive process "allows the student to be an active inquirer and the teacher to be an active guide" (Polman & Pea, 2001, p. 226).

This stage of the study proved to be a very labor-intensive time for coteachers. It would not have been possible for a teacher to work independently with each student to generate a question without a coteacher taking the remainder of the class. Furthermore, considerable expertise was required of the coteacher working with each child in order to manipulate the area of interest each child expressed into an investigable question related to the general theme of "beach," as well as provide helpful hints on how to carry out the investigation. This type of specific knowledge—how to respond appropriately in the here and now of the classroom about a scientific topic—is generally outside the knowledge base of most primary teachers, particularly beginning teachers. As Asoko (2000) noted, primary teachers are generalists and many find their understanding of science challenged by the demands of the curriculum.

Solving the perceived problem of a lack of expertise in primary science teaching will require a range of solutions. One possibility is to adopt a coteaching approach to science teaching that utilizes the expertise of willing scientists. Roth et al. (1999) drew on the notion of *spielraum* (room to maneuver) to understand the nature of masterful practice, which does not need reflection prior to action. Developing *spielraum* means that beginning teachers learn ways of being and acting in the classroom. Beginners develop a feel for what is right at the right moment by seeing and experiencing these modes of operation in practice. As a novice in an elementary classroom setting Donna was constantly learning how to deal with young students. During class discussions, Donna found that a student sitting in the front row would attempt to attract her attention by making loud noises, waving his arm vigorously, almost jumping out of his chair. Donna was unsure how to deal with this distracting behavior without dampening the student's enthusiasm. Donna observed how Trish would acknowledge his enthusiasm by saying "Thank you Peter, but let's hear from someone who hasn't said much today" or by calling on others who were quietly raising their hands, explicitly commenting that "today I will ask people who are sitting quietly with their hands up." Donna utilized this strategy in future class interactions. Donna's acquisition of this teaching strategy was an example of coteachers "becoming like the other" (Tobin et al., 2003, p. 57). The manner in which a person teaches is shaped by the unfolding practices of coteachers and students within the structure of the particular classroom. Family resemblances become apparent in the strategies of actions undertaken by coteachers.

Trish too was a novice in the area of science inquiry. During an activity involving the construction of a hat, one student was using sticky tape to join two pieces of cutout paper together, but had taped an area that should have been left open. Trish began to instruct the student that he had made a mistake, but Donna quietly indicated to Trish that the student should be left to test the viability of the artifact for himself and generate possible solutions to the new problems. Subsequently, when the child thought he had finished he tried to put the hat on and realized something was amiss. He examined the hat and discovered for himself what wasn't working and figured out how to correct it. Donna and Trish's brief interchange was similar to the huddles described by Tobin et al. (2003) where coteachers regularly but briefly interacted during a lesson with the purpose of "touching base and fine-tuning a lesson" (p. 53). Following the lesson Trish and Donna had a longer conversation about this critical incident sharing perspectives on issues such as the nature of inquiry practices compared with traditional approaches, student participation and meaning-making. This and other conversations between Trish, Steve, and Donna were similar to cogenerative dialogues described by Tobin et al. (2003) where coteachers engage in a conversation about shared experiences. The collective purpose of a cogenerative dialogue is to "make sense of and generate theory about the praxis of teaching, focused on building collective responsibilities for learning" (p. 52). Afterward Trish reflected:

I know through experience and reading that children learn in different ways, but this became more evident to me during the science inquiry lessons as I observed the children handling the variety of activities set up in the classroom. The children ultimately came up with the same answers to our questions, but they did so in their own way, and I could see that it was more meaningful for them—empowering them to be in control of their own learning.

Doing inquiry

As students completed inquiry activities in the classroom we continually monitored and evaluated the level and type of scaffolding we provided. The first issue that caused concern was parents' limited understanding of inquiry. We found that parents were not confident about undertaking investigations with their children at home—a component of our program that was borrowed from McGonigal (2000). For example, to assist students and parents to get started on their first inquiry a coteacher spoke to each student individually about a question they might like to investigate based on the introductory activities carried out in the classroom. The coteacher wrote down the question with accompanying notes to act as helpful guidelines for parents to help their child carry out the inquiry over the holiday period. However initial attempts at inquiry rarely involved any kind of manipulation or direct experimentation; completed projects displayed information from books rather than providing evidence that variables were manipulated to collect data that could be used to test particular ideas or hypotheses. Furthermore we surmised that the holiday period was not the best time for parents to attempt to undertake a project with their children. We subsequently made two significant changes for the final inquiry project: we offered students a list of questions to choose from and we scheduled the inquiry during term rather than during the holiday period. We emphasized that students should attempt something that they could demonstrate to the class. We also guided students through a group inquiry in the classroom investigating the best conditions for seed germination. We assumed that with appropriate scaffolding parents could assist their children to generate an investigable question. However we found that only a few parents were able to guide their children through a process that led to an investigable question. For example, one parent reported that

It took a while for S to come up with a topic for this project. She had a friend over for a swim on the weekend and asked me, "Why is she heavy to carry on land, but light in my arms in the pool?" We used a cork in a bowl of water to demonstrate how the water presses back on the cork as it displaces the water, and pops it to the surface. We then had her jump in the pool and try to stay on the bottom without moving. Of course she floated to the surface. We explained how the air in her lungs lifted her to the surface. What started off as a lack of interest on S's behalf, turned out being an enjoyable experience for her, and in turn enjoyable for me. (Parent Michelle)

Offering parents a list of questions to choose from relieved anxiety for some parents and also served to stimulate inquiry style thinking for others. The difficulties parents and students experienced in generating investigable questions alerted us to the mismatch between school science and laboratory science. A scientist working in a laboratory is usually part of an established project that provides a context for investigation. While the scope of the investigation is generally well defined, part of the dynamic of laboratory work is that the occurrence of anomalies and the need to overcome barriers or solve specific problems are scenarios in which the scientist is led to pose the practical questions that need to be answered. In a school setting the students are not usually immersed in a culture of scientific practice or thinking. Unlike the laboratory scientist, thinking scientifically is not part of their daily lives, at least not overtly. While Fleer (1994) suggests that participating in the ritual of asking formal questions is possible from a young age, unless the inquiry emanates from a context-based topic that is embedded in their daily curriculum, it is unlikely that students as young as six or seven will independently generate investigable questions without assistance from an expert or somebody experienced in science inquiry practices.

Communicating findings

Our final concern related to students' attempts at formal communication. While class discussions involved lively question and answer sessions, most children were reticent to present their findings formally, requiring a great deal of prompting from coteachers and/or parents. The limited literacy levels of children at this age and their natural reluctance to stand up in front of a class to talk made formal communication a challenge. We attempted to overcome these barriers by providing written guidelines encouraging parents to assist their children in preparing simple presentations. We also encouraged students to present in pairs, inviting a friend to stand in front of the class with the presenter. Another approach was to sit the class on the floor, creating a less threatening environment for the students to address. Interestingly, this was Trish's usual practice with children's presentations. That we tried alternative formats demonstrated Trish's willingness to trial different approaches as well as Donna and Steve's inexperience with teaching children of this age. With experience through coteaching Donna and Steve tended to adopt/adapt Trish's usual approaches.

The quality of students' final presentations indicated that there had been a shift in understanding of the nature of inquiry. Most students attempted to manipulate materials and many times had extended the inquiry with further questions. We attributed this shift to placing an emphasis on the "doing" part of the inquiry. Nearly all of the students carried out an investigation and there was a domino effect where those students who had not yet undertaken an inquiry were motivated to do so when they witnessed other students' presentations. The final inquiry project involved preparing a small booklet that coteachers assumed would be used by students to help communicate their findings. Yet it was apparent during these presentations that the booklets became a hindrance for most students. Reading was halting and often inaudible and consequently the rest of the class became restless. We achieved a breakthrough in our difficulties with communication of findings when we encouraged students to abandon their prepared booklets in favor of simply showing and telling what they had done. One student in particular had not attempted to write anything in his booklet, but had instead drawn pictures to show what he had done. When he presented his findings to the class he was most articulate and clear about what he had done, and when he demonstrated his inquiry (how to burn a hole through a piece of paper using a magnifying glass) the other students were enthralled. Another student who was typically extremely shy and hesitant to speak in front of the entire class presented his findings through a demonstration. Without uttering a word he showed the class what he had done and what he had found out about mixing colors while the students were extremely attentive.

The idea for including a formal booklet as part of the final project came from Donna who assumed it would assist students in their final presentations. In fact it proved to be a hindrance as one parent reported:

C enjoyed the practical component of this project and discussing what was found and why, but she lost interest when it came to writing it up. I'm sure when she is more confident and independent in writing she will find this easier. She was happier to talk about the project findings when I was recording the information. (Parent Bronwyn)

Again Donna and Steve were struck by the revelation that placing an emphasis on a written artifact might not be appropriate for students of this age. Rather than writing a formal lab report it was more fruitful to emphasize the "doing" part of the inquiry, with the inclusion of some props or posters for demonstration purposes. Another reason Donna included the preparation of a formal booklet in the final project was that she thought parents would be galvanized into action if they knew they had to help their child prepare an artifact. Donna however was surprised at the creativity of students when faced with obstacles. The use of illustrations by a student who had difficulty writing and the expert but silent demonstration by a student who typically avoided public speaking were examples of this creativity. Another student who tested the color absorption capacity of various objects simply taped a sample of each object she had tested into a book and presented her findings using that as a prop. For Donna the most valuable learning to arise from the coteaching project was an understanding of the limitations of parental involvement in inquiry-style activities. While there was much positive feedback from parents regarding the value of the science program, many were not confident enough in their own science abilities to support their child's learning actively. Donna realized that most of the activities had to be classroom-based with minimal input from parents besides complying with deadlines and materials requests. Trish "had reservations" about the types of activities Donna had in mind, but she was supportive and encouraged Donna to implement them because she knew they "were working towards a common goal of improving the way we teach science." Donna was subsequently able to learn from her experience and develop her understanding of parent involvement and student ability through her own perceptions. Trish, who was surprised at the high standard of the final presentations, also developed her understanding of students' capacity to do inquiry in a scientific way. Recent reports suggest that the demands placed on learners and teachers by inquiry projects require considerable support to allow them to do and to learn from these sometimes complex activities (Krajcik, Blumenfeld, Marx, & Soloway, 2000). Within the framework of the coteaching model utilized in this primary classroom the teachers were able to identify difficulties and opportunities as they arose. Donna was able to call on her science expertise while Trish had a wealth of pedagogical knowledge to draw on while they worked together in the classroom. Asoko (2000) argued that primary teachers need to understand science in ways that are appropriate to teaching so that they have a "broad, interconnected, qualitative understanding of important scientific ideas, closely linked to everyday events and phenomena, and embedded within and exemplified through practice" (p. 91).

Removing the barriers

In earlier research we reported how a student teacher struggled with the concept of "experience," a word that practicing teachers frequently used to eschew the often difficult responsibility of sharing their wisdom (Ritchie, Rigano, & Lowry, 2000). The "experience" word became a conversation stopper as teachers used it to assume a powerful position ascendant to the student teacher who was denied the right to probe further. Feldman (1997) made the claim that good teaching practice requires three varieties of wisdom: wisdom-of-practice, deliberative wisdom, and wisdom-in-practice. Wisdom-of-practice and deliberative wisdom can be accessed through formal instruction and individual reflection. However, the development of wisdom-in-practice requires the student teacher to participate in a community of practice. It cannot be accessed by student teachers reading stories, vignettes, narratives, or discussing models of effective teaching. In this chapter we have reported how Donna found herself in the position of a student teacher ostensibly able to complete her long-since-abandoned practicum with the opportunity to explore how the coteaching model could facilitate her learning. While Donna was considered an expert with respect to her broader knowledge of science content, in relation to a primary classroom she was a teaching novice. As Donna, Steve, and Trish worked together implementing a coteaching approach to science inquiry in the classroom Donna became aware of the opportunities for developing her understanding of what it is to teach science in a classroom. It was not surprising that as a novice Donna placed a heavy emphasis on planning. Due to their limited experience novice teachers may devote a large amount of planning to issues that experienced teachers could deal with swiftly, for example planning activities for those students who finished set work earlier than expected. Donna however had the support of Steve and Trish who provided reassurance as well as a fallback provision if necessary. The coteaching framework supported Donna's struggle to focus on developing teaching strategies and techniques rather than maintaining timelines and plans. After reflection on this shift in focus Donna was also able to develop an understanding of how to collaborate and communicate with professional colleagues.

Once Donna was able to focus on learning how to teach science she was faced with the dilemma of scaffolding students' understanding of science inquiry. Effective teachers have both a principled knowledge base and the ability to access and use this knowledge base in the very noisy, interactive, moment-by-moment decisions that constitute teaching. Working within the coteaching framework afforded Donna the space she needed to develop her understanding of how to teach science in a primary classroom. Roth et al. (1999) labeled this space *spielraum*, and other researchers use different terms to describe a similar phenomenon, for example, Russell and Hrycenko (2004) called the process dynamic self-regulation. In any case, there is a knowledge base required for teaching that allows teachers to develop a particular sensitivity for the situation at hand as well as an understanding of how to operate in these situations. Donna routinely encountered issues such as limited literacy, difficulties with posing questions and behavior management, but being in the world of the classroom and being with another teacher helped Donna to develop the shared experience that is fundamental for communication which builds the necessary common ground to construct a viable professional discourse within the community of practice.

Knight (2002) suggested that reliance on event-delivery models of professional development that are located in managerial discourses do not make good sense because such models provide poor fit with learning theories that appreciate the significance of nonformal learning in communities of practice. While the delivery modes of traditional models are cost effective and time efficient, early studies in coteaching (e.g., Tobin et al., 2003) are promising even though it is time consuming and labor intensive. A fundamental change in attitude might be required of policymakers; perhaps there needs to be a shift in thinking from "my work" to "our work" in order to develop a culture of collaboration among and between teachers and university educators. Forming strong collaborative cultures where teachers and university educators study and learn together could provide the scaffold to support more meaningful educational reform.

Coda

An interesting development occurred during the last term of the year. Trish and the two other lower elementary school teachers formed a team for preparing science lessons. The objective was for each teacher to prepare a hands-on science activity suitable for her class. Each teacher taught her own prepared lesson to all three classes so that each class received three different science lessons. The initiative for forming this team came from the teachers themselves who acknowledged that their unfamiliarity with science concepts curtailed their eagerness to try out different ideas from the new science syllabus. They reasoned that with mutual support and a shared workload they would be more likely to experience success with the daunting prospect of hands-on science. Donna sat in on a brief meeting between Trish and the grade 1 teacher Megan who were discussing which topic Megan might choose. Megan expressed interest in a mold growing activity but was concerned that it might be "a bit too messy," a typical concern for elementary teachers. Trish replied that "messy is good" because she had seen how her students had responded eagerly to the seed growing experiment where they were required to make daily observations. While these three teachers were independently pursuing this team effort, it was encouraging to witness a positive influence emanating from the coteaching project where teachers engaged in co-generative dialogue aimed at reaching consensus and negotiating roles. Eager to sustain the perceived benefits of the coteaching model the principal invited Donna to continue working at the school as a specialist coteacher in science following the completion of the project.

References

Abell, S. (2000). From professor to colleague: Creating a professional identity as collaborator in elementary science. *Journal of Research in Science Teaching, 37*, 548–562.

Asoko, H. (2000). Learning to teach science in the primary school. In R. Millar, J. Leach, & J. Osborne (Eds.), *Improving science education* (pp.79–93). Buckingham, UK: Open University Press.

Feldman, A. (1997). Varieties of wisdom in the practice of teachers. *Teaching & Teacher Education, 13*, 757–773.

Fleer, M. (1994). Determining children's understanding of electricity. *Journal of Educational Research, 87*, 248–253.

Gergen, K. J., & Gergen, M. M. (1983). Narratives of the self. In T. R. Sarbin & K. E. Scheibe (Eds.), *Studies in social identity* (pp. 254–273). New York: Praeger.

Goodrum, D., Hackling, M., & Rennie, L. (2001). *The status and quality of science teaching and learning of science in Australian schools. A research report.* Canberra: Department of Education, Training and Youth Affairs.

Knight, P. (2002). A systemic approach to professional development: Learning as practice. *Teaching & Teacher Education, 18*, 229–241.

Krajcik, J. Blumenfeld, P., Marx, R., & Soloway, E. (2000). Instructional, curricular, and technological supports for inquiry in science classrooms. In J. Minstrell & E. H. van Zee (Eds.), *Inquiry into inquiry learning and teaching in science* (pp. 284–315). Washington< DC: American Association for the Advancement of Science.

McGonigal, J. (2000). Transacting with autobiography to transform the learning and teaching of elementary science. *Research in Science Education, 30*, 75–88.

Polman, J. L., & Pea, R. D. (2001). Transformative communication as a cultural tool for guiding inquiry science. *Science Education, 85*, 223–238.

Ritchie, S. M., Rigano, D. L., & Lowry, J. (2000). Shifting power relations in "the getting of wisdom." *Teaching & Teacher Education, 16*, 165–177.

Roth, W.-M. (2001). Becoming-in-the-classroom: Learning to teach in/as praxis. In D. R. Lavoie & W.-M. Roth (Eds.), *Models of science teacher preparation* (pp. 11–30). Dordrecht, The Netherlands: Kluwer Academic Publishers.

Roth, W.-M., Masciotra, D., & Boyd, N. (1999). Becoming-in-the-classroom: A case study of teacher development through coteaching. *Teaching & Teacher Education, 15*, 771–784.

Roth, W.-M., & Tobin, K. (2002). *At the elbow of another: Learning to teach by coteaching*. New York: Peter Lang.

Russell, R., & Hrycenko, M. (2004). The role of metaphor in a new science teacher's learning from experience. In P. Aubusson, A. Harrison, & S. Ritchie (Eds.), *Metaphor and analogy in science education*. Dordrecht, The Netherlands: Kluwer Academic Publishers.

Schön, D. A. (1983). *The reflective practitioner: How professionals think in action*. New York: Basic Books.

Shulman, L. (1987). Knowledge and teaching foundations of the new reform. *Harvard Education Review, 57*, 1–22.

Tobin, K., Zurbano, R., Ford, A., & Carambo, C. (2003). Learning to teach through coteaching and cogenerative dialogue. *Cybernetics and Human Knowing, 10*(2), 51–73.

Zuckerman, G. A., & Chudinova, E. V. (1998). Inquiry as a pivotal element of knowledge acquisition within the Vygotskian paradigm: Building a science curriculum. *Cognition and Instruction, 16*, 201–233.

9 Coteaching in a science methods course: an apprenticeship model for early induction to the secondary classroom

Charles J. Eick and Frank Ware

How soon should teacher education candidates begin teaching in grade-school classrooms? Professionals in university programs, governmental agencies, and public grade schools continue to debate this question from their unique perspectives and needs. Most professional educators agree that a combination of essential knowledge (theory) for teaching and practical teaching experience is crucial in learning to teach, but disagree on the sequencing or integration of it. We take the perspective that learning in practice, through informed practice, must take precedence over other forms of learning to teach. Practice in the classroom in the role of teacher provides opportunities to learn in action, to develop practical teacher knowledge that can only build from practice (Roth, 2002). It also provides concrete experiences that are essential for initiating meaningful dialogue that can shape practice (Korthagen, 2001). In our teacher education program we place candidates in authentic teaching contexts as soon as possible, as early as their first methods course. Coteaching with experienced classroom teachers comprises the majority of their time in schools during the methods course. Candidates are concurrently enrolled in university course work as they progress from early coteaching in their methods course to the full-time student teaching practicum or internship.

In this chapter, we articulate our informed reasoning for coteaching early in our program that is based on situated learning theory and the need to develop practical teacher knowledge (Brown, Collins, & Duguid, 1989). We describe our rationale for using an apprenticeship model of coteaching, how it works in our contexts, and how it compares with other models. Recent research on our model supports the assertion that coteaching develops self-confidence and practical teacher knowledge essential for successfully implementing inquiry lessons in the classroom. Last, we discuss contexts under which our model works optimally in helping candidates learn to teach using inquiry in secondary science classrooms.

Theoretical and practical perspectives for early coteaching

My (Charles) personal experience in education as a practicing secondary school science teacher (grades 6–12) and then as a science teacher educator evoked a sense of duplicity that is often ignored among teacher educators. As a practicing teacher, I implicitly knew that learning to teach with a modicum of effectiveness and expertise came with time in teaching. The small amount of teacher education training that I had before my first teaching job gave me a set of procedures and generalities to apply to get started. This prior training for practice seemed to break down, or at least pale, when faced with what I needed to know and do to effectively manage and teach adolescent students. Through time in the classroom and ongoing advice from colleagues, I learned to make teaching work for me. I think this experience of trial-and-error once in the classroom is universal. Many beginning teachers do not make it through this difficult transition.

Only later, upon entering a graduate program while still teaching, I discovered that my practice could be shaped, even radically changed, through the study and implementation of new methods and approaches, critical reflection on what I was doing, and professional guidance and support. I learned to teach mostly through practice, but my practice was later transformed through new ideas such as constructivist learning theory and its practical implementation in the science classroom. During this time, I began utilizing cooperative learning, discrepant events that were designed for exploring students' conceptual understanding, data-gathering inquiries, performance-based means of assessment, among others. But did my experience in learning to teach have to follow a path that separated theoretical learning from practical learning, or at least ignored this apparent dichotomy?

Program goals in learning to teach using structured inquiry

While becoming a science teacher educator at a large university in the United States, I frequently heard from student teachers that what they had learned at the university did not work in the reality of classrooms. One example of what did not work was teaching through structured inquiry. To student teachers this meant utilizing hands-on approaches for students to observe scientific phenomena, create scientific models, or gather empirical data (or information) to learn science processes and content (National Research Council, 1996). As a former classroom teacher, I understood the difficulties and reasons for our student teachers' views on the disconnection between university learning on campus and learning in the grade-school classroom, as well as their lack of perceived success in using many of the methods that we advocated. They spent little time in real classrooms, and then, only to teach prepared "showcase" lessons to their "audience." Candidates learned to perform many of the skills and methods advocated in the program as guest teachers from their methods course, but not as everyday teachers. The novelty of their limited presence somehow made the classroom environment less real or authentic to what teachers face each and every day. In these situations little could be learned about how to manage and discipline students successfully while teaching through inquiry on a regular basis. Often, the regular classroom teacher was in the room managing the students, and this served to further heighten the air of unreality.

From my experience and candidates' complaints, I felt strongly that they needed to be able to both observe effective science teaching modeled in real classrooms and experience personal success in doing the same before they entered student teaching. In the reality of the everyday classroom they would have to simultaneously integrate their personal abilities to teach with what I called the student factor, the ability to manage and teach students for learning in inquiry-oriented environments.

Situated learning theory as a framework for early teaching

As a new science teacher educator, I began developing closer ties with science teacher colleagues in our local schools. One colleague in particular, Frank, had worked with our program for many years, hosting methods students and student teachers in his classroom. Frank also frequently taught using structured inquiry through cooperative learning teams. Together, we discussed the situation of candidates needing more time in authentic teaching roles and how to best provide this experience within the constraints of a methods class. He pointed out that elementary education candidates follow a model with much more time allocated to actual classroom experience, and we wondered together what we could do to increase time in teaching for our secondary candidates.

Frank and I began brainstorming together as coresearchers with a practical problem in search of a theory of learning in practice that could work in our contexts (Reason & Heron, 1986). We particularly felt that situated learning theory when applied to teacher communities of practice addressed the inadequacies of our traditional approach where learning to teach occurred mostly out of the context and culture of the classroom (Brown et al., 1989). Candidates could not learn to effectively utilize the tools of practice outside of the authentic commu-

nity and culture of practice, which included practicing teachers and their students. We considered how this theory could inform the learning to teach environments that we wanted to establish in the methods course field practicum.

Situated learning theory provided us with a road map for what might work
in our contexts. In our methods course, few candidates came with actual classroom teaching experience. As brand-new teachers to the classroom culture, they
would be viewed as *apprentices* much like a craft apprentice. As apprentices,
they would assume the role of legitimate peripheral participants in observing
teaching practice, modeling it with support, and moving to independent practice.

So the term apprenticeship helps to emphasize the centrality of activity in learning and
knowledge and highlights the inherently context-dependent, situated, and enculturating
nature of learning [to teach (our addition)]. And apprenticeship also suggests the paradigm of situated modeling, coaching, and fading, whereby teachers or coaches promote
learning, first by making explicit their tacit knowledge or by modeling their strategies for
students [candidates (our substitution)] in authentic activity. Then, teachers and colleagues support students' [candidates'] attempts at doing the task. And finally they empower the students [candidates] to continue independently. (Brown et al., 1989, p. 39)

In applying situated learning theory to learning to teach in our methods course,
we decided to set up coteaching arrangements between classroom teachers who
modeled and mentored effective practice and their assigned candidates. Candidates would learn to teach in their methods field placement as an apprentice in
the role of legitimate peripheral participant where they would use coteaching to
bridge the gap between the university and the classroom—theory and authentic
practice.

Encouraging development of practical teacher knowledge

Developmental changes and learning through practice are well documented in
the learning to teach literature (Borko, Bellamy, & Sanders, 1992). These
changes in practical teacher knowledge along with growing teacher expertise
support teachers in effectively enacting their chosen practices. We felt that the
immediate development of practical teacher knowledge while in a preservice
program was essential in supporting candidates' practice as new teachers. New
teachers are overwhelmed with the rigors of their jobs at a time when they are
still developing the practical knowledge needed to effectively teach and manage
students. Without this knowledge from practice new teachers would have an up-
hill battle in implementing more complex teaching practices that supported inquiry in the classroom. We knew that the learning curve in teaching was espe-

cially sharp for beginning teachers and wanted to create a transition to the classroom that integrated the complexities of learning to teach early in the teacher education program. Our hope was that candidates could begin to transition from initial self-concerns about their teaching and the nature of students to a modicum of competency in teaching and managing students if immersed in authentic teaching contexts. By coteaching with experienced teachers who utilized structured inquiry, candidates would tackle the learning curve and begin developing practical knowledge while using methods espoused by our program.

Apprenticeship as a first step in induction to teaching

We chose to take the path of an apprenticeship model for coteaching within the methods course for numerous contextual and practical reasons. Secondary science candidates in our program (undergraduate and graduate) have limited time to spend in schools until the student teaching term. Our program arrangement for secondary teacher education has candidates completing course work concurrent with methods fieldwork in local schools. Often this time is only one or two half-days per week while in a methods course. This limited time reduces the opportunity for collaboration, co-planning, and cogenerative dialoging that is evident in other programs where candidates are immersed in their schools as their primary focus (Roth & Tobin, 2002). Such collaboration is difficult in the methods course with the limited time at the school for cooperating teachers to work with a candidate.

We have also found that cooperating teachers are initially reluctant to share control over planning and teaching with a candidate that they do not know very well. This may not be the case in student teaching where a teacher and candidate often get to know each other well before a candidate assumes full teaching responsibility. Also, many of our participating cooperating teachers choose to coteach under our apprenticeship approach because they do not have to modify their curriculum and teaching. This is an issue in Advanced Placement courses for college credit and courses that are under high-stakes testing pressure (e.g., biology) that determine student graduation.

We also choose to use an apprenticeship model for coteaching for very practical reasons that focus on the nature of induction to the classroom. Most candidates in our methods course enter the secondary classroom as a teacher for the first time. They are often very scared and find the transition from the role of student to the role of teacher a very difficult one to make. At this point in their learning they are most concerned with being able to teach and to assume the role of teacher in the classroom. They desire to spend time observing the teacher at work and gradually trying their hand at teaching through an approach that allows them to teach gradually over time. Cooperating teachers acting in the role as coteacher can support them during this transition. Candidates' early concerns as they begin to teach are expressed through their voracious need for feedback on how well they look, sound, and execute their lessons. They are initially less concerned over the substance of lessons, but first prefer to work on attaining a modicum of technical proficiency and confidence in their role as teacher. These technical and role concerns will transition to concerns about the substance of lessons with more time in the classroom.

In the next section we describe our apprenticeship model of coteaching that we use in the methods course. An excerpt of the dialogue from a coteaching episode is portrayed where the candidate acts in the role of a peripheral participant: observing and assisting during her teacher's lesson in one class before modeling the same lesson in the following class. Some of the benefits of coteaching through this model from the perspective of the candidates are also shared.

Our model of coteaching

Candidates in the methods course are placed in pairs (partners) with a cooperating teacher for one or two half-days each week for twelve weeks. We allow the candidates to choose a partner with whom to work in their placement. Being that the candidates know each other from previous courses, we find that allowing them to choose each other reduces the potential difficulties that can arise due to conflicting personalities and general compatibility issues. Partnered candidates begin their field or school experience for the first two weeks through observing and assisting their cooperating teacher in practice. They complete exercises that focus their attention on classroom procedures and routines, the nature of their students, and their teachers' style and approach to teaching.

During the fourth week of placement, candidates begin to coteach with their cooperating teacher for part of her lesson. They continue to observe and assist their teacher for the first period or class of the day's lessons before each one takes the lead for a portion of the same lesson taught to the second or third period. In this model candidates do not fully coteach with their cooperating teachers during their first observational period. Also, they do not share the lead in coteaching with each other. Each candidate takes the lead in coteaching with the cooperating teacher in a later period while the other candidate continues to observe and assist on the side. In this way, partners share the lead with their cooperating teachers across periods. Candidates as apprentices concentrate on modeling their cooperating teacher and her lesson, and not each other. Cooperating

Figure 9.1. A candidate (right) as lead coteacher is helping students with activity materials while the cooperating teacher assists as needed.

teachers support each candidate when he or she takes the lead during the later periods through ongoing assistance, interjections, and even sharing the lead to keep the lesson on track (see Figure 9.1).

By the sixth week of the placement, candidates are coteaching with their cooperating teachers for an entire lesson, taking the lead for the entire lesson as much as possible during the second or third period. Toward the end of coteaching candidates are given the opportunity to coplan a lesson with their cooperating teacher that the candidates will each take the lead in coteaching without modeling their cooperating teacher. In this way, candidates complete the methods course by beginning to assume a greater role in the planning and teaching in their placements.

The following are parallel excerpts from a coteaching episode over two periods. These excerpts are from a forty-five-minute lesson on fingerprinting taught to a sixth-grade class in a nearby rural school. The excerpts are arranged so that the reader can see the same portion of the lesson from the first period, where the cooperating teacher is leading the lesson, to the next period where the candidate is leading the lesson. During the first period, the cooperating teacher assumes the lead with the candidates present (only one in this case) and acting as peripheral participants. In this role, Jessica is mainly observing her cooperating teacher, Ms. Green, leading the class while she assists in directing students. Jessica does not do any direct teaching during this lesson, but later in the lesson she will help prepare materials for the fingerprinting activity and then assist individual student teams.

In this excerpt students enter the classroom to find it ransacked by a fictitious criminal who has stolen their fish, King Louis, and are instructed to write down all the clues that they observe before sharing their observations with the class. This portion of the lesson is a very engaging opener to the topic of fingerprinting. The students' observations will lead to a discussion of fingerprinting as a way to find a criminal before students conduct a fingerprinting activity. The opening of the lesson is depicted here with Ms. Green during the first period, directing the class what to do when they enter the room.

Ms. Green:	Period science stop. Don't sit down. Don't move anything. Take out a piece of paper. We need to figure out what happened. Don't move anything. Don't touch it. Let's write down our clues and see if we can figure it out.
Jessica:	Write down everything you see.
Both:	Everything! ((Time elapses while students rove about the room recording their observations before being seated.))
Ms. Green:	Raise your hand if you can tell me something that you noticed ((pause)). Shalonda.
Shalonda:	Somebody got mad and threw things around.
Ms. Green:	Somebody got mad and threw things around. Mirissa?
Mirissa:	They came in looking for something and they trashed the room.
Ms. Green:	They came in looking for something and they trashed the room. Josh?
Josh:	They came and took a fish. ((Josh points to message on board of abduction of King Louis, the class fish.))
Ms. Green:	Whaaat?!
Jessica:	Whaaat?! ((Said with same rise in inflection as Ms. Green.))
Ms. Green:	((Reading message on chalkboard.)) If you want to see King Louis alive, start looking for the clues and find him.

During the second period class, Jessica takes the lead in coteaching the entire identical lesson with Ms. Green interjecting and assisting where needed to facilitate the lesson. Teacher interjections often take the form of content insertion for what was forgotten and management directives to the students. Also, occasional huddles between the cooperating teacher and the candidate take place during coteaching (see discussion of huddles, Wassell, this volume). Cooperating teachers and candidates both initiate these huddles. As in Wassell's experience with coteaching candidates (chapter 6), coteachers often discuss the practical aspects of the class, including on-the-spot modifications of a lesson for a particular group of students or to accommodate time constraints.

This episode of the fingerprinting lesson occurs late in the field placement and Jessica is able to retain the lead for a greater portion of the period than earlier in the term. Also, since she has had time to get to know the classroom routine and environment better, she is a better manager by now. Each coteaching arrangement is somewhat different in the amount of interjection made by the cooperating teacher, and the level of interjection with which a candidate feels comfortable. Candidates who are fast studies, easily model their teacher's approach, and handle management well may need less interjection than others. Also, as candidates model their cooperating teacher, they differ in the degree to which they take on the mannerisms of their teacher.

In the following excerpt Jessica clearly takes on her teacher's style of repeating each student's response in recitation. However, she does not know the students' names well so she points to each one that she calls upon. The lesson opens the same as in the period before with the students entering the ransacked classroom. Jessica clearly has a harder time in quieting the class and getting their attention. In her effort to quiet the class she uses a clapping technique that she appears to have learned from her cooperating teacher. Ms. Green interjects in the opening of this lesson to help get students started in searching for clues, raise important terminology, and facilitate the timely movement of the lesson when it seems to be stuck. During the lesson, the following interactions occurred.

Jessica:	Do not touch anything. Do not touch anything. I want you to get out a sheet of paper and in your group I want the recorder to write down everything you see. Everything you see as you enter the room.
Ms. Green:	You can move as a group from area to area.
Jessica:	Do not touch anything. Recorders you can take out a sheet of paper and write down all the clues. Recorders write and everybody moves about as a group.
Ms. Green:	If you can't figure out who the recorder is, then team captains do it. Let's go.
Jessica:	What I want you guys to do is move about the room . . . if you can hear me clap your hands. ((Class repeats the signal and gets quiet.)) I want you to move about the room and record everything you see. You guys have about five minutes to record all the clues that you see, and then come back to your tables.
Ms. Green:	Writing down all that you see, what is that called?
Class:	Clues.

Ms. Green:	No, it starts with an "o.
Class:	Observation.
Ms. Green:	All right, let's observe.
	((Time elapses while students rove about the room recording their observations before being seated.))
Jessica:	O.K., who can tell me, who can tell me what's going on here? Raise your hand if you, what's goin' on? ((She picks student with hand raised by pointing at student.))
Student:	Somebody trashed the classroom.
Jessica:	Somebody trashed the classroom. ((She picks another student.))
Student:	Somebody stole King Louis ((Their fish)).
Jessica:	Somebody stole King Louis. ((She points to the message on the board.)) Who knows what King Louis is and where he is usually kept?
Student 1:	A fish, and he's kept in that tank back there.
Jessica:	He's kept in that, what tank back there?
Student 1:	That aquarium right there. ((He points to it while standing.))
Jessica:	Is he kept in the aquarium? ((Question directed to class; students give mixed response.)) Did they take just the fish? ((Students give mixed response.)) They took the whole thing. [((Student confusion on this statement.))
Ms. Green:	Like the, the beta in the flower,
Student:	like the one that Jeremy gave you?
Ms. Green:	like the one that Jeremy gave me!
Student:	Ms. Green why aren't you gonna do anything?
Ms. Green:	Well, y'all are gonna solve the crime!
Jessica:	Who can give me, who can give me an observation of what you have seen around here that can give you a clue as to what might be going on? ((Students raise hands and she picks one by pointing at the student.))
Student:	The skittle machine.
Jessica:	The skittle machine is flipped upside down.

In our program we try to work with cooperating teachers in our Professional Development Schools (PDS) (Darling-Hammond, 1994). These schools have established institutional links with our university for the placement of candidates for the mutual benefit of improving teaching and student learning. Each cooperating teacher selected for our program utilizes structured inquiry and constructivist practices supporting it to one degree or another. We choose to work with middle grades schools (grades 6–8) because they operate with shorter periods or classes. This allows opportunity for candidates to observe and model their cooperating teachers' practices over two or three periods during one visit. Teachers are instructed to share lesson plans and explain their upcoming lessons before coteaching and to dialogue with candidates on enacted curriculum after coteach-

Figure 9.2. Frank (right) discusses coteaching performance with his candidates at the end of the day.

ing (Figure 9.2). Dialogue focuses on technical feedback for the candidates on ways to improve lesson delivery or management as well as discussion on issues of student discipline and behavior. Candidates continually document their perceived technical difficulties in teaching and develop concrete plans for improvement. They also take time to dialogue with their partners on practice and query their peers and course instructor via an electronic bulletin board for needed practical advice as they reflect on their enacted practice (Loughran, 2002).

Essential knowledge of science before coteaching

Candidates for initial licensure in secondary science begin their first methods course after completing introductory science and most upper-level science in their field of certification. This scientific knowledge, and the deep understanding of it, are vital for candidates' ability to take the lead in coteaching and model, not mimic, their cooperating teacher's practice (Grossman, Wilson, & Shulman, 1989). In our studies of coteaching, candidates consistently describe limited knowledge and understanding of the science in particular lessons for their inability to take and hold the lead in coteaching. This situation is particularly prevalent in candidates with a biology major teaching earth, space, or physical science concepts. Their role in these situations becomes at best one of mimicking their cooperating teacher's earlier performance, but often involves frequent interjections and sharing of the lead with their cooperating teacher. Also, responding to student questioning, though difficult for all beginning teachers, becomes almost impossible in these situations. We attempt to remedy this situation by requiring candidates to meet with their cooperating teachers before they coteach to review the upcoming lesson and its scientific principles, and to acquire books and materials to study (or review) these principles further. Since instituting this practice we have reduced the number of situations where candidates have obviously struggled in taking the lead in coteaching.

Candidate perceived benefits of coteaching

In our research on this coteaching model we continue to ask candidates in each methods course their perceived learning and benefit from coteaching. In every case they have reported learning through modeling their teacher's practice with active teacher involvement in the lesson and through dialogue on practice afterwards with their coteaching partner and teacher. After first tackling getting-started issues such as early trepidation and teacher delivery, candidates learn how to better explain concepts and directions so that students understand them. They learn how to ask more fruitful questions following an activity as well as pace their lessons for the time allotted. They also begin learning how to best meet the needs of particular students, including different learning styles and interests. Although what is specifically learned varies with each candidate and placement context, we can document through class discussions and interviews that coteaching builds candidates' confidence in their ability to teach and use structured inquiry in their future teaching. Their experiences in coteaching close the gap for them between what they are learning on campus and what they are doing in the classroom. In an interview with three candidates who cotaught at the same PDS middle school (grades 6–8), each one shared how coteaching helped them in this regard. The conversation began with a question posed by Charles.

Charles: So the question is: Has your mind changed, or your thoughts changed, or what have you learned? How do you feel about this notion of doing various kinds of student-centered practices now that you've actually been in a classroom?

Brenda: I think I have more confidence. I think that like Dr. Edward's class, they're like either great theories. And you're like "Okay, that's a great idea." I could, you know, that sounds great, but it's kind of like "Can we do that? Can it really work?!" And then you get out of here with this class and you hear about the theory and you hear about constructivism and you hear about hands-on and how great it is and you see it working. And so it goes from being a head thing to knowing it and knowing that it's possible and seeing things to emulate and being able to do it. I think with me that's where I come from that I now have more confidence that I could do this in my classroom as a teacher.

Jessica: I feel the same way. I now have more confidence that I could do this in my classroom as a teacher.

Andrea: I feel the same way– It gives you more confidence to know that you can do different activities and inquiries in a classroom and feel confident that you'll be able to do them.

Candidates' seeming confidence about what they can now do in their own classrooms is a change from past candidates' attitudes where they entered student teaching never believing that inquiry-oriented teaching was ever possible, or possible for them to do. This newly formed attitude and acknowledgment that inquiry is possible may help to sustain them through the difficulties of beginning practice as they attempt to implement it. The teaching skills and practical knowledge that candidates begin developing through coteaching can support them in "hitting the ground running" as they enter student teaching.

Learning how to manage and discipline students in activity-based learning is another perceived benefit that candidates continually cite after each methods course. Candidates get over the initial shock that students are not all respectful to adults and that many do not automatically do what the teacher asks. They begin establishing their teacher presence in the classroom so that students will comply with their direction. They start asserting themselves to secure their students' attention when they need it, often at the beginning of class and again after an activity. They learn how to give better directions for student tasks including expectations for student behavior. They learn to redirect off-task behavior and meet out consequences for student non-compliance. These disciplinary actions are hardest for our candidates to do because they are not yet comfortable with the role of teacher, and fear that they will harm their teacher–student relationship if they discipline their students. They come to learn that establishing teacher presence along with the implementation of fair but firm discipline is essential if activity-based learning is to work.

Impact on developing practical teacher knowledge

After our coteaching model had been implemented with ongoing modifications over many terms, Charles wanted to describe the nature of candidates' increased confidence through the lens of practical teacher knowledge, knowledge learned in practice, or what Roth (2002) calls the *room to maneuver* in the classroom (Eick & Dias, in press). Candidates in the methods course are required to post queries to an electronic bulletin board (webCT) each week after coteaching. In these queries they share episodic stories of their day in coteaching and end their queries seeking feedback or advice on a problematic issue for them in their teaching. Their peers and the course instructor reply with advice that may be helpful to them. The electronic bulletin board helps build a learning community among the candidates and extends the time available for discussion of their individual experiences and support needed (Barab, Makinster, Moor, & Cunningham, 2001). It also provided Charles with a means to study the nature of their struggles in coteaching and the advice shared by peers to support them. The electronic bulletin board provided a means to study learning in practice.

Initial reliance on prior knowledge and observation

Early in coteaching most electronic postings (posts) describe candidates' "reality shock" of coping with their newfound situations of interacting with grade-school students. Candidates write about their alarm over student attitudes and behavior in interacting with each other and with other adults. They initially expect to observe a high level of respect and compliance from their students when they start teaching them. At this time, candidates also write about struggling in technical matters of teaching, how to sound more assertive, how to be clearer in giving directions, how to quiet the students, and how to be cognizant of time constraints, among others. They seek advice from each other on these matters. The candidates give advice from what they have learned so far in their university course work that could apply to their peer's situation or what they observe their cooperating teacher doing that is effective in their classroom. Advice is often given as platitudes or general prescriptions that could work, and in this advice candidates frequently cite specific courses or strategies learned from these courses. They also share advice from their past experience as students in grade school and college classrooms and laboratory. All of the advice at this time comes from ongoing observation and what was learned *outside* of their actual teaching experience in the grade-school classroom. Hence, it lacks the conviction of personal teaching experience.

Below is an excerpt from an electronic posting and two replies that are typical of candidates' postings early in the coteaching term. This candidate cotaught in a sixth-grade classroom at one of our Professional Development Schools where they are using STC inquiry kits (Science-Technology-Concepts™) in their curriculum. Her cooperating teacher, Mr. John, modeled the effective use of these kits and how to manage student behavior during their use. Early in coteaching Sarah was still learning how to get her students quiet after they completed their activities. She received advice from two other candidates who shared from their past learning experiences and current observation and assistance from their cooperating teachers.

Sarah:	All the kids were excited about the thought of a holiday. This didn't really bother me – there was more talking but nothing truly disruptive or unmanageable – however, it did set me to thinking about what different methods teachers use to get back attention of the class. Before, I had just been asking them to please be quiet and listen up; today, with the added volume, I tried out Mr. John's ((the cooperating teacher)) method of counting down from 5 to 1, after which everybody is supposed to be quiet (worked okay). So, I was just wondering what other types of methods teachers use to get back the attention of their classes? Especially with inquiry exercises, with lots of confusion beginning and ending, it would be nice to try out a few options and see which works best for me or for future classes.
Carry:	When the kids were talky with me, I got them quiet for a few seconds with telling them I can only handle one voice at a time. Mrs. Little ((the cooperating teacher)) suggested that after getting them quiet, maintain the quiet for a few seconds, to drive home the message.
Jill:	You can also do like that girl did in the video of coteaching we watched in class, where you raise your hand in the air when you want to speak, so it signals them to be quiet. Also, you can tell them that they can only speak if they raise their hand and you call on them. Finally, if none of these work, you can tell them that they will have to open up their books and read the chapter and answer the questions at the end if they don't quiet down.

Jill's reply and advice, much like other candidates during this time, was a smorgasbord of ideas and approaches that might work for the candidate. The most targeted advice during this time, like Carey's, comes from peers who have observed similar situations in their classrooms and effectively observed their cooperating teacher handling it. Early in coteaching, advice rarely comes from personal experience in successfully handling a similar issue or problem.

Later reliance on experience from coteaching

Later in coteaching, candidates continue to seek advice on technical matters of teaching but posts no longer dwell on the entry-level skills of how to teach, how to give clear directions, how to question students, how to get students' attention, how to present material, among others. The focus shifts away from purely self-concerns to concerns about the lessons at hand, and how to implement them effectively for their particular class of students. Candidates discuss more complex skills in enacting inquiry exercises such as making cooperating learning work better, whether to give students content information before beginning an activity, and working with more difficult students. They develop an understanding of the nature of their classes and individual students within these classes. This knowledge enables them to anticipate and trouble shoot difficulties with a particular lesson in their unique classroom contexts.

Candidates' replies to each other continue to sporadically cite university course learning, personal experience as past students, and what their cooperating teacher does in the classroom. However, the nature of replies and advice that is given comes more from the candidates' actual experience as a teacher in their classrooms. They rely less on what they have learned *about* teaching and more on what they are learning *in* teaching. Candidates begin to discuss issues and problems on a deeper level that goes beyond quick fixes. Some of the issues raised have no easy solutions and could puzzle experienced teachers. In these discussions they show signs of trouble shooting and diagnosing situations much like experienced teachers. Charles finds himself joining these conversations at length and also feels as if he is an equal member of the learning community at this time.

Below is an excerpt of a post on the issue of teaching density with a reply from a partner, a peer, and Charles. Angela was beginning to work with an STC Kit for teaching density to her seventh-grade class. Students are guided through each activity of the kit in order to build their concept of density through conducting multiple small inquiries with the given materials along with teacher-led discussion of their findings and learning. Density is notoriously a difficult concept to teach and learn for students in our schools. Angela encountered student confusion on the onset of teaching with this kit. She had a good understanding of the nature of this confusion, but was not sure which approach to understanding was better or how best to work with learners at different levels of understanding. Her partner, Kelly, shared advice on working with the students at different places in their learning. A peer, Joe, addressed the issue she raised about how much content information should be shared before doing the activity. Charles shared further insights about the nature of the kits and what he viewed as acceptable conceptual confusion and not acceptable procedural confusion.

Angela: This week we are working on mass, volume, and density of various objects. Do you tell them everything without them seeing it ((lab)) and have them be confused? Or do you let them see some stuff ((lab)), be confused and then explain? Either way, the start of this has been confusing. I noticed that many students were lost; they were saying so. Although today was tough, I know that by the end of this week the students will have a great understanding of volume and density due to the remaining lab activities with this section. I guess the question is, how do you manage when some students are behind and some students are ahead during the discussion of a concept?

Kelly: If an advanced student asks a question you feel will confuse those not quite up to the same par, say "good question, we will get to that later" or "talk to me after class and we can discuss your question then." If you jump right on the advanced question in front of class, the half that is confused will only get more confused and the half that understands will only have more advanced questions to ask. With the students who just don't get the concept, ask them to explain to you their understanding of the concept. I think that doing this in front of the entire class can be beneficial.

Joe: We understand inquiry and its components and effectiveness, but now we only need the practice to make it a success the majority of the time. This is only true if you let the students go into the lab before explaining it to them– which allows them to formulate their own ideas about what's going on with density.

Charles: The kit approach takes time to "build" this concept by starting out small with student understanding tied to one principle such as volume, then working to the big concept. You raise a good point about "confusion." Some confusion built into a lesson, that is more confusion about understanding ((not the procedure)), can be a good thing. You really don't want to move to more complicated aspects of learning density until "most" of this confusion is cleared up.

Each candidate shared from a deeper conviction borne of experience in coteaching but was still informed by prior and ongoing university learning about inquiry and conceptual change teaching. This ability to move beyond theoretical knowledge and observation of teaching (past and present) to integrated knowledge developed through teaching may be a source of candidates' growing confidence through coteaching. Our work in coteaching also demonstrates that most candidates, not all, develop the basic skills and habits of teaching and managing a classroom on their own with little coteaching support in the end. Getting over initial fears of teaching and being a teacher, developing the initial technical skills of teaching, and growing in practical knowledge to successfully implement inquiry-based lessons all likely contribute to a greater self-confidence and positive attitude toward teaching and inquiry in our coteaching model.

Conditions that optimize benefits from our model

Strong cooperating teacher-candidate professional relationship

Each new term of coteaching we observe what we call seamless or smooth coteaching arrangements in many of our cooperating teachers' classrooms. We find that these contextual arrangements vary a great deal, but seem to have some common threads. In strong coteaching arrangements we often hear from candidates about how much they like their cooperating teacher's style of teaching, the amount of structure they provide to support them, and the nature of their ongoing feedback and relationship with their teacher. In their apprentice-like role, candidates desire a relationship with their teachers, that is, both professional and caring. Caring means that their teachers enthusiastically take the time needed with them before, during, and after coteaching, so that they feel successful and grow in confidence and competence.

Although all the cooperating teachers in our program are experienced teachers who utilize structured inquiry in their classrooms, not all of them provide a strong coteaching presence or support for their assigned candidates. In these few cases, too much is left for the candidates to figure out because the scaffolding that their teachers provide for coteaching may be too loose. For example, cooperating teachers may not have shared or enacted a clearly visible coteaching role that is supportive of their candidates, including use of ample and appropriate interjections for getting started in coteaching. In addition, cooperating teachers in some instances may not be providing adequate preparation information for lessons before a coteaching episode or inadequate feedback and dialogue on practice after coteaching. Any combination of these situations denigrates the learning experience in coteaching through our model.

Congruent personalities and styles of teaching

Not all difficulties with coteaching are the fault of the cooperating teacher. Like all preservice teachers, our candidates come to coteaching searching for a style and approach to teaching science that fits who they are—their personalities, beliefs, and preferred methods of teaching—when they enter teacher education (McLean, 1999). They do not always find this preference in their assigned classroom. Beyond issues of personality that surely exist, a poorly matched placement for coteaching can manifest itself through candidate-led coteaching episodes that are never smooth. Each semester we observe one or two candidates who never "find their groove" while lead teaching in coteaching. Unlike the rare candidate who cannot enact a teaching practice at all, these few candidates perform very well when enacting their *own* practice, during their own planned and taught lessons in the classroom. In these instances candidates are very honest with us about their difficulties in coteaching and struggle with modeling their cooperating teacher's practice. In these situations, which are often not identified early enough in the term to change placements, Charles tries to intervene with the teacher and candidate so that the candidate has more leeway in planning upcoming lessons through coplanning with the teacher. Coplanning allows the candidate some preference in how the curriculum is enacted, in ways that are more suitable to their preferred style or approach.

Challenging contexts with strong support

We have observed the most dramatic change in our candidates' abilities to teach and manage students in placements with effective classroom coteachers and challenging students. Effective classroom coteachers have a strong professional relationship with their candidates as discussed in the previous section. For example, we have observed that either a difficult class to manage or a class with a few unresponsive students have led candidates to hone skills of behavior management that they would not have to do otherwise. Most of our candidates will encounter some degree of challenge in their attempts to manage and discipline students while conducting structured inquiry activities. However, classes as a whole that perform well under the candidate's direction do not provide the dissonance that can lead to further reflection and growth in managing abilities. Candidates in these situations may or may not be able to immediately handle a more challenging class of students when they finish coteaching. Effectively managing a classroom doing inquiry and handling individual student discipline is one of our goals in learning to teach in coteaching.

Future directions

We will continue to coteach using our model in the methods course. Recently, we have teamed up our coteaching model with one of our Professional Development Schools as a form of colearning and cosupport for our cooperating teachers in their ongoing use of new inquiry science kits (STC kits). Candidates and cooperating teachers will receive in-depth training in the new inquiry kits that they will use in coteaching. Candidates will continue in their role as peripheral participants in providing "extra hands" support for cooperating teachers in use of the kits, but also they will be learning along with the cooperating teacher how best to implement the kits. We are curious to see if this collaboration

around new science kits begins to move candidates' roles closer to equal participation in coteaching.

References

Barab, S. A., Makinster, J. G., Moore, J. A., & Cunningham, D. J. (2001). Designing and
    building an on-line community: The struggle to support sociability in the inquiry
    learning forum. *Educational Technology Research & Development, 49*, 71–96.
Borko, H., Bellamy, M. L., & Sanders, L. (1992). A cognitive analysis of patterns in sci-
    ence instruction by expert and novice teachers. In T. Russell & H. Munby (Eds.),
    Teachers and teaching: From classroom to reflection (pp. 49–70). London: Falmer.
Brown, J. S., Collins, A., & Duguid, P. (1989). Situated cognition and the culture of
    learning. *Educational Researcher, 18*(1), 32–42.
Darling-Hammond, L. (1994). *Professional development schools: Schools for developing
    a profession.* New York: Teachers College Press.
Eick, C., & Dias, M. (in press). Building the authority of experience in communities of
    practice: The development of preservice teachers' practical knowledge through
    coteaching in inquiry classrooms. *Science Education.*
Grossman, P. L., Wilson, S. M., & Shulman, L. S. (1989). Teachers of substance: Subject
    matter knowledge for teaching. In M. Reynolds (Ed.), *Knowledge base for begin-
    ning teachers* (pp. 23–36). New York: Pergamon.
Korthagen, F. A. (2001). *Linking practice and theory: The pedagogy of realistic teacher
    education.* Mahwah, NJ: Lawrence Erlbaum Associates.
Loughran, J. J. (2002). Effective reflective practice: In search of meaning in learning
    about teaching. *Journal of Teacher Education, 53*, 33–43.
McLean, S. V. (1999). Becoming a teacher: The person in the process. In R. P. Lipka &
    T. M. Brinthaupt (Eds.), *The role of self in teacher development* (pp. 55–91). Al-
    bany: State University of New York Press.
National Research Council (1996). *National science education standards.* Washington,
    DC: National Academy Press.
Reason, P., & Heron, J. (1986). Research with people: The paradigm of cooperative ex-
    periential inquiry. *Person-Centered Review, 1*, 456–476.
Roth, W.-M. (2002). *Being and becoming in the classroom.* Westport, CT: Ablex Pub-
    lishing.
Roth, W.-M., & Tobin, K. (2002). *At the elbow of another: Learning to teach by coteach-
    ing.* New York: Peter Lang.

10 Coteaching as an approach to enhance science learning and teaching in primary schools

Colette Murphy and Jim Beggs

A few years ago, Loretta, a principal of a local primary school, invited us (the two authors) to come and discuss with her ways in which the school could improve science learning and teaching. We asked her what she thought she most needed. "I need your science student teachers, who could work alongside our teachers in class, I need some of the college resources and I need you guys to provide practical workshops for our teachers in science areas they find difficult."

So began our first venture into coteaching. We set about putting together a proposal for funding to see whether implementing Loretta's request in a group of twenty schools would work. Could coteaching by science student teachers and more experienced classroom teachers result in an enhanced science learning and teaching experience for children, student teachers, classroom teachers, and science teacher educators?

In our use, coteaching involves two or more teachers who plan and teach lessons, and who subsequently evaluate their teaching together with the aim of providing the most effective and enjoyable learning experiences for the children, whilst at the same time, learning from each other to improve their own practice. As Roth and Tobin pointed out in the introduction to this book, when two (or more) teachers begin working together, and share the full responsibility for planning, teaching, and reflecting on lessons, there is "automatically a greater range of action possibilities" and collective activity enables each individual to develop since "any individual can now enact teaching practices not available in individual teaching."

Some of the main challenges in primary science teaching are the low levels of confidence of many primary teachers to teach aspects of the science curriculum, teaching inquiry-based science, maintaining pupil interest in school science and the difficulty of some science content. We give a brief background to these issues, which serves as the broad context for our work on coteaching. We then illustrate the local context with descriptions of some of the project schools. We describe the level of enjoyment and learning from all participants that has been brought about by coteaching. Finally we explore some of the processes that may underlie effective and less successful coteaching scenarios.

The context—challenges for teaching primary (elementary) science

There is much evidence from research and from government reports worldwide that highlights the problem of primary school teachers' lack of confidence in science and technology teaching. Many elementary teachers lose their confidence during their first year in the classroom (Soodak & Podell, 1997); many primary teachers also lack confidence in their ability to teach science and technology (Harlen, Holroyd, & Byrne, 1995). A third of the teachers in the latter study identified their own lack of background knowledge as a source of their problems.

   The main problems in preparing teachers for science in primary schools arise from the situation that the majority of student teachers are not science specialists. There is an urgent need for such individuals to become confident and effective science teachers. Many have an inordinate level of fear for dealing with difficult science questions from children such as, "How does the sun stay hot?" or "What *is* electricity?" New teachers are also anxious about conducting science investigations with children due to time and resource management in addition to explaining anomalous results. Reports from the USA (Fulp, 2002; Weiss, Pasley, Smith, Baniflower, & Heck, 2003) and the UK have highlighted inadequacies in the preparation of teachers of science for primary schools. In the USA, elementary school teachers are lacking in science content preparation, especially in the physical sciences. Almost three-quarters of the 5,728 science and mathematics teachers in a national survey perceived that a substantial need for professional development was to deepen their own science content knowledge (Fulp, 2002). Primary student teachers are judged not to be scientifically literate and yet would be teaching science in U.S. elementary schools (Abell & Smith, 1994). Some of our own work showed that even third-level student teachers, including those who experienced compulsory school science from the ages of eleven through sixteen and some with post-sixteen science qualifications, could not correctly answer questions on some primary science tests that had been written for eleven-year-olds (Murphy, Beggs, Carlisle, & Greenwood, 2001). These problems, when taken together with the emphasis of national tests on content knowledge, may have contributed to science frequently being taught as facts or as a body of knowledge in the final two years of primary school. Teachers feel the need to prepare children for the tests by ensuring that they can recall the required content knowledge. Attention to constructivist theories of learning science and to scientific inquiry has diminished by this stage. The UK Office for Standards in Education reported that some teachers' understanding of particular areas of science, especially the physical sciences, "is not sufficiently well developed and this gives rise to unevenness of standards, particularly in years 5 and 6 (age 10 and 11)" (OFSTED, 1995, p. 6–7). The Office further reported that in the upper years of Key Stage 2 (which represents children seven to eleven years old) "shortcomings in teachers' understanding of science are evident in the incorrect use of scientific terminology and an overemphasis on the acquisition of knowledge at the expense of conceptual development" (p. 10).

In the USA there has been major concern about the standard of preparation of science and mathematics teachers (Barufaldi & Reinhartz, 2001). During the 1980s and 1990s more than 500 national reports addressed various inadequacies in science curricula and in the preparation of teachers. Many of the resultant reforms centered on collaborative efforts to effect change. Innovations in science education are currently aimed at encouraging more practical and relevant science teaching. An overview of an Organization for Economic Co-operation and Development (OECD) study of innovations in science, mathematics, and technology education stressed that the critical point determining the success or failure of innovations is the classroom interaction between teachers and pupils (Atkin, 1998). Other scholars commenting on the case studies carried out in the OECD study concluded that the teacher is at the heart of curriculum innovation and that innovation depends on a "more thorough-going and comprehensive view of teacher professionalism" (James, Eijelhof, Gaskell, Olson, Raizen, & Saez, 1997).

Maintaining pupils' interest in school science as they get older is another challenge for primary teachers. Most researchers agree that the erosion in pupils' interest in school science occurs between the ages of nine and fourteen (e.g., Hadden & Johnstone, 1983; Schibeci, 1984), even though they retain positive attitudes toward science generally and acknowledge its importance in everyday life. The problem of declining interest in school science is international and many reasons have been put forward to explain it, including the transition between primary and postprimary schooling, the content-driven nature of the science curriculum, the perceived difficulty of school science and ineffective science teaching, as well as home-related and social-related factors. We carried out an extensive survey of primary children's attitudes to science and found that most of the older pupils (ten to eleven years) had significantly less positive attitudes than younger ones (eight to nine years) toward science enjoyment, even though the older pupils were more confident about their ability to do science. The effect of age on pupils' attitudes was far more significant than that of gender. Girls, however, were more positive about their enjoyment of science and were a lot more enthusiastic about how their science lessons impacted upon their environmental awareness and how they kept healthy. There were also a few significant differences in the topics liked by girls and boys—girls generally favored topics in the life sciences and boys preferred some of the physical science topics (Murphy & Beggs, 2003).

A third challenge for primary science teachers is the curriculum. The contemporary science curricula in the USA were considered to be "overstuffed and undernourished" (Nelson, 1998, p. 4). A prescriptive set of specific learning goals (benchmarks) from K–12 was recommended in *Benchmarks for Science Literacy* (AAAS, 1993), which suggested reasonable progress toward the adult literacy goals laid out in a sister report *Science for All Americans* (AAAS, 1990). In the UK it has also been recognized that there is still an overemphasis on content in the school science curriculum. Much of this content is isolated from the contexts that could provide relevance and meaning. Further problems include the lack of an agreed model for the development of pupils' scientific capability from the age of five and upward and the fact that assessment in science is geared toward success in formal examinations (Reiss, Millar, & Osborne, 1999). A two-year study, *Beyond 2000* (Nuffield Foundation, 1998), has made ten recommendations regarding the implementation of the Science National Curriculum in England and Wales. Essentially, it is suggested that the curriculum should be redesigned to enhance general scientific literacy as opposed to the current curriculum that is geared toward the small proportion of pupils who will become scientists.

Coteaching science in Northern Ireland primary schools

The work we discuss in this chapter was carried out in the full range of primary schools in Northern Ireland, many of which are very small rural schools (less than one hundred pupils), whilst others are large urban schools with up to 1,200 children enrolled. Our flagship school is St. Teresa's Catholic Primary School, a large urban primary school with about 600 children, situated in West Belfast (Figure 10.1). Loretta is the school principal. She has a strong interest in promoting primary science, not just in her own school but also in schools all over Northern Ireland. St Teresa's has a mixed catchment area with about 40 percent of pupils coming from backgrounds that would be assessed as socially deprived. More than 50 percent of staff members graduated as teachers prior to the intro-

Figure 10.1. Picture of St Peter's catchment area.

duction of the *Common Curriculum* (1990) that raised science to one of three core subject areas in primary school and enhanced its priority within teacher training courses. Few of these teachers would have studied science. In this school, even teachers teaching the oldest pupils may not have an adequate background in science, which is a typical situation in many schools throughout Northern Ireland.

St Peter's is also quite a large school with nearly 500 children enrolled. It is situated in the Lower Falls area of West Belfast. Its catchment area is inner city. The vast majority of the pupils live in the area. Employment prospects are largely limited to low-paid service-type work. The majority of the pupils receive free school meals. There are no science specialists among the teachers, however, the science coordinator has a postgraduate qualification in the teaching of science. The staff has had to become knowledgeable and proficient in science through their own endeavors, interest, and staff development. It is those teachers who teach Primary 6 and 7 (nine to eleven year olds) who have the steepest learning curve with respect to teaching science. Teachers in the school have also developed their science knowledge and teaching expertise by participation in our coteaching projects.

The student teachers involved in the coteaching are preparing to become primary school teachers via completion of the Bachelor of Education (B.Ed.) degree. All B.Ed. student teachers study a specialist subject to degree level in addition to Education Studies and Curriculum Studies. Coteaching is an element of preparing science specialist student teachers for teaching. The science teacher educators and research associate worked closely with student teachers and schools to enhance the opportunities afforded by coteaching science.

To enable coteaching to work most effectively, we devised a model that would promote equal roles for student teachers and teachers and more effective learning and teaching of science for all participants. Equal roles were promoted by means of shared responsibility for, as opposed to sharing of, all tasks. However, student teachers and teachers planned, taught, and evaluated all lessons together. More effective science learning by pupils was addressed by freeing student teachers from mentoring, supervision, or assessment of their work and encouraging them to concentrate on experimenting with a wide variety of teaching approaches as they concentrated the coteaching on science investigations (inquiry). Student teachers' and teachers' own learning was brought about via the sharing of science and classroom expertise and by the completion of reflective diaries during the coteaching placements.

Coteaching in practice

In this section, we outline some of the lessons to give an impression of what coteaching looks and feels like and we illustrate, using transcripts of classroom discourse, the different roles between student teachers and the more experienced classroom teachers. (Names of schools, teachers, student teachers, and children have all been changed.)

The following extract from the observation notes of the research fellow, Karen, reveals the complexity of the coteaching context. As with all teaching situations, there is a host of factors external to learning and teaching that are going to have a huge impact on what goes on in the classroom. In this case, we are looking at a student teacher's first coteaching session but the regular classroom teacher is absent for the lesson and there is a substitute teacher in her place. At the moment when the field notes begin, the class is very boisterous and the room is cramped.

This primary school is situated in South Belfast. It is average in size (just over 400 children on roll) with two Primary Five (P5) classes (pupils are of ages 9–10) who are taking part in the project.

We are in a P5 class taught by Susan (substitute teacher) and Emma (student teacher). The science lesson had just started and Emma was giving an introduction to senses and the sense of taste. The children were sitting at their desks and the teacher, who was substituting (Brenda was off sick), was sitting at the front of the class. The children seemed quite restless and had to be subdued by the student teacher/teacher/classroom assistant throughout the lesson. I later found out that the class was known to be a "difficult" one.

The student teacher put up a picture of a mouth with the tongue sticking out (homemade—very good and colorful) and began describing the sense of taste and taste buds. The children were able to remember scientific terms that their teacher had used in previous weeks. Emma talked about different tastes and how different parts of the tongue can taste sweet, salty, sour and bitter. She got one person from the class to put 'taste buds' on the tongue to show the different parts of the tongue that taste sweet etc.

After the introduction Emma began explaining the investigation. The children would be given a plate of food and they had to taste the food and decide whether it was salty, sweet, sour or bitter they also had to try and identify the food. Before beginning the investigation they were encouraged to predict what each food would taste like. The children were very boisterous and the instructions had to be repeated a number of times to make sure the children understood what they were to do. The children worked in groups (each table of 4–5 was a group) and one person from each group was responsible for collecting the materials for the investigation. The teacher, student teacher and classroom assistant were all working together making sure the children knew what they were doing and didn't misbehave. The children seemed to enjoy tasting the food, trying to guess what it was.

The teacher was a sub but was very interested in the project. He supported the student teacher in discipline matters and helped out during questioning and throughout the investigation. He admitted that she was coping very well with the class considering how difficult they were.

Emma was very nervous as it was her first day and she did have problems with discipline, however she did have the support of the other adults in the room that made things a little easier. She was very well organized and had good visual aids, the plates for the taste investigation were all set up and she also provided work sheets for the children to record their findings. The children mostly were attentive although there were a few that had to be repeatedly asked to keep quiet (by all adults).

The classroom is very cramped, over 25 children in the small classroom. I think Emma has her work cut out for her. Generally the class respond well to her but there are a few which may cause problems. There was no one person who was dominant when Emma was introducing the lesson the teacher was not doing other work but observing and making comments were necessary. It will be interesting to see how they teamwork when the teacher comes back.

This is my second visit to Freshfield Primary School. I had brought my camera to take some stills of the lessons. The secretary has a child in one of the P5 classes taking part and informed me that every Tuesday her child comes home raving on about science and how much they are enjoying the investigations (very encouraging!!).

On my first visit to this class the teacher was off sick, however, today she was there along with the classroom assistant and Julian (science teacher educator). The student teacher was explaining the investigation at the front of the class, the classroom assistant was sitting with the children (who were at their desks) and the teacher was walking around the room, preparing for the investigation. The children were much better behaved this time. The teacher had informed them they would have some visitors today so I think that had something to do with it!

Emma began the lesson with an introduction to the investigation, which she had written on the board as a mission: *"Your mission*: 'Keep u dry' is a leading umbrella manufacturer in Northern Ireland and due to recent weather conditions they are having to make hundreds more umbrellas. They have asked you to decide what material they should make these umbrellas from! Remember they must keep the customers dry and be long-lasting!"

The children were then given out a number of plastic cups and different materials to test—plastic, kitchen towel, cotton, cloth and newspaper. Each group had to pour some water on the materials that were placed over the top of the plastic cup and secured using an elastic band. They then had to decide how quickly the material passed through the material. Before starting the investigation they had to make a prediction on which material they thought would be most waterproof.

As the children worked the teacher and student teacher walked around the groups helping and answering any questions they had. Julian also helped out. The children, through the investigation and prompting by the teacher and student teacher, were able to determine which material was the most waterproof. The student teacher finished up the lesson by asking the children to report on their findings and decide which material would be the most suitable for making umbrellas.

The teacher was pleased with her student teacher and felt that although she had a very rowdy class she was doing well and getting the children interested in science. She commented that she couldn't really approach some of the investigations on her own and appreciated that she had been able to try different things. Throughout the lesson she worked with small groups of children and took on some of the discipline. She let the student teacher lead the lesson.

The student teacher was more at ease today and I felt her confidence with the children had grown from the first week. She knew all their names and was more assertive when they got boisterous. She took a good lesson, very simple idea but effective.

In this next extract from Karen's field notes also describing a student teacher in her first coteaching session, we see an entirely different scenario. The school is well resourced for science teaching. There is even a dedicated science room. The teacher is a more experienced science coteacher, having worked with a different student teacher in the previous year:

We are in P6 (ages nine and ten) class. Sinead is the teacher and Ciara is the student teacher. The science lesson was taking place in a specially designated science room; this room is only used for science and has been laid out specifically for investigations. There are a lot of displays on the walls, most of the equipment and furniture is new and it is a very bright welcoming room. The children are sitting in groups at their desks. The student teacher and the teacher are sharing the lead in the lesson, the student teacher gives a brief introduction and the teacher fills out what she has said. The class is very noisy but the chat is mostly about the investigation.

The topic of the investigation is materials and whether they are transparent, opaque or translucent. The student teacher and teacher describe the words and refer to previous work they have done to ensure they understand the terms. The children are given a number of materials, a piece of card and a torch and with minimal instructions they have to find out whether the materials are transparent, translucent or opaque. The children work in groups at their desks; the teacher and student teacher work with the groups. The children are very engaged in the investigation and this is reflected in the noise level!! The teacher tells the class to quiet down a number of times; the student teacher doesn't deal with any discipline issues. After the investigation individual children come to the front of the class to report their findings to the rest of the class. During this the teacher and student teacher ask them questions about the investigation to check their understanding.

The teacher had taken part in the project last year and I have noticed how much more confident she is. She is participating more, using more scientific language and in some cases more able than the student teacher to explore the children's ideas regarding the investigation. The teacher is fairly at ease with the student teacher and they have had some opportunity to plan the lessons. This year there is a more equal partnership between the teacher and her student teacher.

The student teacher, whilst having a fair amount of scientific knowledge, lacks confidence when trying to control the class. This is almost entirely left to the teacher. She leads the introduction but allows the teacher to follow through any areas that she hasn't covered. It works well as both have a different viewpoint. Throughout the group work the student teacher walks around the groups talking ideas through with the children.

Overall this team works well, the teacher is more dominant, mainly because of her increased confidence, although when I pointed this out to her, she said she wasn't aware of it. The children are very keen; this may be due to the culture in the school and the promotion of science. The teacher pointed out that in the practice transfer test, the children (even the weaker ones) scored well in science.

As the student teachers and teachers progressed with coteaching, we noticed that they effortlessly seemed to work together in many different ways. The following transcript of classroom discourse shows the teacher, Niamh, and student teacher, Simone, in a question and answer session with young children (five- and six-year-olds) about plant life cycles. The teacher's interventions reveal her greater knowledge of the children and concern with the learning of individuals. Niamh uses names more frequently than Simone, although Simone does seem to subconsciously pick up on this and tries to use the children's names more. Niamh uses prompts and cues to help the children with their vocabulary development, whereas Simone's less experienced approach assumes greater familiarity of the children with the scientific terminology.

The teacher and class are covering the topic of "spring" and they have been looking at plant life cycles. Today the student teacher and teacher are going over the life cycle and then they are going to plant sunflower seeds. The children are sitting on the floor at the back of the class facing the student teacher and teacher. The student teacher is leading the lesson with active support from the teacher. There is also a classroom assistant who will be assisting with the practical aspect of the lesson.

Niamh:	Everybody, listen for a second, sit down so that everybody will be able to see.
Simone:	I'm going to test you all today. Who can remember the parts of the flower? I'm going to take these all down ((labels on a picture of a sun flower)) and jumble them up. I'm going to start with Paul, what are these things called, the things that go down into the soil? They are the first things that grow.
Niamh:	Listen to the sound of the start of the word . . . r, roo . . .
Paul:	Roots.
Simone:	Very good, roots.
Niamh:	Afric, what's this big long part here?
Afric:	The stem.
Simone:	Ryan, these two things here.
Ryan:	Leaves.
Simone:	Good boy! What about this thing here?
Child:	The bud.
Simone:	And this?
Child:	The petals.
Simone:	Good girl. Does anybody know another name for the petals?
Child:	The flower.
Simone:	Good girl, the flower. Now what are the roots for?
Child:	For sucking up the water.
Simone:	And the stem?
Child:	Keeping it steady.
Niamh:	What were you going to say Brian?
Brian:	Holding it down.
Niamh:	Yes, it keeps it steady and in the ground.
Simone:	What does the stem do?
Child:	When you pour water in it goes up into the root . . .
Simone:	So what is the stem for?
Niamh:	Seamus, what do you think?
Seamus:	The stem holds the flower and the leaves.

Simone: Good! That's right.
Child: And the buds.
Child (another):   The roots suck up the water go into the stem and the flower.
               ((Student teacher shows the children a diagram of the life cycle of the plant.))
Simone: Do you remember what we called this?
Niamh: This is a hard one, remember how the word starts off . . . l, l . . . life . . .
Child: Life cycle.
Simone: What does it show us?
Child: It shows you what happens to the flower.
Simone: Yes, will we let Maria do it? So what comes first?
Maria: Seed.
Simone: And then what comes out of the seed?
Maria: Roots.
Simone: And what comes out of the top?
Maria: Bud?
Niamh: Sh . . . Sh.
Maria: Shoot!
Simone: If we have the shoot coming up, what comes next?
Child: Stem?
Child (another): Bud?
Simone: Yes, the bud comes next. And what comes out of the bud?
Maria: Flower.
Simone: Will we see if Maria's got it right?

Our observations and conversations with children, student teachers, teachers, and other science teacher educators indicated that everybody seemed to be gaining from the coteaching experience. Children were really enjoying science investigations. Student teachers discussed the massive increase in their confidence to teach and highly valued the more equal relationships they had developed with the teachers and university tutors. Classroom teachers appreciated the opportunity to reflect in diaries they completed and greatly valued their own increase in confidence in teaching investigative science. The science teacher educators also appreciated the improved relationships with student teachers, the increased dialoguing with both student teachers and classroom teachers about science and the opportunity to reflect more on their own practice. In the next section we present some of the evidence we collected to determine whether, indeed, there was enhanced learning as a result of coteaching, or whether we were just observing isolated instances of good practice and hearing what participants thought we might like to hear!

Children's enjoyment and learning

We carried out a survey of children's enjoyment of science about six months after the placement. We were interested to see if the coteaching had a long-term effect and if the teachers' reported increase in confidence in investigative science teaching translated into a more enjoyable experience of science for the children. We compared children who had been cotaught science investigations with those who had been taught science more traditionally.

We found that the children who had been cotaught were significantly more positive than other children about their science lessons. The chart in figure 10.2 represents the percentage of children in each group who agreed with the statements (a) science lessons are fun, (b) solving science problems is enjoyable, and (c) I look forward to science lessons. The fact that the survey was carried out six months after the placement indicates that the student teacher involvement appears to have positively influenced the science experience of the children in the longer term. Many children commented in the free response section of the questionnaire on their enjoyment of science lessons when the student teachers were in the schools, for example: "I liked it when we were doing dissolving" and "It was good fun making circuits."

Comments from the teacher journals also reflected children's enjoyment of the experience. They said, for instance, "I feel that the children really enjoyed the practical experimenting and testing. I think they have learned from their experiences and I enjoyed watching them progress." Student teachers also highlighted children's enjoyment of the experience in their journals. When reflecting on children's enjoyment of their learning, most student teachers linked this with their progress. As one student teacher said, "They loved the practicals, it added to their enjoyment . . . they listen more and take more in. We tested them through questioning at the end—they all seemed to take it in a lot better than previous classes I have taught who haven't had as much practical work."

There were also fewer differences between girls' and boys' preferences for different science topics in the classes that had been involved in the coteaching project. Project children also showed much less of a decline in enjoyment of science in the more senior primary classes (nine- to eleven-year-olds) than those who had not been involved (Murphy, Beggs, Carlisle, & Greenwood, 2004). This was exemplified by a teacher's comments during his interview:

In P6 [children nine and ten years of age], the investigation side takes a back seat because of the transfer [test]. I would not have done as much investigations without being part of this project, so it was great that way. When [the pupils] did the experiments and saw with their own eyes what happened—that was great!

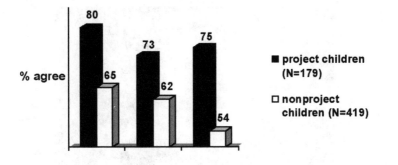

Figure 10.2. Prevalence of children agreeing with the statements (from left to right): science lessons are fun; solving science problems is enjoyable, and I look forward to science lessons.

Teachers commented about the children's learning in their journals and interviews: "They learned about the skill of predicting, and that predictions don't always have to be correct" and "When I tested the kids I couldn't believe how much they'd picked up from her, even the weakest of the children knew what she'd been doing."

We asked student teachers and teachers to prioritize another aspect of children's learning, which was that of encouraging children to talk science. The following extract is from a nine-year-old girl, Sarah, who is talking about the water cycle to the whole class, prompted by the student teacher, Aisling. Sarah has a large diagram of the water cycle on a flip chart and her "talk" is aided by constant reference to the picture (Figure 10.3).

Sarah:	The sun heats up the river.
Aisling:	Good girl!
Sarah:	And it goes up ((Sarah moves her hand from the river up toward the clouds)).
Aisling:	What goes up?
Sarah:	The steam.
Aisling:	Or the–?
Sarah:	Water vapor. Water vapor goes up into the sky and it gets colder and colder and forms clouds.
Aisling:	Why? What happens to the water vapor? Why does it form clouds?
Sarah:	Because the sky is cold.
Aisling:	Yes, so what happens when it gets colder? What does the water vapor do? It goes into.

Figure 10.3. Picture of Sarah giving her "presentation."

Sarah:	The clouds.
Aisling:	And then they join together, don't they?
Sarah:	Yes, and the clouds grow bigger and bigger and when it gets too heavy it goes down and forms rain and then it goes back down into the oceans and rivers and it goes again and again. ((As she says the last phrase, Sarah draws an imaginary circle from the river to the sky, clouds, rain, and back to the sky several times to demonstrate the cycling of the water.))
Aisling:	That's brilliant! I think we should give Sarah a clap. Excellent!

Sarah's description of the water cycle commences with short answers to the student teacher's questions. After plenty of encouragement, she launches into her description of clouds forming rain, the rain moving back down to sea level and its evaporation from rivers and oceans to start the process again. The attention of the rest of the children was intense—they were hearing the water cycle described by one of their peers in words and phrases with which they were familiar. Their clapping at the end of Sarah's short presentation was really enthusiastic!

These findings imply that the work carried out by children in science lessons that involved a science student teacher coteaching with the classroom teacher—both clearly focusing on investigative science—was more enjoyable for pupils and enhanced their science knowledge and skills.

What did student teachers get from coteaching?

Most student teachers reported a highly positive experience of coteaching, which developed their own confidence in teaching science and other subjects. Figure 10.4 shows data from surveys of student teacher confidence before and after the coteaching project. It seems that although the student teachers were concentrating on developing science they "grew" in overall teaching confidence as a consequence of planning, teaching, and evaluating lessons as a "team" with the classroom teacher. The data also revealed increased student teacher confidence in developing children's scientific skills and concepts, as well as in more general pedagogical areas such as ensuring equal participation of girls and boys, explaining ideas to children, questioning to stimulate children's thinking, organizing practical work, and all aspects of integrating ICT into their teaching of science (Murphy & Beggs, 2003).

In her post-coteaching interview, Emma talked about coteaching and her overall teaching confidence:

I had a real opportunity to build confidence in teaching science and this helped me prepare for my teaching practice [internship]. I feel this was a totally worthwhile experience. I built good relationships with all children and enjoyed teaching the lessons. I definitely feel much more confident in teaching practical science and have a clearer understanding of how children learn science. I think the children enjoyed it. They loved getting involved and I could tell they were excited every Tuesday morning. The teacher enjoyed it as well. She let me know this when I was leaving.

Male student teacher confidence in teaching younger children is frequently quite low. We were therefore interested in the experience of a male student teacher, Sean, who was coteaching a class of six- and seven-year-old children (P3):

It gave me a bit of confidence. We seemed to focus on technology itself and physical activities, not just the theory of the thing. It was important for P3s that when you introduce a concept to them you have to have it backed up with something concrete that they could get involved in so it would reinforce the learning. It kept me on the ball for my approach to the lesson the following week and the week after, not just adopting my approach to the lesson but adapting to the other teacher's method of introducing and progressing. We did work in partnership and it worked out well, it gave me the confidence to contribute and to listen and it also was useful, because I was listening to a teacher that was in the situation and I was picking up on her cues all the time. I was learning from her approaches.

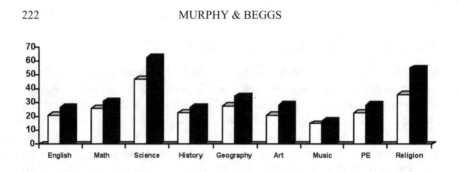

Figure 10.4. Student teacher confidence to teach different primary subjects.

In a few instances the student teacher experience was not as positive. We learned from our first coteaching project that two types of factors could obstruct the potential of coteaching for both student teachers and teachers. First, factors external to coteaching, such as school politics and prolonged teacher absence, and second, when there were relationship problems between student teachers and teachers. In subsequent planning for coteaching we tried to match student teachers and teachers, which worked very well. We teamed student teachers who were confident with teachers who expressed fears about teaching investigative science. We placed less confident student teachers with experienced teachers who volunteered to support them.

What did the regular teachers get from coteaching?

The main teacher learning about science seemed to come from their observation of and participation in simple, classroom-based science investigations. They commented on how easy this was in practice—as opposed to reading about do-ing it—and how well student teachers used the resources that had been provided for science. The following extract from an interview with a teacher a few months after the student teacher had been in the schools illustrates the teacher's appreciation of the student teacher's confidence with investigative science and how she was able to take forward the work they had carried out together. She was asked whether she had picked up any new ideas:

Yes, I got a lot of new ideas—practical ideas of the use of the resources. I just felt she had great ideas and things that I'd never used before. I think you're inclined whenever you are doing the same class or classes every year to get into the same mold of teaching things and I just felt she introduced ideas that I hadn't thought of. I probably gave her a few ideas as well, so when we put the whole lot together she learned from me and I learned from her.

It would have been the practical ideas that I enjoyed the most because it was a fresh new approach just gave me a totally different idea. One of the things coming up to Christmas we did was which material would be best for Santa's coat to keep him warm. So we did an experiment using all sorts of materials to see which one would keep him the warmest and that was great for fair testing. Afterward I was able to follow it up with lots of artwork and the children were able to bring it into their writing, how they did [the investigation], which [coat] would be best, and why. It had that fun aspect to it as well.

Many of the teachers also commented on the development of their science knowledge as a result of coteaching with the student teachers, particularly the physical science areas, as the following interview extract reveals. The teacher was asked what she thought she might gain from her work with the student teacher:

I thought I was going to have an experienced student teacher in my room who had more knowledge in practical science than I had in regards to P6 [nine- to ten-year-old children] which, as it turned out, she did. Katie was very good. It was so new to me the whole [pause] and the reason why I chose electricity was because I wasn't confident in that area at all. I was fine with the human body and all that but I really didn't know where to begin. I didn't know how to set up a circuit or how to teach it methodically and start at the beginning, which she was great at. She knew exactly where to start and had it all progressed from that. I have it all and all the worksheets and will use it again next year.

Another very important area for teacher learning was expressed by the following teacher as she reflected on how she observed critically some aspects of the student teacher's teaching whilst pondering that she probably did the same things and how she had now been made more aware and would be able to avoid such slips in the future. She was responding to the question of what she thought she might have gained from coteaching:

One of the main things that I gained was that you could sit back and watch your children responding to somebody teaching them. Obviously you're normally the one who's in there doing the teaching and I thought the benefit was that, okay, you are involved in the lessons, but a lot of the times you were secondary. You weren't up there totally organizing and in charge of everything. So it gave you an opportunity to watch how children responded. You could see there was sometimes that there were children in the classroom continually getting the attention from the student teachers because they were the loudest, who were always coming up with answers, always being funny. They were getting the attention and there were children who were being completely ignored throughout some of the lessons because they were quiet and sitting not making a sound but not showing any interest. It made me aware that I'm probably doing that in my teaching but I would be aware even with the younger children that there are the ones that do get all the attention, sometimes it's for the right reasons, sometimes they deserve it but at other times you're so busy disciplining children that the other ones get left out. To be able to see someone else teaching, because you never do that, you are in doing all the teaching. Also just with ideas and things some of the practical things they came up with I'd never done before, like making the lungs and things so that was good to see and getting new ideas.

What underlies successful coteaching?

We feel that it is very important to try to analyze those factors that appeared to produce good coteaching and those which seemed to be the cause of problems. Initially we thought that if both student teachers and teachers were concentrating on the children's learning, then it was less important that they needed to "get on well" for effective coteaching to take place. Evidence from the student teacher and teacher reflective diaries and from our interviews with them suggested that the teachers were more positive about the impact of coteaching on children's learning even when they felt that the student teachers with whom they were coteaching required a lot of support. For example, when asked about whether coteaching contributed toward his own professional development, a teacher working in a class with two student teachers reflected:

Yes just having to encourage, support, and talk them through that aspect of the counseling side of it for them. Discussing lesson plans, discussing at the end of it what had been good and what had not been good and trying to support them through times when they felt that it didn't go just quite as they expected. They needed a lot of that and I'm not good at that so it was nice to make me do that positive reinforcement. . . . The nicest thing about the whole thing was that the children were totally engaged in what they were doing, every Thursday afternoon.

Harmonious coteaching

By far the main factor influencing satisfaction with the experience of coteaching was the relative perception by student teachers and teachers about the symmetrical nature of their roles. Student teachers complained if the teacher was not joining in enough or giving constructive feedback on their teaching. Teachers were highly tolerant of student teachers' less-than-perfect teaching skills but commented negatively when they felt that student teachers were leaving too much to the teachers.

When roles were perceived to be symmetrical, both student teachers and teachers were highly positive about the benefits of coteaching for themselves and the children. Here are some comments from the student teacher's diaries:

I found we worked well as a team overall. It was great learning experience for me and her. We established a great rapport within the classroom environment. We were able to help each other in areas of teaching science. We shared, altered, and experienced lessons and kept coordinating the coteaching throughout the whole experience.

I think we worked well as a team. It seemed quite natural to everyone. One teacher would take the introduction and then all teachers would overlook group work and guide groups when required helping them to achieve higher levels of thinking and learning than they would be able to independently

I feel that our teamwork skills have grown. Coteaching involves a range of different skills such as communicating, compromising, idea sharing, planning, and executing each lesson. Certainly I believe that I have learned a lot and also that each pupil benefited from our joint approach and input into each lesson

Since the diaries were completed during the placement, we were also interested to hear the lasting reflections of participants. The following three examples of responses to the questions our research fellow Karen asked, show how positively these participants viewed their coteaching experience six months after it had occurred.

Karen: What were the positive aspects of the experience?
Ben: I think it was very valuable to actually work along with someone to be able to cooperatively work to serve the needs of the children. We tried out different things, I consulted with the teacher to see what sort of ideas or what she would like and together we decided what we thought was best for the children at their level.
Karen: Do you think your teaching ability improved?
Marita: Yes because it was coteaching with the teacher and she was always there and watching, because she admitted herself that she wasn't very up in science. She boosted my confidence. She would have at the end of the lesson said, "What about we do this as a wee round up?" or "Would you mind going back over that?" because she knew the class better and she could say, "Could you redo that because I don't think they got it?"
Karen: What were the positive aspects of the experience?
Maura: To coteach with somebody was really good, it was good to discuss everything and how we both saw the lesson working out. Every week we took ten minutes before I left and we talked about what we would do for the next day. She knew the class better whereas I had the science background. It did balance itself really well.

The teachers were also appreciative of the benefits of coteaching when they perceived equality of responsibility between themselves and the student teachers, as revealed in some comments from their diaries:

Emma and myself worked well as a team. I managed to reassure her that I did not mind the mess of scraps of paper or noise while the children were doing this. I think she was annoyed at how long it did take and just how messy it was but I knew they were learning and didn't mind. As a nonscience specialist I was unsure how we would pull our skills together, I did find however that the student teacher could share her science skills and I could show her good classroom management. Practical science, with help, gives me the chance to move about the room and discover what my children know and how they use their thinking and investigative skills.

Teachers were interviewed six months after the student teachers had been coteaching with them. Their interviews highlighted the advantages of the experience primarily in terms of the children's learning and how the coteaching might influence their future practice.

Karen: What are the main strengths of the coteaching?
Teacher   With the student teachers there it gave the children much more opportunities to be doing. We had smaller groups, the number of adults around and the amount of talking and listening that was going on and not having to worry about who was where doing what, knowing that it was all going to be dealt with. The whole bit on vibrations, the children came up with those words themselves in their groups and I'm thinking, "This is wonderful." There was an adult always to develop that thought with them. When you are on your own, by the time you've got round to them, that thought has moved on and they're onto something else. So at the time the thought came it was able to be taken forward and developed with them and challenged that at that point. That challenging of their thinking was an important point.

Karen: Overall did you consider that working with the student teacher promoted your own professional development in any way in relation to science and technology?
Teacher: It taught me to be more diplomatic when working with others. I realized how difficult it is and it takes time to build up. I enjoyed coteaching—this is the way forward to teach investigative science. It is a major strength of coteaching. The coteaching aspect allowed me to explore different types of assessment of the children. I was able to question them in small groups. I was able to watch them all carrying out the investigations. It was a more

thorough form of assessment—it allowed me to help the children who needed the extra help.

Disharmonious coteaching

Disharmonious coteaching occurred in the few situations where the roles between student teachers and teachers were not perceived to be equal. Our analysis of comments from the diaries and interview from both student teachers and teachers revealed that the least harmonious situations were those in which the teacher took a leading role in the teaching. When student teachers were taking too much of the lead they were sometimes delighted with the level of freedom they experienced, but in other situations, complained about teachers not contributing sufficiently to the coteaching experience, as the following diary entries reveal.

I don't feel that we worked well as a team at all. This was partly due to the fact that I arrived with a detailed plan of what I was going to do with no room for possible input from the teacher.

Teamwork could not describe our lesson today as the whole lesson was conducted by me. My fellow student teacher did not participate at all in the lesson; instead she sat at the back with a group and helped them build their lighthouse (this group was not incapable of doing so themselves). If a child had a query they were sent to ask me. The class teacher left the room as soon as we arrived and went to mark work. He was meant to be building a sample model of the lighthouse and photocopy sheets but he had failed to do so. He did not arrive back until after the class had gone home. Therefore he was unable to comment on the lesson.

The worst-case scenario was when teachers took the leading role in teaching the lesson. Student teachers felt disenfranchised when this was the case and teachers felt that student teachers were "not pulling their weight." This comment from a student teacher interview illustrates Deirdre's strength of feeling about not being taken seriously enough by the teacher:

Karen: How did you get on in the school?
Deirdre: I hated it. I think it was because the teacher I was with was a young male teacher and he didn't take it seriously enough and it left me very awkward because I was supposed to be writing up lessons that I was supposed to be taking and he wasn't taking it seriously enough. He thought he was doing me a favor and I tried to say to him, just let me get on with it everybody else is doing plenty of work for it. Even when I was teaching—he would just take over and he was the kind of character, it wasn't my place to start interrupting. He just liked to run the show and I was left like a twit more

times than enough, I suppose, in a different school it would have been different.

The teacher who was working with Deirdre, however, seemed unaware of her feelings. His interview recalled a positive experience of working with Deirdre:

Karen: What did you think you were going to gain?
Teacher: My student [teacher] was very knowledgeable, very helpful, and very eager. She was one of the better ones, no clash of personalities. If I had asked her to do something she would have no problem doing it. I worked well with my student teacher and as far as I know the other teachers worked well with their student teachers. We worked it out that the start was teacher led and the student teacher helping and then she would take the latter half of the lesson.
Karen: Any weakness?
Teacher: I honestly can't say there were any negative points there was that uncertainty at the start. I had enough time with Deirdre to talk over what we had to do the next week.
Karen: Did you get any new ideas from the student teacher?
Teacher: A couple of lessons Deirdre would have said well what about this and she gave me an idea. Probably nothing new, nothing original; one example that she came up was the gases and she did all the work herself. . . .

This scenario illustrates the importance of open communication between coteachers. Clearly, Deirdre felt that Dominic did not hear her voice; he seemed to be blissfully unaware of her predicament. We were able to learn from this situation and in future coteaching arrangements we encouraged student teachers to talk confidentially to their tutors if they were feeling uncomfortable in any way with their coteacher. In addition, as mentioned earlier, we made deliberate attempts to match student teachers and teachers. These measures proved very successful.

Content analysis of the data from diaries and interviews relating to harmony in coteaching revealed that there was most harmony in the relationship between student teachers and teachers when the respective roles were perceived as equal, less harmony when the role of the student teacher was perceived to be dominant, and least harmonious of all when the role of the teacher was perceived to be dominant. This is summarized in Figure 10.5.

Conclusion

In this chapter we have described coteaching science in primary schools. The potential benefits for all participants are immense and we have been able to provide substantial evidence of this. We have also been able to pinpoint situations leading to less successful coteaching scenarios and have suggested ways of overcoming these constraints. We feel strongly that, whilst we have been discussing and analyzing the coteaching of science in primary schools, that coteaching provides the way forward for preservice education in all subject areas, both primary and secondary. This year, we extended our work to include a

Equal Roles: most harmony
- we were aware of each other's roles
- we planned together
- we had a sense of shared responsibility
- we interacted positively with each other
- we helped each other to promote children's learning
- we bounced ideas off each other
- the lesson was ours rather than mine
- she was pleased that the children had the opportunity to experiment for themselves
- she was pleased that the children worked in groups . . . pupils had not done this type of work before
- they had the freedom and independence to design and plan . . . teacher thought it was excellent

Student-teacher-led: less harmony
- I felt it was my lesson
- she relied on me, thought I knew a lot of science
- the teacher helped out with the practical activity
- my teacher gave me free reign and I took it
- I used to encourage my teacher to work alongside me more

Teacher-led: least harmony
- the teacher interrupted
- we both agreed we should have spent more time planning together
- I just helped out—there were no practical activities
- he made alterations to my planning . . . I felt it had too much writing
- the teacher totally dismissed my ideas, led her own lessons with myself as an onlooker

← decreasing harmony →

Figure 10.5. A content analysis of diaries and interviews revealed a correlation between levels of harmony and symmetry in roles that coteaching participants experienced.

virtual learning environment that could be used by all teachers and student teachers on the project. The virtual learning environment enabled participants to communicate "live" or asynchronously, despite being in schools that were, in some cases, over 100 miles apart. We moderated the student teacher conversations on the virtual learning environment and advised them if they wished for privacy in any of their conversations, to use e-mail. A snippet between two student teachers, which we picked up recently, reinforced our belief of the potential of coteaching beyond science in primary schools:

I'm doing "sound" for my visit for science– gonna split the class in half, half make an instrument and the others investigate vibrations with tuning fork, drums, rice, etc. The height of originality! Any other ideas?

Can't help on the ideas really, but that sounds grand. Sure it's all in the way you teach it– which will be class. We are taking the coteaching to the extreme and doing everything together, it's good, it works well. That's all, hope you all get on well.

References

Abell, S. K., & Smith, D. C. (1994). What is science? Pre-service elementary teachers' conceptions of the nature of science. *International Journal of Science Education, 16,* 475–487.

American Association for the Advancement of Science (AAAS). (1990). *Science for all Americans.* New York: Oxford University Press.

American Association for the Advancement of Science (AAAS). (1993). *Benchmarks for scientific literacy: Project 2061.* New York: Oxford University Press.

Atkin, J. M. (1998). The OECD study of innovations in science, mathematics and technology education. *Journal of Curriculum Studies, 30,* 647–660.

Barufaldi, J. P., & Reinhartz, J. (2001). The dynamics of collaboration in a state-wide professional development program for science teachers. In D. R. Lavoie & W.-M. Roth (Eds.), *Models of science teacher preparation: Theory into practice* (pp. 89–105). Dordrecht, The Netherlands: Kluwer Academic Publishers.

Fulp, S. L. (2002). *Status of elementary school science teaching.* Chapel Hill, NC: Horizon Research.

Hadden, R., & Johnstone, A. (1983). Secondary school pupils' attitudes to science: The years of erosion. *European Journal of Science Education, 5,* 309–318.

Harlen, W., Holroyd, C., & Byrne, M. (1995). *Confidence and understanding in teaching science and technology in primary schools.* Edinburgh: Scottish Council for Research in Education.

James, E., Eijkelhof, H., Gaskell, J., Olson, J., Raizen, S., & Saez, M. (1997). Innovations in science, mathematics and technology education. *Journal of Curriculum Studies, 29,* 471–483.

Murphy, C., & Beggs, J. (2003). Children's perceptions of school science. *School Science Review, 84*, 109–116.

Murphy, C., Beggs, J., Carlisle, K., & Greenwood, J. (2004). Students as 'catalysts' in the classroom: The impact of co-teaching between science student teachers and primary classroom teachers on children's enjoyment and learning of science. *International Journal of Science Education, 26*, 1023–1035.

Murphy, C., Beggs, J., Hickey, I., O'Meara, J., & Sweeney, J. (2001). National curriculum: Compulsory school science—is it improving scientific literacy? *Educational Research, 43*, 189–199.

Nelson, G. D. (1998). Science literacy for all: An achievable goal? [online]. Available from http://www.project2061.org/research/articles/opa.htm (Accessed June 15, 2004)

Nuffield Foundation. (1998). *Beyond 2000: science education for the future.* London: Author.

Office for Standards in Education (OFSTED). (1995). *Science: A review of inspection findings 1993/94.* London: HMSO.

Reiss, M. J., Millar, R., & Osborne, J. (1999). Beyond 2000: Science/biology education for the future. *School Science Review, 79*, 19–24.

Schibeci, R. A. (1984). Attitudes to science: An update. *Studies in Science Education, 11*, 26–59.

Soodak, L. C., & Podell, D. M. (1997). Efficacy and experience: Perceptions of efficacy among pre-service and practicing teachers. *Journal of Research and Development in Education, 30*, 214–221.

Weiss, I. R., Pasley, J. D., Smith, P. S., Baniflower, E. R., & Heck, D. J. (2003). *Looking inside the classroom: A study of K–12 mathematics and science education in the United States.* Chapel Hill, NC: Horizon Research.

11   Gender issues in coteaching

Kathryn Scantlebury

I had become involved with coteaching through working with Ken Tobin and his colleagues at the University of Pennsylvania in Philadelphia. During that time, I discussed with Pam, a chemistry teacher and science department chair at Biden High School in Delaware, how the researchers and teacher-researchers in Philadelphia had restructured student teaching such that cooperating teachers remained involved with the teaching of their classes, while working with the interns from the University of Pennsylvania. In previous conversations, Pam had shared that several teachers at her school did not want to supervise the University of Delaware's student teachers because it meant "giving up their kids." That is, in the traditional student teaching approach, cooperating teachers typically assumed a minor and very peripheral role in teaching their classes when supervising a student teacher. For Pam, the coteaching approach provided opportunities to work with and learn from beginning teachers while remaining actively engaged with her high school students. She encouraged me to consider using coteaching as the model for my interns; I saw the benefits and disadvantages of coteaching from Penn's model.

We adapted the approach used by Tobin and his colleagues at Penn and utilized some of those who were instrumental in developing the Penn program as consultants. For the most part coteaching was highly successful in the way we enacted it, however, contradictions arose from the gendered nature of socialization and the salience of gender in coteaching assignments was apparent.

Laying the foundation for coteaching

I have coordinated the University of Delaware's secondary science education program for over ten years. For most of that time Pam has worked with the program in a variety of roles, such as cooperating teacher, methods instructor, and teaching assistant. During my discussions with Pam about Ken's research on coteaching and changing the student teaching model, she offered her classroom and those of her colleagues as sites for coteaching for the interns from the program I coordinate. The opportunity to establish a structure that would offer interns an extended support system while they learned to teach and also provide an enriching professional development opportunity focused on reflective practice for cooperating teachers along with Pam and Ken's support were the main reasons I decided to change the program's approach to internship.

In the fall, Pam and I visited City High School in Philadelphia, the primary site where Ken initiated coteaching. Our visit provided Pam with information on how teachers and administrators viewed coteaching, which she could share with her colleagues and administrators. We approached Pam's administrators to ascertain if they would consider the placement of a cadre of science interns in their school to conduct coteaching. As science department chair Pam was sufficiently networked and had the social capital to negotiate with her building administrators and peers to establish Biden High as a site.

I attended the science department's meeting before the commencement of the school year, presented the department with the proposed plan, and invited teachers to participate. Pam reported what she had learned about coteaching from her visit to City High and her discussions with that school's teachers and administrators. Six of the eleven science teachers at Biden agreed to become coteachers. Pam was the only teacher with experience as a cooperating teacher. Two teachers, Mary and Tim, had graduated from the University of Delaware's science education program and I had been their methods and student teaching supervisor. All of the cooperating teachers had traditional student teaching experiences.

The University of Delaware's secondary science education program had six interns scheduled to student teach in spring of 2004. Thus, I decided that we would place all the interns in Pam's high school, three seeking certification in biology and three in chemistry. Pam assumed more responsibility within the science education program by becoming a coteacher with me during the methods course, by coordinating the field observations and the on-site coteaching experience for the interns, and by participating in the weekly seminar that we held during student teaching at Biden High School. Pam also efficiently dealt with the daily minutia of questions and concerns that teachers and interns raised during the year.

Arranging coteaching

Science education students at the University of Delaware attain a Bachelor of Arts degree in biology, chemistry, earth science, or physics and complete all of the College of Arts and Science's content and liberal arts requirements, in addition to the professional studies courses in education. In their final semester of their senior year, the students complete a fifteen-week internship in a public high school. Interns must complete the degree requirements before this extended field experience.

Secondary education programs at the University of Delaware are independent from each other and the elementary program, thus changing the secondary science student teaching model did not adversely impact other secondary or elementary education majors. Although the science education program is within the College of Arts and Sciences, our field placements are arranged through a central office housed within the School of Education. The director of the School supported our plans and completed the necessary paperwork to assign all interns to Pam. Rather than assign interns to individual teachers we had planned to discuss the coteaching placements with interns after they had had the opportunity to visit the science teachers.

The interns take a science methods course, "Teaching Science in the Secondary School," which they take in the fall semester of their senior year. It is their first opportunity to meet each other, even if they are in the same content major. Pam and I cotaught "Teaching Science in the Secondary School," which met for three hours two afternoons each a week. At the first meeting, we introduced the concept of coteaching, showed the interns video from Penn's program, and outlined how we envisaged the model would work at Delaware. During the methods course, the interns read articles about coteaching written by Ken Tobin, Michael Roth, Cristobal Carambo, and others. We described our plans as "written in smoke" and teaching assignments would evolve as the interns began to build relationships with teachers at Biden High School.

Throughout the fall, interns conducted their field observations in a supportive or assisting role in a variety of Biden High School's science teachers' classrooms, observing ninth and tenth grade coordinated science classes, chemistry, biology, anatomy and physiology, environmental science, and chemistry and biology Advanced Placement courses. In some classrooms the interns were not involved in coplanning, however, they were actively involved in the lessons. Pam coordinated the visits of teaching interns at Biden. Interns either e-mailed or talked with Pam after class to arrange their visits. Our plan was to allow interns time to work with each other and the teachers at Biden, thus the coteaching assignments for the spring student teaching experience were not made until early in December.

Three issues dictated the interns' coteaching arrangements. First, because there were only six interns, coteaching partnerships were arranged by major. All the interns were white. All three chemistry interns and a biology intern were male and two biology interns were female. Second, Pam and a colleague—a retired, high school science teacher and an adjunct faculty member who has assisted with student teaching supervision for the past seven years—had emphasized the importance of the interns assuming solo teaching responsibilities for at least one class. Hence we decided that interns would teach five of the seven periods per day, coteaching four and solo teaching the fifth. Solo teaching occurred when one intern worked with one cooperating teacher. The intern assumed sole responsibility for a class with the cooperating teacher offering support and advice. During the solo teaching experience the cooperating teacher observed the lessons and acted as a consultant for the planning. In contrast to coteaching, there was no collective responsibility established for the teaching and learning of science. We decided that interns needed at least one assignment that would reflect the traditional student teaching model to offset possible concerns from prospective employers regarding the interns' ability to manage students and assume teaching responsibilities.

The third issue dictating the coteaching arrangements arose when one of the biology teachers took maternity leave early in the student teaching experience. In late fall, Pam and I met with school administrators to discuss how the science faculty and interns could maintain the high school students' science learning while the teacher was on leave. We raised concerns regarding the legal implications of interns assuming primary responsibilities for teaching the classes. The principal solved this problem by designating the interns as substitute teachers. This status provided the interns with the same insurance and legal coverage as the regular teachers in the school. When the interns assumed teaching duties without supervision, the school paid them as substitute teachers. All interns completed the paperwork to become substitute teachers and the school listed their names on the daily roster to the district office. Overall, having the interns assume the teaching responsibilities for these classes proved beneficial to all stakeholders. The high school students had qualified (and nearly certified) biology teachers for the full academic year. Accordingly, the teacher knew she was leaving her students and classroom in good hands and building administrators were confident that learning would continue in those classes.

The biology interns completed their solo assignments in anatomy and physiology; this commitment determined their other teaching assignments and those of their chemistry colleagues. Although initially concerned about assuming the sole responsibility of teaching one anatomy and physiology class per day, the interns enjoyed the opportunity to adopt the role of a regular teacher. Another cooperating teacher taught one class of anatomy and physiology. Two of the interns cotaught anatomy and physiology with this teacher and she co-planned the course with them. The school also provided the interns with building and classroom keys, access to the computer system—which teachers used for attendance and grade keeping—and a unique e-mail account on the school's system.

In the latter part of the fall semester, colleagues from the University of Pennsylvania and the School District of Philadelphia presented a workshop on coteaching and cogenerative dialogues to the interns. Biden High School science teachers and various personnel from the University of Delaware attended the meeting. I also invited teachers who had previously been cooperating teachers in the program and other district personnel. It was important to involve other cooperating teachers in the new process we were using because we would have to scale up from one school site when the number of interns increased in the future.

Methodology

The study is a mesolevel exploration of coteaching from a sociocultural perspective. Data were collected from a wide range of sources throughout the ten-month study. We interviewed the interns during their fall methods course, three weeks into student teaching, and after completing the program. Video data were also collected regularly during the study. Each intern provided at least ten hours of footage, and the weekly seminar associated with practicum was videotaped. Finally, weekly lesson plans, student journal entries, researcher field notes and anecdotal conversations served as additional data resources. All interviews and seminar video footage were transcribed, and the video data were reviewed using the Macintosh iMovie software. All data were coded to produce segments or vignettes, and then further analyzed for themes and patterns. Two interns and Pam also participated in the data analysis, thus providing an emic, or insider, perspective on the data constructions and interpretation.

Data sources and evidence

We collected multiple sources of data during the ten-month study. The six science interns were interviewed at three points: during their fall methods course, three weeks into student teaching during the spring semester and after completing the program. Video data were also collected regularly during the study; approximately ten hours of footage was taped for each teaching intern; this included examples of solo teaching, coteaching, and the weekly seminar associated with the student teaching experience. The seminar participants included the interns, cooperating teachers, university-based research assistants, student teaching supervisor, and methods course professors. Finally, interns' weekly lesson plans and journal entries, and researchers' field notes served as additional data resources. We transcribed the interviews and reviewed video data that produced coded segments and vignettes. Two interns also participated in the data analysis, thus providing an emic, or insider perspective on the data constructions and interpretation.

The setting

Biden High School is located in a community that is swiftly changing from an emphasis on small farming to a larger and more commercial town. The school has a growth rate of approximately 8 percent per year. The high school was built in 1997 and designed for 1,600 students. Currently there are over 1,700 students in the building. In 2002, an additional wing was added to the school to help alleviate overcrowding. The school has limited diversity, as the student population is 80 percent white, 16 percent African American, and 2 percent Hispanic and Asian populations. Low-income families make up 9 percent of the school population. Ninety one percent of the staff are White, 61 percent are female.

There are eleven science teachers at Biden, seven women and four men: one male teacher is of African-American origin; the other teachers are White. Several of the teachers either have or are seeking their teaching certification through an alternative route program. All teachers have at least one class of coordinated science. Three teachers are assigned to the ninth-grade academy, three teach biology, two are chemistry teachers, and there is one physics and one environmental science teacher.

To maximize the number of teaching experiences with different subject matter and student age and abilities, the chemistry interns were assigned to work with each other and up to four different cooperating teachers. For this chapter, I focus on their coteaching with Pam, Tim, and Joan.

Participants

This study focuses on the coteaching experiences of the three chemistry interns. Sam had recently completed his chemistry degree and worked for a short period of time in the industry before returning to the university to complete the coursework he needed to attain a university endorsement for his teaching certification.

Chris and Pat were seniors, majoring in chemistry education. During the spring, the chemistry interns cotaught with Pam, Joan, and Tim in either chemistry or tenth-grade coordinated science.

Pam and Tim, the school's certified chemistry teachers, have only taught at Biden High, Pam for sixteen and Tim for nine years. In addition to her bachelor's degree in chemistry, Pam has a master's degree in curriculum and instruction. Coteaching rather than the traditional student teaching appealed to Tim because he did not have to give up his students. He coaches sports and graduated from the university's science education program. Tim, who taught chemistry and coordinated science, referred to the three chemistry interns as the *Chemies*. Joan is in her second year of teaching and completed her special education certification through an alternative route program. She was working with Pam in two tenth-grade science classes as an inclusion teacher. Joan had a bachelor's degree in chemistry. In the fall semester, before the interns began their teaching experiences at Biden High, Pam and Joan coplanned and cotaught tenth-grade coordinated science.

Establishing social networks and garnering social capital

The interns established social networks and built social capital with each other and coteachers through a variety of experiences. Pam had established social and cultural capital with the interns during the fall semester because she cotaught the university methods course. She was a key resource for all the interns during the fall, but particularly the chemistry interns because she offered them advice and assistance with a major assignment during methods. The interns had to coplan three units in chemistry, which they would implement during student teaching. This activity gave the group time to establish their social capital with each other and Pam. In the following sections I address some of the problems that arose during the field experience, highlighting those associated with gender roles, and the use of cogenerative dialogues to resolve contradictions as they arose.

Emerging problems

The interns visited Biden High about once per week during the fall semester. But as they had different course schedules, they often did not visit the school at the same time or on a regular basis. The interns were not assigned specific classes or teachers to work with; but the three interns expected to coteach with the two chemistry teachers—Pam and Tim. Whenever possible, they visited the classes of those two teachers. Pam had an Advanced Placement chemistry class,

Tim taught regular chemistry and they both taught coordinated science. During the fall, Tim had limited interaction with the interns.

Pam and Tim had the same planning period, which I assumed would provide an advantage to the chemistry interns during student teaching. This arrangement meant that all five teachers had the same planning period. The expectation was that the coteachers would assume collective responsibility for the planning and teaching of coordinated science and chemistry classes. It was assumed that coplanning would be convenient because there was a common time scheduled into the day where teachers could meet for coplanning to occur. In a post-student teaching interview, Tim noted how quickly he related to the chemistry interns:

In terms of [planning with] the three Chemies—and it's also the nature of the units that we've done. We sat down and laid out the gas laws unit—boom. We had some tweaking to do, but we were set for a month. And once we got to the end of that unit we set out from there to spring break. We came back from spring break. We finished out the rest of the unit. And you know, right at the end of the unit we started this . . . [W]e do an okay job working together around what we need to do. (Interview with Tim, 5/04)

Tim saw that the interns quickly assumed responsibility for teaching chemistry and actively engaged with coteaching. However, this contrasted dramatically with their work ethic in tenth-grade coordinated science with Pam and Joan. Several factors contributed to the interns' reticence in assuming responsibility in the course. First, when the interns began their student teaching practicum, Pam and Joan were teaching astronomy. There was a resistance by the three chemistry interns to learn the science being taught because the content was out of field for them—as it was for all the teachers. Second, two of the interns cotaught a class that had a large number of students assigned *Individualized Education Programs* (IEPs) and after several weeks it became apparent that the interns were not comfortable dealing with these students. The interns stepped back and allowed Pam and Joan to deal with the students, the course, and the class.

Instead of being "up and going," as Tim had observed, Joan felt she had to had to "put a foot in their tooshes, telling the interns, 'You need to do this [assume responsibility for teaching].'" There were four teachers in a class that had nineteen of twenty-six students on IEPs. Originally, we thought placing multiple coteachers in the class was an excellent arrangement because students would have access to four teachers. However, the strong working relationship that Pam and Joan had established by teaching together in the fall and the difficulty the group had in building successful social interactions detracted from a successful coteaching experience for the teachers.

A lack of communication and coordination between the coteachers contributed to this problem. Sam explained:

Today went really well up until sixth period. We are still having real problems in sixth and seventh with who should be doing what and when. I'm not sure how to fix it either. I want to say that a lot of it is because Pam, Chris, Joan, and myself do not have enough planning time together, but I don't even know if this will fix everything. In some ways, I think that there are way too many people in the class at once. We have problems every day with who should take the lead, who should pass out papers, who should check homework, who should take attendance, who should submit the attendance, and who should sign passes out of the class. Also, and probably more detrimental, we have problems knowing what work is late because everyone is grading and we have not worked out a system to fix this problem. (Sam, journal entry, 2/26/04)

At the beginning of the field experience, coteachers' time for coplanning became a critical resource. Although assigned the same planning period, Pam had a major commitment with the stage crew for the school's drama production. Often, she was working with students during her free time during the day and after school. She was available early in the morning but the interns arrived for work at the required time, not earlier. Time was also a limited commodity for the interns, as two of them (Sam, Chris) participated on university athletic teams during student teaching, and often they left immediately after school ended to attend practice sessions. The third intern was employed at a retail store in a part-time position. Pam's time commitment to the play ended by the fifth week of the internship but, by then, several patterns had developed which led to the erosion of the co-respect and ease of communication between Pam and the interns. The interns exacerbated these issues by spending their planning period in Tim's room, talking with him and each other, and planning their lessons. This may have been due to them being closer in age to Tim and having similar interests, such as sports and socializing after work.

The interns had high levels of respect for Tim because of his teaching style and ways of interacting with his students. In their journals and interviews, the interns mentioned Tim's ability to provide multiple examples and analogies to help the students understand chemistry. Sam's comment is illustrative of this respect and the high cultural capital the interns afforded Tim: "I really like how Tim has examples for EVERYTHING in chemistry. He just has a way to make the kids see what he's talking about" (Sam, journal entry, spring 2004).

The interns had less respect for Pam. They assumed that she should be available on their schedules, and initially did not change their practice of not scheduling with her a time for coplanning. Pam became frustrated when the interns would appear five minutes before the next cotaught lesson and ask what the plan was. She began to lose respect for them because they were not coplanning and appeared to disrespect her. Moreover, Pam inferred that their habit of leaving the school building immediately at the end of the day signaled that they were not dedicated to teaching. The failure of the interns to show Pam the respect for her chemistry teaching may have been due to them not having the opportunity to see her teach chemistry. Because of their teaching assignments, the interns' observations and collaborations with Pam were limited to the coordinated science classes. In contrast, the interns observed Tim's teaching of chemistry. These difficulties appear to be associated with gender, an assertion I address in the following sections.

Gender issues in coteaching

We can use feminist and sociocultural theory to understand the interplay between the female cooperating teachers and male interns. Women are often expected to develop social networks, but these efforts are to garner social capital for others, such as family members, not themselves. Similarly in the workplace, women's social capital and networks are used to promote and provide status to others, typically men, such as their administrators rather than for themselves. At the start of student teaching, the chemistry interns expected that Pam would arrange her schedule to suit their needs. Although Pam was the senior chemistry teacher in the school and potentially had most to offer the chemistry interns as a resource for their learning to teach science, they chose to spend most of their time with Tim, possibly because of the comfort they had with him in terms of dispositions and interests.

Pam and Joan's observations of the interns' practices, such as not being prepared for class, meant that the interns were not getting the most from their experience of coteaching with the two female teachers and at the same time they were losing their respect. Because Pam and Joan had both completed undergraduate chemistry degrees, they were not impressed with the status of the interns (i.e., because of their degrees and associated knowledge) and instead lamented their lack of preparedness to teach, which they regarded as unprofessional. Pam had worked in the industry before raising her children and returning to the workforce several years later as a teacher. Joan had been involved in research and had planned a graduate career in chemistry before life events changed her plans and she, too, moved into teaching as a second career.

Female and male science teachers are positioned in different paradoxical dilemmas. In the mid-nineteenth century, Catherine Beecher called teaching
"women's true profession" (Hoffman, 1981). Yet, science, with its strong masculine image has never welcomed women into its ranks. Women are not viewed
as producers of scientific knowledge and for many years were consider unsuit-
able and incapable of participating in science even as observers (Harding, 1986;
Potter, 2001). Gender is a "socially variable entity" and as such participants do
not garner gender capital, but gender may impact an actor's accruement of symbolic capital within a field (Moi, 1999). Further, the importance of gender codes
is field dependent, subject to power relations, and as such may be uneven and
discontinuous (McNay, 2000). But in many science-related contexts, being a
female can be a source of disrespect, while maleness can be a means of gaining
respect. Given that science is a masculine field, women may not be perceived as
belonging in the field. What can become problematic for female science teachers
is an unconscious belief by others—peers, students, administrators, and parents—that they may not be as credible teaching science compared with their
male peers. In this way their gender contributes negatively to their acceptance
by peers and the respect they are given. From their perspective, Pam and Joan
had more resources to effectively teach their class and because they were resident teachers at Biden High, they had more agency and power than the interns
when planning, teaching, and overseeing the class. Hence lack of respect was a
central construct in the failure of collaborative arrangements flourishing in the
coteaching of the three male interns and the two female resident teachers. Any
solution to this problem would necessarily address the roles of gender in collaboration between male and female coteachers and the primacy of all participants being able to earn and show respect for one another during coplanning and
coteaching.

Coteaching seeks to minimize the power differential between intern and cooperating teachers. One limitation of coteaching and coplanning is that teachers
lose their individual flexibility in diverting from the planned lessons. But Pam
and Joan as the resident teachers could exert their power by teaching their
classes with little or no input from the interns. As the women lost respect for the
interns because they did not contribute to teaching the astronomy unit, Pam af-
firmed her status and power over the interns by not discussing with them her
ideas for changing a lesson. Reflecting upon the previous day's lesson on her
drive to work, she decided to change the approach. But she made no effort to
talk with her coteachers during the planning period about the change in plans.
Pam's disrespect annoyed the interns, but Pam and Joan were frustrated by the
interns' reluctance to accept responsibility for preparing, teaching, and disciplin-

ing the class. This is just one example of a downward spiral in the co-respect among the five coteachers. If there was to be a way out of this rapidly escalating problem it was essential for the five teachers to identify and discuss the problem.

Using cogenerative dialogues

In a conversation with me, Pam requested that we discuss the issue during the next seminar. I brought the apparent lack of co-responsibility and co-respect to the foreground by using a cogenerative dialogue. We showed several video vignettes of the interns coteaching with Pam, where I posed the question, "Is there coteaching happening in this class?" In the ensuing discussion, the coteachers showed courage acknowledging that they had struggled in structuring a successful coteaching setting. Chris and Sam observed that they had not become as involved with the coordinated science course for several reasons, they did not know the science content and had not spent time out of class learning the subject matter. Also, they were fearful of working with the inclusion students and uncertain as to the authoritative role they should assume. Pam noted her frustration with the interns' unwillingness to step up and used this to justify the two women reassuming the responsibility for teaching the class, taking back the teaching space and the classroom authority from the interns.

After the cogenerative dialogue, the coteachers developed several strategies to improve their teaching and collaboration. They unofficially assigned students to a coteacher by reading through a class list and deciding which coteacher could meet the students' needs. When the content changed from astronomy to chemistry, the interns were no longer teaching out-of-field and they became more comfortable and confident in their teaching. And, as the interns spent more time working with Pam and Joan, they began to recognize their strengths and teaching prowess, that is, they began to show them respect. At that point, social networks began to grow and there was more evidence of collaboration among the coteachers. Several weeks later, Chris commented,

Working with Pam has been great. Ever since I realized I don't know everything and she realized that I don't know everything, we have gotten along great. She is getting used to the fact that telling one of us [interns] does not always mean she told all of us. I think that is why she was surprised and mad when we said she had never told us before. (Chris, journal entry, 4/19/04)

The coteachers reached this stage because they were willing to critically reflect upon their practice, the importance of co-respect and co-responsibility in a coteaching model. After the cogenerative dialogue cleared the air, the interns assumed more responsibility for the class. For next year, Pam and Joan have decided that they would change the topic sequence in the course, so that the chemistry interns would begin coteaching chemistry, which may possibly minimize the interns' nervousness when they begin to teach and allow them to build and consolidate coteaching strategies.

Building collaborative relationships

Schools are entities that engage in cultural reproduction and gender stereotypes are often reinforced rather than challenged or changed. Schools rely on the interactions between individuals and groups to function and thus, gender becomes a factor in shaping those interactions and relations. Joan was one of several female science teachers and the two female interns who daily ate their lunch together at a time when Pam taught. During lunch the women would discuss personal matters, issues related to teaching science, and any student concerns. These daily interchanges provided the women with time to get to know and respect one another. They created social networks that could potentially extend to creating opportunities for professional growth.

Similarly, the men ate together and in so doing developed a camaraderie and companionship that rarely involved conversations about school, teaching, or reflective practice. But they did build social networks through their participation in what is know at Biden High as "boys' lunch." All the male interns at Biden High School, with up to seven males teachers, gathered together for lunch in a lab adjacent to Tim's, where they watched videos of an animated comedy, "Family Guy," or movies that appealed to the group, such as "Tommy Boy" and "Fast Times at Ridgemont High." All the male interns, including the biology intern, chose to participate in the boys' lunch group and in so doing the interns split their lunchtime discussions along gender lines and formed professional affiliations along those same boundaries.

A spiral effect began to reinforce gendered roles because the male interns established strong social connections with their male coteachers and other male teachers at the school. Language and gendered images constitute sites for gender relations. Although "boys' lunch" provided space for the male interns to bond and build social networks with those in the group, it led to the disenfranchisement of the interns with their two female coteachers and limited their opportunities to build social networks with the female science teachers. My research shows that the gendered nature of the lunchrooms was so evident that even the high school students noted them. As is apparent from the analysis of the coteaching of the chemistry interns with Pam and Joan the lack of respect and

social networks among the five coteachers was central in shaping what transpired as an unsuccessful experience. Participating in social exchanges over
lunch, across the boundaries of gender might have contributed to the development of co-respect and social networks on which more successful coteaching
might have been built.

Conclusion

If there is any misleading concept, it is that of coeducation: that because women and men
are sitting in the same classrooms, hearing the same lecture, reading the same books, per-
forming the same laboratory experiments, they are receiving an equal education. They are
not, first because the content of education itself validates men even as it invalidates
women. Its very message is that men have been the shapers and thinkers of the world, and
that this is only natural. (Rich, 1979, p. 241)

Coteaching relies heavily upon social interactions between teachers, and as such
it becomes a gendered activity. As we promote coteaching as a model for learning to teach, we must also turn a critical eye on the division of labor, the interchanges between coteachers, teachers' assumptions about co-responsibility, and
how teachers garner and give co-respect. Taking heed from Rich's (1979) comments about coeducation, those involved with coteaching need to carefully examine the social interactions and networks that are built to ensure that one group
of coteachers constitute the primary "shapers and thinkers." We need to examine
with a critical perspective teachers', students', and other stakeholders' conscious
and unconscious assumptions about who is perceived as having the cultural
capital to teach science and why that is the case.

   There is a large body of research on the gendered nature of linguistics, discourse and conversation styles (Tannen, 1994). A discussion of these patterns
and what this may mean for a group of coteachers will be important for preservice and inservice teachers to consider. For example, men tend to have a
combative approach to discussions. They are more likely to interrupt or turn-
shark a female teacher, because she is perceived as having less status, than another man. Videotaping coplanning sessions and a careful analysis of the roles
coteachers take in the division of labor—for example, are male coteachers more
likely to take center stage and teach the students than the female teachers? One
promising avenue for research on gender and interactions is the prosody of male
and female coteachers. Just as Ken and Michael used PRAAT software in their
analyses of coteachers' synchrony (see chapters 2, 7), this software could also be

used to examine coplanning sessions and the interchanges between and among coteachers and students during science lessons.

Because teaching is traditionally an isolated practice, there are no gender studies of interactions between coteachers. However, as coteaching becomes more commonplace in teacher education programs and is used as a model for professional development, researchers need to consider how participants' gender is related to coteaching, coplanning, and cogenerative dialogues. Are there differences in the way women and men assume individual and collective responsibility? Are women delegated to the support roles, such as grading papers, entering grades in teaching the class? Do men assume authoritative roles in the classroom? Do women assume nurturing roles?

Women are socialized to consider others and place the well-being of others before their own needs. It is possible that without careful monitoring that coteaching may provide two very different teaching experiences for women and men rather than "co-" (shared) experience. If gendered patterns occur within coteaching and coplanning, we need to address and challenge these patterns to interrupt the cycle of stereotypic gender roles for women and men for several reasons. First, there may exist an inequity in the division of labor between women and men teachers and such gendered practices may reinforce students' perceptions of sex-role stereotypes for women and men. Second, the careful examination of coteaching and coplanning from a gender perspective provides teacher educators a context to discuss these issues with beginning and experienced teachers.

To date, most of the research related to coteaching has focused on the classroom events and how coteachers work together, or not, with the students and each other. Our research also needs to examine how coteachers work with each other to build corespect and to assume coresponsibility, in fields outside of formal teaching, that is, coplanning sessions, cogenerative dialogues that occur between coteachers outside of the school day and in nonschool settings where they begin to build respect and rapport with each other. We strive for gender-sensitive coteaching, that is, one that takes gender into account when it is important and ignores gender when it does not. And, we also need to consider how other social categories, such as race, age, and socioeconomic status, mediate the enactment of coteaching.

Coda

Although problems arose during the practicum for interns, coteachers, and me as researcher and supervisor, overall the experience was successful and we plan to continue using coteaching as the model for student teaching. However, coteaching concurrent with coplanning requires that the teachers involved assume co-responsibility for students' learning and the teaching, and have co-respect of each other and the students. When teachers engage in these actions they establish and build upon social networks between each other and their students.

References

Harding, S. (1986). *The science question in feminism*. Ithaca, NY: Cornell University Press.

Hoffman, N. (1981). *Woman's "true" profession. Voices from the history of teaching*. Boston: The Feminist Press.

McNay, L. (2000). *Gender and agency*. Malden, MA: Polity Press.

Moi, T. (1999). *What is a woman?* New York: Oxford University Press.

Potter, E. (2001). *Gender and Boyle's law of gases*. Bloomington: Indiana University Press.

Rich, A. C. (1979). *On lies, secrets, and silence: Selected prose, 1966–1978*. London: Norton.

Tannen, D. (1994). *Gender and discourse*. New York: Oxford University Press.

Epilogue

Kenneth Tobin and Wolff-Michael Roth

In our work, coteaching and cogenerative dialoguing have evolved as we continuously attempted to adapt teaching practices to diverse needs teachers face in the classroom. We expect such evolution to occur wherever the two practices, as any practices, are enacted. In part, the important message of this collection for our readers is that there is not one right way to do coteaching and cogenerative dialoguing, but there is an underlying intention and spirit that are enacted by those who subscribe to these practices. In our Canadian context, coteaching emerged as a way of allowing elementary teachers to learn to teach science by participating in science teaching with someone comfortable with the subject matter. In the Philadelphia context, coteaching initially emerged when the principal at an urban high school put two interns in charge of one class and thereby recognized them as legitimate resources in the teaching of students. Cogenerative dialoguing, too, emerged from our (debriefing) meetings that followed coteaching experiences and evolved into a practice that allows all stakeholders to legitimately participate in shaping the conditions of the classroom. From their humble beginnings, coteaching and cogenerative dialoguing have continuously evolved, not in the least because of our efforts to develop explanatory discourses for what was happening in addition to the practical understandings that arose from our research. It turned out that the two forms knowledge, practical understanding and explanation, mutually presupposed one another. To explain what was happening in coteaching and cogenerative dialoguing, we needed to have a practical understanding of these practices, which we developed through our participation in teaching and making sense. At the same time, to develop our practical understanding, we needed to articulate our practices, many aspects of which were tacit and had been acquired without our consciousness. The cogenerative-dialoguing sessions constituted the context in which we, together with new teachers, cooperating teachers, and students articulated what happened with the intent to plan what to do the next day to improve the conditions of learning and teaching.

Cogenerative dialoguing in particular has had a tremendous impact not only on the way we conduct research but also on the genres we use to write research. To reflect the collaborative way in which we made sense and learned from having participated in the same events, we began drawing on dialogic forms to present our research. These dialogic forms themselves constituted the grounds for new learning to occur. To represent this form of learning about learning in our writing, we made use of the *metalogue* as a genre (Bateson, 1972); in our informal talk, we referred to this as "ratcheting up." In the beginning, conversations about teaching are at a descriptive level, what we each experienced. There then comes a point where someone makes the comment that we need to ratchet up, meaning, we need to look at commonalities and differences between our experiences or at the processes that allow different experiences to come about.

In its initial conception, the metalogue was defined as a conversation about some problematic subject, whereby the structure of the conversation is relevant to the subject. Thus, in our use, the metalogues reflect our work both in content (i.e., learning) and process (i.e., its dialogic production). In the following, we use the metalogue genre to begin conversations about topics that have become salient to use in the various chapters. Using the metalogue format here appears particularly fitting, as the term epilogue itself etymologically derives from the Greek *epi-*, after, and *logos*, speech, that is, the ending part of a speech. Gregory Batson alone and together with his anthropologist daughter (Bateson & Bateson, 1987), based their metalogues on father–daughter interactions, frequently beginning with "Daddy why. . .?" The metalogues are not necessarily continuous, but may jump to a related but new issue within some topic.

As we edited the chapter contributions, we identified four topics as sufficiently important to be pulled out and further developed here. These include the collective orientation concerning responsibility and respect, interactions that produce and reproduce gender at the collective level, new roles for different stakeholders in the educational enterprise, and new methods in and for research associated with coteaching and cogenerative dialoguing.

Collective orientation: responsibility, respect

M: Reviewers of our early manuscripts often suggested that coteaching has a long history, and then conflated it with team-teaching and equated cogenerative dialoguing with reflection on action.

K: They did not seem to engage intellectually with coteaching and seemed only to look at surface features and then to connect to what they understood of their own practices and ways of thinking.

M: In my mind, coteaching and cogenerative dialoguing always have had decidedly different intentions and epistemological underpinnings than team-teaching. Coteaching and cogenerative dialoguing emphasize, for me, the *co*, that is, they are practices based on a *collective* orientation to life in the classroom. Thus, what I do has to reflect collective interest rather than partial interests, my own or those of a group smaller than the collectivity.

K: As I have come to better understand the nature of coteaching it is apparent that the critical unit is the interaction. All participants have to work together to create successful interactions. Clearly this necessity is grounded in lots of constructs that all begin with *co*, the essence of which is being with, together and joint.

M: It is in this ensemble of constructs that I see the essential difference with team-teaching, the practice with which some readers of our early work confused coteaching. In team-teaching, teachers most frequently cut up the work such as to lessen their loads or to teach what they find more convenient to teach. For example, two elementary teachers, one specializing in science and the other in reading, might pool their classes; they take turns teaching the combined class science and reading and thereby free up preparation time for the other. In my view, this constitutes a division of labor, not coteaching, for they have lessened the opportunities for learning from one another. They also may not have taken collective responsibility for planning, enacting, and evaluating the lesson. In this way, they reproduce their preferences and differential expertise. In our chapter 1, Christine and Brigitte truly took collective responsibility in the sense that they planned every lesson together, taught together, learned from one another, and so on.

K: Creating collective responsibility involves focused discussions in which what is agreed upon and shared is discussed in a context of what has happened recently or what happens routinely. These conversations can occur in a context of video-based vignettes, which can serve as a resource for focusing discussion and associated *cogenerated* resolutions.

M: Here again, the important part of the word cogenerated is the *co*. To me, the term *collective* in collective interests, collective responsibility, collective generation of meaning, or collective respect truly means pertaining to or including everybody, that is, all stakeholders and not just some, or even the majority of a group (Holzkamp, 1980). Playing majority interests against minority interests, or the partial interests of different stakeholder groups and subgroups can only lead to the reproduction of differences, different access, different gains, and so on. Both Jennifer Beers (chapter 4) and Sarah-Kate LaVan (chapter 5) articulate the tremendous potential that lies in cogenerative dialoguing when students are included as partners.

K: We have tried to enact cogenerative dialogues with a whole class and they have been successful—but they pose challenges because not everyone can get a chance to talk, argue, and eventually buy in to a cogenerated outcome. We have had most success with up to two representatives from each stakeholder group and about six or seven participants. Hence the group involved in the discussion is small and a rule structure can be set up to equalize power relations in the group. Usually we say, "What gets said here stays here," and the only rules are to be a good listener, show respect for one another, and make a serious effort to cogenerate outcomes.

M: This respect, too, has to be a collective issue. It is insufficient for a student to show respect for a teacher, or for a researcher to respect the needs of teachers and students. And it involves all the others, not just some of them. Respect is not only mutual but also collective and encompassing. Thus, it is not consistent with my understanding when male new teachers show respect for male but not for the female teachers, as this has happened in the study Kate Scantlebury reports here (chapter 11). I am not scolding them here from up high. Rather, if I had been in the situation, I would have attempted to have a cogenerative dialogue about it.

Kate Scantlebury: We did in fact have a cogenerative dialogue about the apparent lack of co-respect and co-responsibility but not in the context of gender because at the time, it hadn't struck me as a gender issue. It was not until the summer research meetings that I began to realize the implications of boys' lunch etcetera.

M: Jennifer Beers shows that such issues as respect can also be addressed with students to the great benefit of the collective classroom climate and, therefore, to the emotional toning of the events.

K: I agree. Showing respect for others and being respected by them is a critical condition for creating and maintaining successful interactions. If anybody feels disrespect or notices instances of it, then the topic should be a high priority for cogenerative dialogue, with an expectation that corespect will be an emergent outcome. There is a collective responsibility for maintaining mutual respect within a community.

M: Collective responsibility to me does not just mean that I am doing the best I can concerning *my* part in the division of labor, but also that I am taking responsibility for the actions of others: in collective responsibility, I am responsible for the collective as a whole. Thus, as a coteacher, if I see that something another teacher has done can be improved, then I attempt to deal with the issue then and there rather than wait for the cogenerative dialogue and evaluate or blame the other. Because my primary intention is to achieve the best science teaching, I do everything I can to maximize the learning of the students. Seeing what I do, my coteaching partner(s) can already get a hint of a possible omission, or at least, that there is some difference. Then we can talk about the event and whether my intervention has in fact improved the situation.

K: I agree. It is imperative that each participant buy in to what has been collectively agreed to and supports others to do what they said they would do. As a participant practices should be synchronized with others' practices in an effort to facilitate the objects of the activity. It can be hard if you think that a particular course of action should have been followed and was not. In such cases you can do whatever is needed to get the outcome you feel is unlikely given the flow of events. Sometimes this may necessitate a short conversation in a huddle to ensure that key participants are on the same page.

M: These huddles, as Beth Wassell shows, have such a tremendous potential in producing and reproducing intersubjectivity between the teachers and keeping them thereby aligned with respect to the directions that the unfolding classroom events might or ought to take.

Interactions and gender

M: Although only chapters 1, 3, and 11 raise gender issues explicitly, I believe the issues to be pervasive enough to be made more salient. On the one hand, when the new teachers from the University of Delaware entered the school context, they also entered the social networks that were already gendered. In this, they contributed in reproducing the existing differences. More so, they produced and reproduced respect in different ways and along gender lines. The situation is aggravated in that even students began noticing the segregation of male and female science teachers.

K: In some ways Kate Scantlebury's research (chapter 11) shows how insidious gender issues can be. The lunchtime meetings seem to have emerged based on dispositions to participate in areas of interest. Because the male science teachers tended to meet separately and watch movies a structure existed for men to do men's things and for women to do women's things. Of course in small gender-defined groups forms of solidarity emerged and social networks were created that extended into the professional realm. But gender-related patterns were evident in your work too.

M: That is true. Brigitte and Christine (chapter 1) had made gender issues their top priority. But changing culturally received ways to act and interact does not come easy. Gender issues are continuously reproduced in everyday interactions, which are, as Randall Collins (2004) shows, really interaction rituals. The gender issue at the teacher level therefore interacts with that existing at the student level, as our own examples in chapter 1 show. Thus, although the two female teachers attempted to increase the number of responses from girls, they met with resistance of both boys and girls. That is, by resisting their teachers' efforts, the boys *and* girls reproduced participation patterns characteristic of other science classes.

K: This issue may have been dealt with in cogenerative dialogues. Perhaps the patterns were not oppressive to females, but probably they were and as forms of hegemony they were accepted by the oppressed females and the oppressive males as forms of practice that were normal and therefore they ought to be sustained.

M: This comment about oppressed females makes me think about actions, on the one hand, and the contribution of the oppressed to their oppression, on the other. What our actions do is so interesting, because they never have singular meaning. Rather, like text, they can be interpreted differently by different individuals, and even by the same individual over time, who understands what she or he has done in different ways as time passes by. Whether our actions oppress some is therefore an empirical matter, both for the participants, who need to ascertain what their actions do to others, and for researchers, who need to look closely at the situation to see what sense the participants themselves make of actions, those of others as well as their own. Furthermore, there is a responsibility not only for the male teachers to ascertain that their actions are not oppressive, but also for the female teachers to make salient those actions that they experience as oppressive . . .

K: . . . with the caveat that females may be oppressed and not recognize the oppression . . .

M: . . . like the soldiers from the inner-city of Flint, Michigan, shown by Michael Moore, who go to war and thereby reproduce a society that has pushed them into the inner city . . .

K: . . . feeling that it is just a case of them striving harder or creating new forms of culture. All participants in a community have a responsibility to recognize and address oppression with the collective goal of it being removed.

M: Simply applying one or the other new strategy does not eliminate gender differences. Separating boys and girls as part of instruction, while giving the latter more opportunities, does not eliminate the differences but reproduce them. Such a practice may be a temporary step, but other practices—such as cogenerative dialoguing—are required to meet gender issues head on, even with the youngest of science students.

K: This is absolutely the case. We have found cogenerative dialogues to be fields in which hegemony can be identified and forms of practice that cut across gendered boundaries (for example) can be produced. So, if males are to learn to interact successfully with females, cogenerative dialogues might be a good place to start. In the case of coteachers not coplanning and not stepping backward and forward synchronously, these issues could be identified as salient and then discussions of possible new roles for the participants could be discussed, negotiated, and agreed to.

New roles for stakeholders

M: We both had done qualitative research, but coteaching changed the way in which we practiced and thought about research. I had come to realize that in order to build an understanding of what was going on in some classroom, I needed to participate rather than pretend to be a fly-on-the-wall observer. The contingencies of an unfolding lesson—making us act in one rather than another way—are seldom evident when we look at the classroom from the remove of the detached observer.

K: Although I was unaware of it at the time, Jim Gallagher routinely cotaught as he did interpretive research when we began to collaborate as researchers back in 1984. He saw this as participant observation. I can assure you he was continuously teaching and otherwise interacting with the students. He rarely assumed a central role, but routinely taught peripherally.

M: Regrettably, many of us in the science education community were not aware that he had conducted his research in this way, and in fact, changed the way research can be done. But researchers are not the only ones who are changing or have to change the ways in which they participate as stakeholders in educational practice, change, and research.

K: I agree with you. In our research we have routinely had teachers as researchers and they have participated in coteaching and cogenerative dialogues with telling effects. Jen Beers (chapter 4) is a good example of a teacher researcher who routinely participates in coteaching and cogenerative dialogue in her own classroom.

M: Unfortunately, the demands on the participants in both teaching and research practices are so tremendous that it is often not feasible for teachers to write up their work so that it can be made available to the scholarly community.

K: We have had astonishing success with students participating as researchers and to a lesser extent as teacher educators and curriculum designers. Jen Beers (chapter 4), Sarah-Kate LaVan (chapter 5), and Beth Wassell (chapter 6) have all undertaken research that has involved students as researchers. We benefit from their perspectives but they build new culture as they interact with us across the boundaries of economic status, class, ethnicity, and sometimes gender.

M: This is true, and as a community, science educators have not yet drawn on the potential that lies in including students or student representatives on their research team. Your teachers and researchers in the Philadelphia context really constitute a new culture, which blends research and teaching despite the demands of both. In particular, the cogenerative dialogues that include students appear to me a step in the right direction to bring about change both in teaching and research.

K: The new culture students develop in cogenerative dialogues greatly expands their agency and we have seen them use this culture in the classroom and in life out of school.

M: In this book, more chapters focus on coteaching than on cogenerative dialoguing. I would argue though that the possibilities of each are enhanced if they are practiced together. This changes the roles of additional stakeholders such as students, who now have a voice in the structuring of their classroom environment, articulation and resolution of perspectives and conflicts, and planning additional instruction to deal with the particular needs of all students.

K: I see dangers in using coteaching without cogenerative dialogue. One becomes like the other by being with the other. Much of the cultural production that occurs is beyond consciousness and for that reason it may or may not be consistent with schema about which you are conscious. It is important in cogenerative dialogues, in the presence of multiple stakeholders, to discuss practices and how they afford the social life of all participants. In this way potentially harmful practices that have developed can be identified and either extinguished or changed.

M: As you are talking, I am thinking about the ways in which many aboriginal peoples had dealt with issues that we now would categorize as psychological. Thus, the mental health of the individual was not distinguished from the mental health of the group (e.g., Kidd, 1998): one person is ill, the group is ill. Issues were frequently worked out by bringing the community together and resolving issues collectively. In my way of thinking, this expresses a dialectical relationship between individual and collective, they mutually presuppose one another. This also means, that any one individual has and recognizes his or her responsibility for the health of the generalized other. I see the role of cogenerative dialoguing in a similar way, as a forum in which issues that arose during a lesson come to be owned by the group. Although a number of chapters do not explicitly address close relationship that does or can exist between coteaching and cogenerative dialoguing, practicing both in the same context enhances teaching, learning, and research and further changes the roles of the different stakeholders. We can conceive of the two practices as mutually presupposing one another, that is, as standing in a dialectical relationship (Roth, Lawless, & Tobin, 2000). For future research and practice, I would like to see more emphasis on the concurrence of the two to enhance their respective possibilities for changing the conditions and understanding them.

K: It seems that in cogenerative dialogues schema and practices are created and can subsequently be enacted in the classroom—by any of the participants. Also, whatever is enacted in the classroom can be recalled in cogenerative dialogues or it can be brought back in the form of video and audio excerpts, thereby creating objects for discussion and cogenerated outcomes. As you say the two are mutually enhancing.

M: This, in my view, leads us back to collective responsibility, which includes the students as agents. Unless students can take active responsibility for the planning, enactment, and evaluation of the curriculum—in the way I have seen the children of Moussac do (Roth, 2002) and those of similar schools—I do not see the kind of altered structure necessary for changing schools from the Fordian institutions that they are to the educational places that they can and perhaps have to be.

K: The underpinnings of coteaching acknowledge the multiple strengths of all participants. The idea that new teachers are resources that can add to the learning potential of any classroom and do not rob the classroom of its best teacher, opens the door for fully utilizing the strengths of all participants to increase learning opportunities of all. The example of Donna Rigano (chapter 8) being asked by the school to head up a curriculum development team is similar to our experiences in the USA. Also Jim and Colette's experiences with the principal in Ireland (chapter 10) show that coteaching was seen as a wonderful way to bring new teachers into a school to enhance professional development and the curriculum.

M: Here again we see that principals, too, will take different roles when they facilitate coteaching and cogenerative dialoguing in their schools. City High School in Philadelphia is one of those prime examples, where a practice, cogenerative dialoguing, has been adopted widely as the central means to mediate differences and conflict between students and teachers. The principals actively promote the use of cogenerative dialoguing.

K: Not only the school-based stakeholders have to change their roles: science educators in universities also should consider changes. For example, it seems imperative for science education methods instructors to consider the ways in which field experiences can be merged with other ways of learning about science education. Cogenerative dialogue and coteaching can be central parts of all science education courses for new teachers. One way to do this is to have a field component within the regular course structure (as Charles Eick and his colleagues did [chapter 9]). Alternatively, we have made the field experience central and we have developed theory and related it to "outside" research and theory through cogenerative dialogues. To do this all participants need to assume the roles of teacher researchers.

M: Which will build continuous renewal of teaching staff into the culture of teaching. Fostering such a culture begins at the university.

K: We have endeavored to model coteaching and cogenerative dialogues in all courses taken by new teachers in the university. This has been especially easy to do in methods courses and in some science courses taught by colleagues in Arts and Sciences.

New methods for researching coteaching and cogenerative dialoguing

Stakeholders as researchers

M: We already began talking about the new roles students can take by becoming researchers, which mediates their student roles as well. The new roles of the different stakeholders, who become participants in the research, itself constitutes a change in method. We learn by participating in teaching, reflecting on teaching and participation, and by generating new observational and theoretical descriptions of the coteaching and cogenerative dialoguing practices. All of this is closer to a form of inquiry that also advocates a cause rather than simply observes.

K: The new forms of participation that arise for students and coteachers can be associated with shifts in identity that seem to afford the learning of science and create horizons of opportunity that were previously not available to some of the students we have worked with. For example, most of our student researchers have gone on to college, even though we selected them because they were in a category of students thought by their teachers to have the highest levels of risk of dropping out of high school.

M: This appears to me a very important role in transformational research. One can think of this research as a new form of participatory action research, in which temporarily participating outside researchers also are considered as legitimate practitioners. Most importantly, participating in such efforts allows students, too, to generate understanding and, with it, transform themselves. A number of the students from City High School in Philadelphia, whom I have come to know more closely because they conducted research and authored papers with us, have created for themselves new opportunities by going to college.

K: Just speaking for myself, coteaching has transformed my perspectives on teaching and learning. Although I never felt that I judged teachers harshly from the side, my involvement as a researcher-coteacher suggests to me that all of my from-the-side assessments of teaching were jaundiced. As a coteacher it is so apparent when doing the research on my own practices that perhaps most of what was happening was beyond my conscious awareness and that any thought to be fully in control of the quality of the teaching that occurred is pure folly. A teacher can only be successful when students "have his back."

M: One interesting issue arising as possibility from coteaching and cogenerative dialoguing is that of doing multiple ethnographies in the same school. Such ethnographies, of which part II of this book and including my chapter 2 are examples, have the potential to contribute to our understanding of coteaching and cogenerative dialoguing as they can be used to tease out contingencies at the classroom level versus cultural processes that are characteristic of the school. There lies a tremendous potential for disconfirmation and confirmation, which is often not used in qualitative research.

K: I agree. By now, our longitudinal studies of teaching and learning science in urban schools has produced a rich yield of insights into what stakeholders need to be represented to produce high quality schools and science education programs within schools. The boundaries between fields are porous and we cannot fail to include parents and the local community in decisions about teaching and learning and of course it makes little sense in many contexts to exclude school building administrators.

M: This is just what we had done in my teaching and research in a middle school in Victoria, British Columbia, where parents and community played central roles in facilitating the children's participation in environmentalism (e.g., Roth & Barton, 2004). What we have not yet done is include them in the research efforts, which is where education would truly become transformative at the community level.

K: The design for our ongoing research on the teaching and learning of science in urban schools also calls for the involvement of parents and community members as researchers. We will include them in cogenerative dialogues and they will be participant researchers in similar ways to the teachers and students who participate as researchers. All researchers will participate in a multitude of ways, including coteaching and cogenerative dialogues.

Microanalytic techniques

M: Coteaching and cogenerative dialoguing also require the adoption of analytic techniques that either exist or have to be developed to be suited to the collective nature of the practices. Thus, the chapters Sarah-Kate LaVan (chapter 5), you (chapter 7), and I (chapter 2) contributed all make use of microanalysis, which in fact turns up the conscious and unconscious ways in which stakeholders interact and relate to one another.

K: The microanalyses clearly show that being with others is a sure way to become like them, especially as the time together increases. Just how alike is somewhat surprising and it seems that an essential part of the toolkit of new resident teachers are the digital camcorders, computers, and software, like QuickTime Pro and PRAAT, that affords video analysis at the microlevel. Once teachers become aware of the ways in which they access and appropriate resources they can begin the process of making changes when contradictions suggest that changes will be fruitful.

M: The analysis of prosody using PRAAT goes beyond linguistic issues. Because emotions are individually exhibited in part through prosodic means—through which we come to know emotions in the first place—the analyses of pitch and speech intensity provide us with access to new phenomena. These include, for example, the classroom collective emotional climate, which is both produced by individual articulation of emotion and mediates these individual articulations. That is, individual and collective emotions presuppose one another; they stand in a dialectical relationship; and the new technologies allow us to provide evidence for it.

K: The focus on interactions and especially prosody allows us to explore the extent to which interactions are successful and unsuccessful and are associated with emotional energy. The research of Randall Collins (2004) on interaction ritual chains has high significance for the work we do and I wonder if emotional energy might be a wonderful barometer for all participants to use when reviewing whether or not learning environments are productive?

M: I believe that the analysis of prosodic features will give us new inroads to, for example, gender issues, how differences between gender are both produced and reproduced, and how these issues arise from different emotionalities that characterize individual students and groups.

K: While I agree with you I suggest too that such differences between males and females are only the tip of an iceberg. We have seen many instances of teaching and learning that are culturally adaptive occurring in the same rooms that students sit motionless, unable to find structures that resonate with their cultural capital. I believe the analysis of prosodic features will allow us to better understand difference as it plays out across borders defined by ethnicity and class.

Coda

There lies tremendous transformative potential in coteaching and cogenerative dialoguing not only as it concerns schools and schooling but also for the way we conduct research and for society as a whole. If schools are no longer viewed and treated as institutions that keep children and students off the streets and reproduce an inequitable society but as legitimate participants in the development of society and culture as a whole, they will to come closer to their true transformative potential. Coteaching and cogenerative dialoguing, together with their ideological underpinnings that value the collective interests rather than individual and partial interests, are practices that can assist us in reaching this transformative potential. The chapters in this book show that these practices are not only feasible in a single setting, but also are transportable to different national settings. Whether these practices have equal potential in other cultural settings is a matter that future research needs to address. We expect additional transformations in these practices to occur to make them work in the new settings.

Coteaching and cogenerative dialoguing have come a long way from their humble beginnings of making arrangements in which participants cover each other's backs, learning from one another while teaching, and learning together while making sense together during cogenerative dialoguing. Increasingly, the tremendous importance of collective responsibility has become salient, in fact serving as a conceptual organizer for what we do and how we do it. Collectively, we have tried different coteacher configurations—two or more new teachers without a cooperating teacher; new teacher(s) and cooperating teachers; seasoned resident teachers; researchers and resident teachers; new teachers, cooperating teachers, and university supervisors; and other combinations. Alongside with coteaching, some of the researchers contributing to this volume have developed cogenerative dialoguing. This practice, too, has evolved as we tried different configurations—initially including a combination of new teachers, cooperating teachers, university supervisors, and researchers; later adding student representatives; and to doing it with a whole class.

There is room to try out new configurations in both practices and to integrate them more tightly. For example, rather than evaluating their teachers through a singular observational visit, school principals might participate in coteaching and cogenerative dialoguing and facilitate the construction of a collective report. Parents, too, can become integral part of coteaching, as we have already seen in our Victoria-based research on coteaching; but they can also become part of cogenerative dialoguing. We have made initial steps to include other members of the community in coteaching, such as environmentalists who cotaught lessons in an environmental science unit and then participated in cogenerative dialoguing. How such additions mediate the processes and products of coteaching, cogenerative dialoguing, and doing research might be interesting avenues for future work.

References

Bateson, G. (1972). *Steps to an ecology of mind*. New York: Ballantine.

Bateson, G., & Bateson, M. C. (1987). *Angels fear: Towards an epistemology of the sacred*. Toronto: Bantam Books.

Collins, R. (2004). *Interaction ritual chains*. Princeton, NJ: Princeton University Press.

Holzkamp, K. (1980). Individuum und Organisation. *Kritische Psychologie, 7*, 208–225.

Kidd, M. (1998, April). *Aboriginal mental health and economic rationalism: The great misunderstanding*. Paper presented at the Social Justice, Social Judgement Conference, Sydney, Australia. (http://www2.fhs.usyd.edu.au/bach/2033/kidd98.htm)

Roth, W.-M. (2002). Learning in Moussac. In L. M. Richter & R. Engelhart (Eds.), *Life of science: Whitebook on educational initiatives in natural sciences and technology* (pp. 45–55). Copenhagen: Learning Lab Denmark.

Roth, W.-M., & Barton, A. C. (2004). *Rethinking scientific literacy*. New York: Routledge.

Roth, W.-M., Lawless, D., & Tobin, K. (2000). {Coteaching | cogenerative dialoguing} as praxis of dialectic method. *Forum Qualitative Sozialforschung/ Forum Qualitative Social Research*, 1(3). Online Journal. [http://www.qualitative-research.net/fqs-texte/3-00/3-00rothetal-e.htm]

Contributors

Jennifer Beers is teaching at a charter school in Philadelphia. Three years after being awarded a degree in Biology from the University of Pennsylvania, she entered the school's Masters of Education Program at the University of Pennsylvania, seeking a secondary certification in science. Here, she was introduced to coteaching and cogenerative dialogue as part of her science teaching method's course and her requirements as a teaching intern. After completing her degree, Jennifer began working at a small urban charter high school where she initially struggled as she worked alone in her classroom. Once situated in this context, she became a cooperating teacher for two teaching interns and a teacher researcher as part of a grant on the teaching and learning of science in urban classrooms. While serving as a cooperating teacher, she revisited the practice of coteaching; however, it was not until working in a collaborative research team with a university researcher and student researchers that she began to see the power of both coteaching with another adult and using students as resources in the classroom. Through video analysis of her teaching and crucial reflection in the presence of other stakeholders, the process of coteaching and cogenerative dialogue became both a critical aspect of her practice and a cornerstone of her inquiry as a teacher researcher.

Jim Beggs is head of science at St Mary's University College, Belfast. He taught chemistry and general science in a secondary school before he was appointed lecturer in chemistry and science education at St Mary's. His principal research area is in primary science teaching and he is currently codirector (with Colette Murphy) of coteaching research projects in primary science funded by the AstraZeneca Science Teaching Trust. Since 2001, Jim and Colette have worked on several projects years that have been very successful in raising children's love and enjoyment of science. In their current project, they incorporated an e-element: Preservice teachers placed in schools all over Northern Ireland (some more than 100 miles apart), compare their coteaching experiences and share data, presentations, photographs, even lesson plans using a virtual learning environment. Science educators from St. Mary have also become involved in the coteaching when they visit the schools.

Trish Bell completed her teacher training at the Townsville Teachers' College, which later amalgamated with James Cook University. For the majority of her twenty years of teaching, she has taught in the lower primary school. Witnessing children's natural curiosity for all things, Trish was particularly interested in participating in coteaching research with Donna Rigano and Steve Ritchie that focused on science inquiry. Trish is keen to see science become an experience that primary school children relate to hands-on and to explore support structures—like the scientist-in-residence initiative at her school—that might improve science teaching and learning.

Charles J. Eick is an assistant professor of science education in the Department of Curriculum and Teaching at Auburn University. Charles became interested in science in middle school where he had the opportunity to participate in the environmental awareness and cleanup movement of the 1970s. After obtaining his undergraduate degree in plant sciences, Charles entered an early alternative certification program in South Carolina that placed him immediately in the classroom. Over time and through much struggle, he learned how to build rapport with his students in order to better teach them. After nine years in the middle and high school classroom, Charles began collaborating with local university professors and their preservice teachers. This work led him to higher education where he understood from experience that learning to teach had to take place in secondary classrooms with supportive and knowledgeable colleagues. Therefore, Charles set up early field experience for his students, and gradually converted his methods courses to allow more time in the classroom collaborating with fellow teachers. Coteaching, as described by Ken Tobin and Michael Roth, provided a natural transition to teaching on one's own where learning to teach in "real classrooms" could be accelerated with "less pain." In a preservice-oriented program, Charles implemented an apprenticeship model of coteaching in his methods courses. He has documented in related articles the evolution and effectiveness of this model, and the changes and development experienced by his students. Today, his program students are still coteaching in their methods course as a peer community of learners, as well as coteaching more and more in their student teaching placements.

Sarah-Kate LaVan began her career in education as a graduate researcher at the University of Miami examining cultural and linguistic influences on the teaching and learning of science. Following her stay in Miami, Sarah-Kate taught middle school science in a variety of settings throughout the city of Philadelphia. At the time of this writing, she is completing her doctoral studies at the University of Pennsylvania where she has taken an interest in student–teacher interactions and the formation of classroom learning communities. In examining the struggles that teachers and students from differing backgrounds confront as they structure teaching and learning opportunities Sarah-Kate has developed a niche in employing cogenerative dialogue and coteaching models to enable students, teachers and university researchers to collaboratively research and reflect on teaching and learning practices .

Colette Murphy is directing the pre-service teaching program and lecturing in science education at Queen's University in Belfast, after having been a research scientist and a teacher of biology and chemistry for many years. She conducts research projects in science education, environmental education, and e-learning. Since 2001, she has been working with Jim Beggs on science coteaching projects involving more than 40 primary schools. These projects came about when a school principal suggested to Colette and Jim that she wanted their science specialist primary preservice teachers to work in the classroom alongside practicing classroom teachers. In this way, it was thought that the teachers might pick up more science and the preservice teachers might learn a lot more about teaching. The idea developed into a large project and Collette and Jim were staggered by how well it worked. They then found out about similar work done by Michael Roth and Kenneth Tobin and about the theoretical framework they had established.

Donna Rigano trained as a biochemist at James Cook University in Townsville, Australia, where she was awarded a Ph.D. for research into amino acid metabolism in tumor cells. After working as a researcher and tutor in chemistry and biochemistry, she entered the field of education through a collaborative project between the university and the metal industry. Subsequent involvement in a series of different education research projects led Donna to her particular interest in the practice of science in school settings. She works as a scientist-in-residence, conducting specialist workshops in a primary through seventh-grade setting, where she is pursuing her research interest in the application of the coteaching model to science inquiry teaching.

Stephen Ritchie is an associate professor in science education at Queensland University of Technology. He spent fifteen years at James Cook University where he collaborated with Donna Rigano on several research projects. Of particular relevance to this volume was their coteaching project in a composite year 1–2 classroom with the regular teacher; namely, Trish Bell. This project was inspired by Wolff-Michael Roth and Kenneth Tobin's (2002) book *At the*

Elbow of Another and recent reports in Australia that have drawn attention to the low take-up of authentic science inquiries in Australian primary schools. While Steve's previous research has focused on classroom issues that relate to teaching and learning science, this was his first experience at coteaching science in a year 1 classroom. He was co-author of *Re/Constructing Elementary Science* with Wolff-Michael Roth and Kenneth Tobin. More recent research projects involving these two scholars are concerned with leadership dynamics within high school science departments.

Wolff-Michael Roth is Lansdowne Professor of Applied Cognitive Science at the University of Victoria. Around 1990, while directing the science department at Appleby College, he began, together with his department colleagues, to develop an integrated approach to professional development, including peer visits to one another's classrooms, peer evaluation, and teaching classes together. Over the course of his tenure, even the science teachers most reluctant to professional development had improved their teaching practices. These early efforts subsequently turned into a research program when elementary teachers in Vancouver and Victoria showed willingness to accommodate practices consistent with the then emerging constructivist principles, but did not feel sufficiently prepared to engage in change efforts on their own. Pairing individuals with different forms of expertise (e.g., local and pedagogical knowledge pertaining to the children to be taught versus subject matter knowledge) turned out to be of great benefits not only to the elementary teachers but also to the subject matter experts. Michael described his work in many research articles as well as in books such as *At the Elbow of Another: Learning to Teach by Coteaching* (with Ken Tobin) and *Being and Becoming in the Classroom*.

Kathryn Scantlebury is an associate professor in the Department of Chemistry and Biochemistry and the Secondary Science Education Coordinator in the College of Arts and Sciences at the University of Delaware. After completing a research degree in chemistry, Kate began teaching high school chemistry, science, and mathematics in Australia. She taught high school for seven years, and then moved to the United States for her doctoral studies and became a science teacher educator. Her doctoral research focused on the impact of student teaching on gender issues in preservice teacher education and her first research grant was based on that study. In her role as coordinator for the University of Delaware's Secondary Science Education program, Kate works with preservice and inservice teachers to improve the effectiveness of the science education on preparing science teachers. After working collaboratively for several years with Ken and others at the University of Pennsylvania, Kate introduced coteaching as the model for student teaching. Kate's other research interests focus on gender and equity issues in urban schools and the academic climate and career development for female chemists and chemical engineers.

Kenneth Tobin is Presidential Professor at the Graduate Center of the City University of New York. He has been involved in research on teaching and learning to teach science for more than thirty years in an ongoing study of research that began in Australia in 1973 and continues in the United States to the present day. After teaching high school science in Australia and England, Ken became a science teacher educator and has continued as such for three decades. Presently he is situated in New York City where he undertakes research in urban high schools and the education of science teachers to enact science curricula that are socially and culturally adaptive. His interests in coteaching have been grounded in the practical necessities of being director of teacher education in a large urban university and the theoretical and empirical goals of creating science teacher education programs that are epistemologically and ontologically consistent with cutting-edge scholarship. His recent book with Wolff-Michael Roth, *At the Elbow of Another*, and numerous articles reveal the promise of coteaching and cogenerative dialogues and point to contradictions that are the seeds for further advancement of research, theory, and practice in teacher education. Many of these seeds have germinated and the fruits are revealed in the chapters of this book.

Beth A. Wassell began her career in education as a secondary Spanish teacher, where she began to consider the practicality of traditional teacher education programs. After commencing her doctoral studies at the University of Pennsylvania's Graduate School of Education, she began to investigate the cultural mismatch between teachers and students in urban schools and how teacher preparation programs do little to prepare new teachers to be effective in urban schools. This led to her study of the coteaching model and its application as a field for enhanced reflection and research on teaching practices. She is currently involved in several research projects that examine the effects of coteaching and cogenerative dialogue on teacher practices and the transition from the coteaching arrangement into the first year of autonomous teaching.

Index

accountability, 15, 134
achievement ideology, 87
activity: collective, 18, 30, 67, 68, 69, 104, 207; learning, 117; motives, 30; sociocultural, 85; system, 11, 12, 13, 14, 15, 17, 21, 23, 24
Advanced Placement, 191, 235, 239
agency, 3, 4, 5, 11, 13, 15, 16, 18, 19, 20, 22, 23, 25, 26, 28, 50, 74, 77, 80, 87, 88, 92, 95, 100, 103, 104, 119, 121, 123, 124, 125, 126, 128, 129, 132, 134, 136, 137, 138, 139, 243, 248, 256; power to act, 5
alignment, 30, 38, 45, 47, 49, 50; emotional, 44; temporal, 31, 32
apprenticeship, 66, 76, 187, 190, 191, 192
attunement, 41

barrier, 179, 180, 182
beliefs, 101, 104, 106, 116, 117, 125, 169, 171, 172, 204
Benchmarks for Science Literacy, 210
benefits, 66, 71, 90, 105, 121, 129, 130, 160, 184, 192, 198, 204, 225, 226, 229, 233
Beyond 2000, 210, 231
biochemistry, 169

biology, 18, 20, 31, 62, 93, 191, 197, 231, 234, 235, 236, 238, 245
Bourdieu, P., 25, 26, 30, 46, 50, 61, 65, 76, 82, 94, 98, 99, 100, 118, 123, 130, 138

capital: cultural, 61, 87, 88, 99, 239, 241, 246, 261; social, 68, 70, 115, 124, 129, 234, 239, 242; symbolic, 90, 99, 101, 111, 123, 125, 243
chemistry, 70, 72, 80, 118, 141, 146, 149, 233, 234, 235, 236, 237, 238, 239, 240, 241, 242, 244, 245
code-switch, 87
coherence, 65, 79, 102, 106; thin, 85
Collins, R., 66, 76, 91, 95, 98, 99, 102, 118, 160, 161, 187, 206, 254, 261, 262
Common Curriculum, 210
communalism, 106, 112, 114
communication: miscommunication, 106
community: discourse, 117; learning, 98, 116, 118, 144, 200, 202
complementarity, 9, 30, 32, 33, 36, 47, 63, 146, 159

confidence, 83, 101, 111, 192, 198, 199, 200, 203, 204, 207, 208, 214, 215, 217, 218, 221, 222, 225
conscious, 5, 6, 10, 13, 18, 30, 36, 48, 57, 63, 64, 84, 87, 89, 117, 123, 132, 134, 146, 173, 246, 256, 259, 260
constraints: structural, 62
constructivism, 11, 21, 60, 188, 196, 199, 209
contradiction, 3, 14, 20, 23, 24, 62, 64, 65, 66, 67, 68, 69, 79, 85, 89, 94, 99, 105, 106, 116, 129, 159, 233, 239, 260; disconnection, 98; systemic, 24
contradictions: structural, 24
control, 11, 21, 23, 33, 74, 85, 86, 100, 102, 103, 123, 141, 142, 144, 147, 149, 152, 154, 174, 178, 191, 215, 259
coordination: prosodic, 38
coplanning, 63, 67, 68, 71, 81, 82, 89, 92, 130, 131, 137, 143, 144, 146, 175, 193, 205, 235, 239, 240, 241, 242, 243, 246, 247, 248, 255
critical psychology, 15
cultural reproduction, 3, 11, 25, 28, 29, 38, 40, 46, 47, 49, 62, 87, 94, 245, 252
culture: capital, 61, 87, 88, 99, 239, 241, 246, 261; incongruence, 100, 106; production, 11, 29, 32, 36, 41, 45, 47, 48, 68, 73, 159, 165, 238, 253, 255, 256, 259, 260, 261; repro-duction, 47, 48, 49, 68, 124, 253, 254, 261; sociology of, 56, 64; toolkit, 74, 85

debriefing, 13, 25, 66, 103, 130, 133, 134, 137, 249
dialectics, 3, 4, 5, 14, 16, 21, 29, 30, 37, 47, 48, 49, 121, 123, 257, 260, 263; agency|structure, 28
dialogue, 51, 67, 68, 71, 72, 73, 74, 75, 82, 87, 88, 89, 91, 93, 97, 98, 103,

117, 131, 133, 134, 135, 136, 137, 139, 143, 161, 167, 176, 178, 184, 185, 187, 192, 197, 198, 204, 244, 252, 253, 255, 256, 258
discourse: classroom, 6, 212, 215
disharmony, 227
disposition, 30, 46, 61, 70, 100, 103, 106, 111, 113, 114, 116, 242, 253
division of labor, 11, 64, 65, 67, 68, 70, 89, 104, 117, 121, 123, 129, 131, 137, 138, 142, 149, 246, 247, 251, 252
domination, 98, 100

electronic bulletin board, 197, 200
emotion, 31, 38, 47, 50, 56, 100, 106, 260; alignment, 44; confidence, 83, 101, 111, 192, 198, 199, 200, 203, 204, 207, 208, 214, 215, 217, 218, 221, 222, 225; disappointment, 160; energy, 99, 102, 106, 114, 160, 261; frustration, 98, 100, 103, 134, 141, 144, 160, 244; resentment, 160
enculturation, 36, 46
Engeström, Y., 3, 4, 11, 23, 26, 62, 64, 76, 139
engineering physics, 122, 130, 134, 138
entrainment, 30, 31, 32, 33, 36, 37, 38, 40, 45, 46, 48, 49, 159
environmental science, 235, 238, 262
ethnography, 25, 55, 142, 165, 166; critical, 142
expansive learning, 23, 24

field, 11, 13, 18, 20, 46, 49, 55, 65, 68, 74, 75, 88, 89, 93, 98, 99, 100, 105, 116, 117, 121, 130, 132, 134, 136, 138, 143, 144, 172, 190, 192, 195, 197, 234, 235, 237, 238, 239, 240, 241, 243, 247, 255, 258, 259

gender, 38, 69, 70, 75, 116, 117, 167, 210, 233, 239, 242, 243, 245, 246,

247, 250, 252, 253, 254, 255, 256, 261; balance, 12, 14; bias, 13

habitus, 82
harmony, 31, 47, 48, 57, 228
Heidegger, M., 48, 50
hermeneutic phenomenology, 104
Holzkamp, K., 15, 18, 23, 26, 251, 262
huddle, 67, 89, 130, 132, 133, 137, 178, 194, 253

identity, 76, 79, 85, 88, 184, 259
Individualized Education Programs, 240
induction, 187, 191
inquiry, 57, 80, 101, 121, 138, 165, 170, 174, 176, 177, 178, 179, 180, 181, 182, 183, 185, 188, 189, 199, 201, 202, 203, 205, 206, 208, 212, 217, 218, 222, 258; structured, 188, 189, 191, 196, 198, 204, 205
interaction, 3, 4, 6, 11, 14, 16, 31, 38, 41, 59, 69, 74, 79, 85, 93, 97, 98, 100, 101, 102, 105, 106, 111, 112, 115, 116, 117, 141, 142, 145, 146, 147, 149, 159, 160, 166, 171, 177, 195, 241, 245, 246, 247, 250, 251, 252, 254, 261; student-teacher, 16
interaction rituals, 98, 254
interest, 11, 15, 37, 38, 111, 121, 147, 169, 176, 177, 179, 181, 184, 207, 209, 210, 211, 224, 251, 253
interjections, 193, 194, 198, 204

knowledge: conceptual, 5, 171; practical, 166, 170, 187, 190, 199, 200, 204, 206; prior, 200; procedural, 170; skill, 9, 21, 33, 62, 73, 83, 99, 101, 108, 116, 170, 172, 189, 199, 202, 203, 205, 219, 220, 221, 224, 225, 226; teacher, 170

laboratory work, 179

learning environment, 8, 10, 21, 60, 61, 71, 73, 74, 97, 98, 124, 139, 167, 230, 261

mathematics, 70, 76, 80, 121, 122, 130, 208, 209, 230, 231
methods course, 117, 123, 134, 138, 166, 187, 189, 190, 191, 192, 193, 197, 198, 199, 200, 205, 234, 235, 237, 239, 258
microanalysis, 4, 142, 149, 160, 260
mimesis, 45, 46, 49
modeling, 86, 190, 192, 193, 198, 205
motivation, 11, 21, 30, 67, 87

novice, 66

opportunity, 5, 6, 8, 16, 17, 25, 36, 61, 63, 65, 67, 68, 70, 72, 74, 75, 79, 80, 81, 82, 84, 85, 89, 91, 92, 97, 100, 106, 109, 113, 116, 117, 121, 123, 125, 126, 129, 130, 131, 132, 133, 134, 135, 136, 137, 138, 146, 147, 157, 159, 170, 171, 172, 173, 175, 182, 187, 191, 193, 196, 212, 215, 217, 221, 223, 226, 233, 234, 235, 237, 242, 245, 251, 255, 259; learning, 8, 12, 18, 19, 24, 123, 165, 257

participation: legitimate peripheral, 66; peripheral, 190, 194, 206
pedagogy, 11, 32, 50, 206
peer: interactions, 112
personality conflicts, 48
phenomenological understanding, 174
phronesis, 171
physics, 31, 121, 122, 124, 125, 128, 131, 134, 135, 136, 137, 138, 235, 238
possibilities: subjective, 21
power, 5, 62, 64, 67, 71, 74, 79, 85, 86, 88, 89, 100, 103, 104, 117, 125, 127, 133, 134, 166, 185, 243, 252

PRAAT, 160, 161, 246, 260
practice, 12, 13, 17, 18, 23, 25, 28, 29,
    30, 33, 37, 45, 46, 47, 48, 49, 50, 56,
    60, 61, 62, 63, 64, 65, 66, 67, 68, 69,
    72, 75, 76, 79, 80, 81, 82, 83, 84, 85,
    87, 88, 89, 91, 92, 94, 97, 98, 100,
    101, 104, 105, 106, 107, 112, 116,
    117, 118, 119, 121, 123, 124, 125,
    126, 129, 130, 132, 133, 134, 137,
    138, 149, 159, 160, 165, 166, 167,
    169, 170, 171, 172, 173, 176, 177,
    179, 180, 182, 183, 184, 187, 188,
    189, 190, 192, 196, 197, 198, 199,
    200, 203, 204, 205, 206, 207, 212,
    215, 217, 221, 222, 226, 230, 241,
    242, 244, 247, 249, 251, 253, 254,
    255, 256, 257, 258, 259, 260, 261,
    262; authentic, 190; inquiry, 178,
    179; pedagogical, 101; reflective,
    171, 206, 234, 245; wisdom in, 169,
    170, 171, 172, 174, 182; wisdom of,
    182; wisdom-in-practice, 169, 170,
    171, 172, 174, 182
praxis, 5, 15, 16, 19, 21, 25, 48, 64, 65,
    66, 68, 91, 94, 117, 175, 178, 185,
    263
prosody, 4, 31, 38, 40, 41, 142, 159,
    160, 161, 246, 260, 261; pitch, 28,
    37, 38, 39, 40, 41, 42, 43, 44, 45, 47,
    49, 50, 56, 102, 108, 109, 113, 148,
    153, 154, 158, 160, 260; rhythm, 31,
    40, 49, 50, 102, 107, 108, 111, 147,
    160

race, 117, 145, 173, 247
research: collaborative, 91, 103, 106,
    117, 121, 122, 129, 130, 134
resistance, 69, 98, 99, 100, 240, 254
resonance, 106, 114
resource, 6, 15, 16, 18, 24, 25, 29, 33,
    35, 36, 47, 48, 60, 61, 63, 64, 72, 85,
    88, 90, 92, 99, 101, 104, 105, 106,
    108, 109, 111, 112, 114, 116, 124,

    126, 132, 137, 138, 141, 143, 144,
    145, 146, 147, 149, 150, 151, 152,
    153, 156, 158, 159, 161, 166, 167,
    207, 208, 222, 237, 238, 239, 241,
    242, 243, 249, 251, 257, 260
respect, 13, 14, 17, 19, 29, 30, 31, 32,
    68, 70, 73, 74, 75, 84, 85, 88, 90, 92,
    114, 115, 142, 147, 148, 182, 200,
    211, 241, 242, 243, 244, 245, 247,
    250, 251, 252, 253; collective, 160,
    241, 244, 246, 247, 248, 252
responsibility: collective, 3, 5, 6, 8, 14,
    19, 20, 64, 65, 67, 68, 74, 75, 84, 86,
    106, 112, 117, 160, 236, 240, 244,
    246, 247, 248, 251, 252, 257, 262;
    individual, 19; shared, 5, 14, 65,
    135, 212; solo teaching, 236
Ricœur, P., 66, 76, 104, 119, 134, 139
role, 64, 70, 71, 79, 81, 83, 85, 90, 92,
    93, 111, 113, 116, 117, 123, 125,
    126, 128, 129, 131, 137, 139, 143,
    157, 160, 165, 170, 173, 185, 187,
    190, 191, 192, 193, 194, 198, 199,
    204, 206, 227, 228, 233, 235, 237,
    244, 255, 257, 259
room to maneuver, 10, 16, 18, 20, 177,
    183, 200

scaffolding, 178, 183, 204
schema, 29, 47, 48, 79, 80, 83, 85, 87,
    88, 89, 98, 103, 104, 117, 124, 137,
    138, 256, 257
Science for All Americans, 210
self-concerns, 191, 202
self-consciousness, 111
self-narrative, 174
Sewell, W., 5, 26, 28, 50, 64, 76, 79,
    95, 98, 99, 119, 121, 123, 124, 139
similarity, 7, 18
small learning community, 69, 80, 144
sociology: cultural, 56, 64
solidarity, 41, 44, 47, 77, 91, 106, 117,
    253

speech: intensity, 147, 148, 149, 152, 153, 154, 158, 160, 161
speech rhythm, 31, 40
stakeholders, 67, 81, 87, 90, 91, 92, 98, 104, 105, 116, 117, 132, 145, 165, 236, 246, 249, 250, 251, 255, 256, 257, 258, 259, 260
STC kits, 205
stories: episodic, 200
strategy, 14, 73, 76, 87, 99, 100, 118, 130, 170, 172, 175, 176, 177, 183, 190, 200, 244, 245, 255
structure, 3, 4, 5, 9, 11, 15, 16, 21, 24, 26, 28, 29, 50, 73, 74, 79, 80, 82, 85, 87, 89, 90, 92, 93, 95, 98, 99, 101, 103, 104, 105, 106, 107, 108, 109, 111, 113, 114, 115, 116, 117, 119, 121, 122, 123, 124, 125, 126, 128, 129, 132, 133, 134, 135, 136, 137, 138, 139, 141, 146, 149, 160, 175, 177, 204, 234, 250, 252, 253, 257, 258, 261
subculture, 87

teacher: as learner, 117; cooperating, 31, 45, 59, 60, 63, 64, 65, 66, 67, 70, 71, 80, 82, 85, 92, 121, 122, 132, 166, 191, 192, 193, 194, 195, 196, 197, 200, 201, 202, 204, 205, 233, 234, 236, 237, 238, 242, 243, 249, 262; new, 28, 31, 32, 36, 38, 45, 56, 59, 60, 61, 62, 63, 64, 65, 66, 67, 68, 69, 70, 71, 72, 75, 79, 80, 82, 85, 90, 92, 93, 94, 117, 141, 142, 143, 144, 166, 190, 249, 252, 253, 257, 258, 262; preservice, 172, 174; resident, 72, 167, 243, 260, 262; student as, 117
teaching: solo, 236, 238; team, 64, 250, 251
theory, 3, 5, 8, 10, 12, 14, 15, 21, 26, 28, 50, 64, 67, 84, 95, 118, 119, 123, 128, 134, 138, 139, 175, 178, 187, 188, 189, 190, 199, 206, 221, 242, 258; cultural-historical activity, 3, 10, 15, 16, 64; situated learning, 187, 189, 190; sociocultural, 79
transformation, 68, 72, 80, 106, 107, 113, 137, 172, 176, 188, 259
trouble shooting, 202

unconscious, 18, 28, 30, 32, 48, 67, 84, 87, 89, 100, 104, 117, 123, 128, 133, 146, 171, 243, 246, 260
university supervisor, 64, 65, 68, 71, 94, 262

verve, 106, 107, 108, 111, 114, 147, 150, 156, 160
violence: symbolic, 98, 100

workload, 184

Studies in the Postmodern Theory of Education

General Editors
Joe L. Kincheloe & Shirley R. Steinberg

Counterpoints publishes the most compelling and imaginative books being written in education today. Grounded on the theoretical advances in criticalism, feminism, and postmodernism in the last two decades of the twentieth century, Counterpoints engages the meaning of these innovations in various forms of educational expression. Committed to the proposition that theoretical literature should be accessible to a variety of audiences, the series insists that its authors avoid esoteric and jargonistic languages that transform educational scholarship into an elite discourse for the initiated. Scholarly work matters only to the degree it affects consciousness and practice at multiple sites. Counterpoints' editorial policy is based on these principles and the ability of scholars to break new ground, to open new conversations, to go where educators have never gone before.

For additional information about this series or for the submission of manuscripts, please contact:

Joe L. Kincheloe & Shirley R. Steinberg
c/o Peter Lang Publishing, Inc.
275 Seventh Avenue, 28th floor
New York, New York 10001

To order other books in this series, please contact our Customer Service Department:

(800) 770-LANG (within the U.S.)
(212) 647-7706 (outside the U.S.)
(212) 647-7707 FAX

Or browse online by series:
www.peterlangusa.com